PLACING AND DISPLACING ROMANTICISM

Placing and Displacing Romanticism

Edited by
PETER J. KITSON
University of Dundee

Ashgate

Aldershot • Burlington USA • Singapore • Sydney

Published by
Ashgate Publishing Limited
Gower House
Croft Road
Aldershot
Hampshire GU11 3HR
England

Ashgate Publishing Company
131 Main Street
Burlington, VT 05401-5600 USA

Ashgate website: http://www.ashgate.com

British Library Cataloguing in Publication Data
Placing and displacing romanticism. - (Nineteenth century
    series)
    1. Romanticism 2. English literature - 19th century - History
    and criticism 3. Place (Philosophy) in literature
    I. Kitson, Peter
    820.9'007

Library of Congress Control Number: 2001096533

ISBN 0 7546 0602 3

Printed and bound in Great Britain by MPG Books Ltd, Bodmin, Cornwall

Contents

List of Figures

List of Contributors

Michael Charlesworth is Associate Professor of Art History at the University of Texas at Austin, and specializes in cultural studies. He is author of *The English Garden: Literary Sources and Documents* (1993), various essays on nineteenth century photography, book illustrations, and mapping, and is just completing a three volume study of *The Gothic Revival, 1720-1870.*

Angela Esterhammer is Professor of English and Chair of the Department of Modern Languages and Literatures at the University of Western Ontario. She is the author of *Creating States: Studies in the Performative Language of John Milton and William Blake* (1994), *The Romantic Performative: Language and Action in British and German Romanticism* (2000) and other publications on Romanticism and comparative literature.

Tim Fulford is Professor of English at Nottingham Trent University. He is the author of *Coleridge's Figurative Language* (1991), *Landscape, Liberty and Authority* (1996), *Romanticism and Masculinity* (1999) and has edited, with Peter J. Kitson, *Romanticism and Colonialism* (1998).

Peter J. Kitson is Professor of English at the University of Dundee. His most recent publications are *Coleridge Keats and Shelley: Contemporary Critical Essays* (1996), (with Tim Fulford) *Romanticism and Colonialism: Writing and Empire, 1780-1830* (1998), (with Debbie J. Lee), *Slavery, Abolition and Emancipation* (1999), (with Tim Fulford) *Travels, Explorations and Empires* (2001).

Philip W. Martin is Professor of English and Director of the English Subject Centre, based at Royal Holloway, University of London. He is the author of *Byron: A Poet before his Public* (1982) and *Mad Women in Romantic Writing* (1987) and the editor (with Robin Jarvis) of *Reviewing Romanticism* (1992). He is the editor of the journal *Literature and History* and is currently the President of the British Association for Romantic Studies.

Thomas McFarland is Murray Professor of English Literature Emeritus at Princeton University. His eleven books include most recently *Paradoxes of Freedom: The Romantic Mystique of Transcendence* (1997) and *The Masks of Keats* (2000).

Lucy Newlyn is Fellow and Tutor in English at St Edmund Hall, Oxford. She is the author of *Coleridge, Wordsworth and the Language of Allusion* (1986), *Paradise Lost and the Romantic Reader* (1993) and *Reading, Writing, and Romanticism: The Anxiety of Reception* (2000).

Michael O'Neill is Professor of English at the University of Durham. His recent publications include *Romanticism and the Self-Conscious Poem* (1997) and, as editor, *Keats: Bicentenary Readings* (1997) and *Literature of the Romantic Period: A Bibliographic Guide* (1998). He is currently co-editing Shelley for the Oxford Authors series with Zachary Leader.

Mary Anne Perkins is currently a Research Fellow at Birkbeck College and the School of Advanced Study, University of London. Her publications include *Coleridge's Philosophy* (1994) and *Nation and Word, 1770-1850* (1999), the latter of which was supported by the Humanities Research Board of the British Academy. Her current research explores the tensions between European and national identity in the nineteenth century.

Lynda Pratt is a Lecturer in Romantic Literature at Queen's University, Belfast. She is General Editor of *Robert Southey: Poetical Works, 1793-1810* (forthcoming 2003), for which she is producing volumes on *Joan of Arc, Madoc* and *Shorter Poems and Plays*. She has published widely on Southey and his literary circle in the 1790s. She is currently working on a book on Romanticism, nationalism and the epic.

Michael Scrivener has taught at Wayne State University (Detroit, Michigan) since 1976. He is the author of *Radical Shelley: The Philosophical Anarchism and Utopian Thought of Percy Bysshe Shelley* (1982), and *Poetry and Reform: Periodical Verse from the English Democratic Press 1792-1824* (1992). His new book, *Seditious Allegories* (2001) is a study of John Thelwall and literary Jacobinism.

Philip Shaw is a Lecturer in English at the University of Leicester. His most recent publications include an essay on the relations between Romantic writing and the Revolutionary and Napoleonic Wars, in *A Companion to Romanticism*, ed. Duncan Wu (1998) and a study of Leigh Hunt and the aesthetics of post-war liberalism in *Romantic Wars: Studies in Culture and Conflict*, 1793-1822, ed. Philip Shaw (2000). A book on Waterloo and the Romantic Imagination is due for publication in 2002.

Paul D. Sheats is Professor Emeritus at the University of California at Los Angeles. He has published widely on Wordsworth and Keats and is the author of *The Making of Wordsworth's poetry, 1785-1798* (1973). He is currently working on a project dealing with romantic formalism.

John Williams is Reader in Literary Studies at the University of Greenwich. His *Literary Life of William Wordsworth* was published by Macmillan in 1996 and his essay on Wordsworth's 'The White Doe of Rylestone' was published in *Writing the Lives of Writers* (1998). His *Literary Life of Mary Shelley* was published by Macmillan in 2000.

Acknowledgements

The editor is most grateful to the following for their help and advice: Linda Jones, Tim Fulford and Nicholas Roe.

The illustrations in this volume are reproduced with the kind permission of the following institutions: *Plans and Views in Perspective of Building Erected in England and Scotland*; Plate no. 14 by Robert Mitchell and *Explanation of the Battle of Waterloo* by John Burnet by permission of the Yale Center for British Art; *Fort Augustus* by Thomas Sandby is reproduced by permission of Royal Collection Enterprises; *View of London from Greenwich* by J. M. W. Turner by permission of The Metropolitan Museum of Art; and *L'Exposition universelle, Paris 1867* by Edouard Manet is reproduced by permission of Nasjonalgalleriet, Oslo.

The editor and publisher would like to thank the following for permission to use copyright material: Tim Fulford 'Wordsworth's 'The Haunted Tree' and the sexual politics of landscape' by permission of the on-line journal *Romantic Praxis*; Peter J. Kitson's 'Romantic Displacements: Representing Cannibalism' by permission of Michael Eberle-Sinatra and the on-line journal *Romanticism on the Net*. An expanded version of Michael O'Neill's 'Keats and the "Poetical Character"' appeared in Michael O'Neill, ed. *Keats: Bicentenary Readings* (Edinburgh University Press, 1997) and in Michael O'Neill, *Romanticism and the Self-Conscious Poem* (Clarendon: Oxford, 1997).

List of Abbreviations

GM	*Gentleman's Magazine*
Howe	*The Complete Works of William Hazlitt*, ed. P. P. Howe. 21 vols (London: J. M. Dent and Son, 1930-34)
Joan 1793	Robert Southey, 'Joan of Arc'. Houghton Library, Harvard MS. Eng 265.3
Joan 1795	Robert Southey, 'Joan of Arc'. British Library, London. Add. MS. 28,096
Joan 1796	Robert Southey, *Joan of Arc, An Epic Poem* (Bristol: J. Cottle, 1796)
Joan 1798	Robert Southey, *Joan of Arc*. Second edition. 2 vols (Bristol: J. Cottle, 1798)
KL	*The Letters of John Keats, 1814-21*, ed. Hyder Edward Rollins. 2 vols 2nd edition (Cambridge, Mass: Harvard University Press, 1972 [1958])
LCRS	*The Life and Correspondence of Robert Southey*, ed. Rev. Charles Cuthbert Southey, 6 vols (Longman: London, 1850)
LPR	Samuel Taylor Coleridge, *Lectures 1795 On Politics and Religion*, ed. Lewis Patton and Peter Mann (London and Princeton: Routledge and Princeton University Press, 1971). CC, I
LS	S. T. Coleridge, *Lay Sermons*, ed. R. J. White. (London and Princeton Routledge and Princeton University Press, 1972). CC, VI
LY	*The Letters of William and Dorothy Wordsworth*, ed. E. De Selincourt, *The Later Years, 1821-1853*, revised Alan G. Hill. 4 vols (Oxford: Clarendon Press, 1978-88)
Marrs	*The Letters of Charles and Mary Lamb*, ed. Edwin J Marrs, Jr (Ithaca and London: Cornell University Press, 1975)
McGann	Jerome J. McGann, *The Romantic Ideology: A Critical Investigation* (Chicago: University of Chicago Press, 1983)
MM	*Monthly Magazine*
MY	*The Letters of William and Dorothy Wordsworth*, ed. E. De Selincourt, *The Middle Years, 1806-11*, revised Mary Moorman (Oxford: Clarendon Press, 1969); *The Middle Years*, 1812-1820, revised Mary Moorman and Alan G. Hill (Oxford: Clarendon, 1970)
NLRS	*New Letters of Robert Southey*, ed. Kenneth Curry, 2 vols (New York and London: Columbia University Press, 1965)

PJK	*The Poems of John Keats*, ed. Jack Stillinger (Cambridge, Mass: The Belknap Press of Harvard University Press, 1978)
Prelude	*The Prelude: 1799, 1805, 1850*, ed. Jonathan Wordsworth, M. H. Abrams and Stephen Gill (New York: W.W. Norton and Co, 1979)
PWC	*The Poems of William Cowper*, ed. John D. Baird and Charles Ryskamp. 3 vols (Oxford: Clarendon Press, 1980-95)
Rochester MS	Robert Southey, 'Joan of Arc'. Department of Rare Books, University of Rochester Library, MS AS727
SCPB	*Southey's Common-Place Books,* ed. J. W. Warter. 4 vols (London: Longman, Brown, Green and Longmans, 1849-50)
SiR	*Studies in Romanticism*
SLRS	*Selections from the Letters of Robert Southey*, ed. J. W.Warter. 4 vols (London: Longman, Brown, Green and Longmans, 1856)
SLSP	Robert Southey, *Letters Written During a Short Residence in Spain and Portugal* (Bristol: Biggs and Cottle, 1797)
SPP	*Shelley's Poetry and Prose*, ed. Donald H. Reiman and Sharon B. Powers (New York: W.W. Norton, 1977)
TLS	*The Times Literary Supplement*
TT	S. T. Coleridge, *Table Talk*, ed. Carl Woodring, 2 vols (London and Princeton: Routledge andPrinceton University Press, 1990). CC, XIV
WPW	*The Poetical Works of William Wordsworth*, ed. E. De Selincourt and Helen Darbishire. 5 vols (Oxford: Oxford University Press, 1940-49)
WW	*William Wordsworth*, ed. Stephen Gill (Oxford: OxfordUniversity Press, 1984)

The Nineteenth Century Series
General Editors' Preface

The aim of the series is to reflect, develop and extend the great burgeoning of interest in the nineteenth century that has been an inevitable feature of recent years, as that former epoch has come more sharply into focus as a locus for our understanding not only of the past but of the contours of our modernity. It centres primarily upon major authors and subjects within Romantic and Victorian literature. It also includes studies of other British writers and issues, where these are matters of current debate: for example, biography and autobiography, journalism, periodical literature, travel writing, book production, gender, non-canonical writing. We are dedicated principally to publishing original monographs and symposia; our policy is to embrace a broad scope in chronology, approach and range of concern, and both to recognize and cut innovatively across such parameters as those suggested by the designations "Romantic" and "Victorian." We welcome new ideas and theories, while valuing traditional scholarship. It is hoped that the world which predates yet so forcibly predicts and engages our own will emerge in parts, in the wider sweep, and in the lively streams of disputation and change that are so manifest an aspect of its intellectual, artistic and social landscape.

Vincent Newey
Joanne Shattock

University of Leicester

1 Placing and Displacing Romanticism

PETER J. KITSON

The essays collected in this volume interpret the critical issues of 'place' and 'displacement', 'placing' and 'displacing' in their figurative and their literal senses, responding to these key terms in contemporary criticism with imagination and subtlety. Romanticism, of course, has always been heavily concerned with the literal sense of 'place'. Often described as an anti-metropolitan and anti-urban phenomenon, British Romanticism has variously been placed in the West Country, the Lake District, North Wales, the Wye Valley and Scotland. Romantic period writing also shows a concern with 'place' in an antithetical sense, imaging the city as an artificial and corrupting phenomenon. Suitably, therefore, a number of essays in this volume approach Romantic period writing's concern with the sense of 'place' and its relevance to other literary, political and historical concerns.

'Placing' Romanticism is, however, also a vexed issue, impinging upon debates about taxonomies and issues of canon-formation. Whether Romanticism should be placed within extra-literary contexts, such as those of the political and social, or of other art forms, such as that of visual art, is a theme that recurs within the pages of this volume. So does the constitution of the Romantic canon itself for although Wordsworth, Blake, Coleridge and Keats figure large, other writers and contexts also appear. Notably, Robert Southey features in several of the essays as a figure inhabiting a space which is not canonical, yet neither is it merely contextual. His works are often outside the aesthetic scope of what we have come to define as Romantic, concerned with the prosaic, the quotidian, and seldom with the transcendent, even in his most heroic writings.

The case of Southey serves to remind us that 'Romanticism' is a critical construct, a term not used by the artists and critics of the period 1790 to 1830 in the specialized sense of signifying an adherence to certain aesthetic ideas and concerns, or 'symptoms', in the formulation of René Wellek.[1] We are also conversant with the ways in which Romantic poets were 'canonised' by their devoted adherents in the nineteenth century. Mary Shelley edited and promoted her husband's work, James Henry Leigh Hunt marketed Keats for a Victorian audience, stressing elements of his verse, such as passion and sincerity, which influenced the reception of the poet's work for many years. William Michael Rossetti and Algernon Swinburne rediscovered a much aestheticized William Blake in the latter part of the nineteenth century, and John Stuart Mill and Matthew Arnold established the reputation of William Wordsworth as a poet concerned with human suffering and the therapeutic values of feeling and reflection. The role of anthologies such as the popular F. T. Palgrave's *Golden Treasury* (1861-88) in establishing a the Romantic canon was important.[2] What is not so often pointed out, however, is the Romantics' own concern with their posthumous reputation and their interest in canon formation. Coleridge's *Biographia Literaria* (1817) attempted to establish Wordsworth's true strength and significance as a poet, as well as the reputation of the poems that he should be most revered for. Vindicating Wordsworth's 'best' poetry also sustained Coleridge's genius as a critic, and affirmed the value of his own poetic theories for futurity. Shelley's 'Adonais' served as a vehicle to vindicate the poetry of John Keats for posterity, constructing a canon of great poets 'the splendours of the firmament of time' who climb 'like stars to their appointed height' (lines 389-91: *SPP*, pp. 403). The poet of 'Adonais' himself takes his place among these splendours. Andrew Bennett has recently shown how Keats's poetry is saturated with its own sense of audience and posthumous reputation.[3] Romantic writers, as Bennett indicates, were influenced by a 'cult of posterity' that held that a great poet should write for an audience of the future, an audience that would fully appreciate the poet's work as the debased contemporary audience could not. Wordsworth famously made this appeal in his 'Essay Supplementary to the Preface' of 1815 where he wrote of a great author '*creating* the taste by which he is to be enjoyed' (*WW*, p. 657-8). Lucy Newlyn's essay in this volume examines in more detail the anxieties that haunt Wordsworth's construction of this audience.

'Place' and 'displacement' have long been important terms in post-colonial theory occupying a more central and crucial space than they have in Romantic studies. It has been argued that the post-colonial crisis of identity and the interest in developing or recovering a sense of identity between self and place is especially relevant to societies marked by a material and psychological processes of dislocation. Yet the dialogue of place and displacement is also a feature of Romantic period writing, which has been often regarded as a response to the great historical movements of urbanization and industrialization that marked late eighteenth- and nineteenth-century British life. One thinks of Wordsworth's 'Poems on the naming of Places' and 'Tintern Abbey' as well as the many other Romantic poems which feature specific topographies and buildings. One also thinks of Byron's representations of exile in poems such as *Childe Harold's*

Pilgrimage Canto III and the drama *Manfred* (1817) where the physical displacement of the poet from his homeland contributes to the existential angst suffered by the poems' heroes amidst the violent, sublime, alpine landscapes in which the poems are set. By and large the wish to recapture a sense of identity with a rediscovered or revisited place, in Wordsworth at least, indicates a wish to establish the unity in continuity of the self over time and through memory, a process that Geoffrey Hartman and Paul De Man have famously ironized. More recently, as the Romantic canon has opened up, we confront more often the literal fact of dislocation. This resulted from migration and the experience of enslavement in the writings of those such as the ex-slave Olaudah Equiano whose *Interesting Narrative* (1789), for instance, is now commonly taught on Romantic literature courses.[4] It is to be expected that other voices from the margins of the period will feature more prominently in future discussions of Romanticism.

'Displacement' as alienation brings us to the most significant usage of the term in Romantic criticism from the 1980s to the present. A number of critics have focused on the phenomena of Romantic alienation, a concern obviously expressed in the number of solitary wanderers found in Romantic poetry; in the Romantic concern for the journey as a unifying theme which M. H. Abrams found so suggestive; and in the Romantic and Gothic concern with the divided self and the psychologically aberrant.[5] Marxist critics, such as Raymond Williams, suggested that this concern with the self and its disunity, along with the stress on the creative act and imagination, were protests against the materialism of the times.[6] More recent critics, also informed by Marxist thought, have been less generous to Romanticism's preoccupation with the aesthetic realm than Williams. They generally use the term 'displacement' in a manner closer to its origins in Freudian thought than to the Marxist notion of alienation. Freud hypothesised that in dreams there is a dislocation between the dream thoughts and the dream content, whereby the dream-content is torn from its context and transformed into something alien. This process is one by which the unconscious produces a distorted form of the dream-wish filtering out the elements of the dream-wish that are unacceptable to the psyche.[7] 'Displacement' is thus an unconscious mechanism of repression by which anxieties resulting from desires that cannot be admitted are sublimated into acceptable dream-thoughts, marked only by their uncanny intensity. This is a matter of psychic defence rather than of bad faith or false consciousness; nevertheless, in a social context it could indicate both, as anxieties relating to class and gender are displaced into the realm of the aesthetic. Williams, following Adorno, found something like this in the construction of an aesthetic realm untroubled by consciousness of social pressures: 'while the immediate evidence is direct, the plausibility of the relation depends not only on a formal analysis of the historical social process but on the consequent deduction of a displacement or even an absence'.[8] This is akin to Lucien Goldmann's structural notion of the 'homologies' which exist between class situations, world views, and artistic forms. This notion that literature presents displaced anxieties and fears in the form of popular narratives has become a staple of recent criticism of the Gothic novel. As Franco Moretti puts it, 'Marxism and psychoanalysis thus converge in defining the function of this literature: to take up within itself determinate fears in order to present them *in a form different from their real one*: to transform them into *other* fears, so that readers do not have to face up to what might really frighten them'.[9] As even a cursory reading of recent criticism of Bram Stoker's *Dracula* (1897) demonstrates this notion of displacement is accepted as a truism, as the fifteenth-century Wallachian noble becomes a figure of polyvalent excess, standing for a variety of contemporary fears relating to Stoker's own position as a Anglo-Irish male writing at the height of the British Empire.[10]

Although Raymond Williams was keen to avoid the reductionism associated with the notion of displacement, stressing instead the complexity of the creative act as itself constitutive, others have been less forgiving. The defining moment for the theory of displacement in Romantic studies was the publication, in 1983, of Jerome J. McGann's *The Romantic Ideology*. McGann argued that 'the scholarship and criticism of Romanticism and its works are dominated by a Romantic Ideology, by an uncritical absorption in Romanticism's own self-representations'. McGann argued that the 'poetry of Romanticism is everywhere marked by extreme forms of displacement and poetic conceptualization whereby the actual human issues with which the poetry is concerned are resituated in a variety of idealized localities' (*McGann*, p. 1). McGann's conception of ideology is close, in this usage, to that of the Marx of *The German Ideology* (1845), in that he postulates a 'false consciousness' or act of bad faith, by presenting an idealistic image of an organic society and a progressive history which serves the interests of the ruling class and helps to maintain the status quo:

> Out of these assumptions emerges that familiar argument of Romantic and Romantic-influenced works: that poetry, and art, in general, has no essential relation to partisan, didactic, or doctrinal matters. Poetry transcends these things. The field of history, politics, and social relations is everywhere marked in the Romantic period by complex divisions and conflicts previously unprecedented in Europe. Romantic poetry develops an argument that such dislocations can only be resolved beyond the realm of immediate experience, at the level of the mind's idea or the heart's desire. The Romantic position – it

is an historically limited and determinate one – is that the poet operates at such levels of reality, and hence that poetry by its nature can transcend the conflicts and transciences of this time and that place (*McGann*, p. 69).

The notion that the Romantic ideology displaces the historical, social and political tensions of the time into an ideal realm of imagination, or nature is one that has encouraged an extensive debate in Romantic studies and has been catalyst to the production of a substantial number of books and articles. Paul Sheats's essay in this volume is a direct response, from a formalist perspective, to McGann's analysis of Wordsworth's 'The Ruined Cottage', for McGann 'an exemplary case of what commentators mean when they speak of the "displacement" that occurs in a Romantic poem' (*McGann*, p. 84).

Generally associated with McGann in what became known as the 'new historicist' school of Romantic studies are the names of David Simpson, Marjorie Levinson, Marilyn Butler and Alan Liu. David Simpson's *Wordsworth's Historical Imagination: The Poetry of Displacement* (1987) argued that as 'the Wordsworthian Imagination is social, and defined even in its isolation by relation to others, so it is also historical, defined in relation to particular others and at specific moments'.[11] Simpson argued that the political and sociological themes in Wordsworth's writing actually constitute 'a major strategy, one that holds together a number of otherwise disconnected gestures'. The strategy must, however, be looked for not in its explicit manifestations but 'traced in the forms of its displacement, as much in its radical incoherence as in its life within the tidy language of propositional argument'.[12] Simpson's use of the term borrows something from its Freudian antecedents as the Wordsworth he deals with is a fractured and ambiguous subject haunted by anxieties concerning poetry, property and labour, yet it is closest to the Marxist formulations:

> Wordsworth is thus the poet of displacement or alienation in the same sense that Blake's poems are *of* innocence or *of* experience. That is to say his poems expound and occupy a range of positions pertaining *to* alienation. It may be imaged critically, or reproduced passively, whether in the self or in others; and, in the case of a dramatic speaker, the self may be presented as an other. But whatever point on the spectrum the poem seems to occupy, the element of *pertaining to* is preserved. Even visionary epiphany experienced as a desired extinction of the social self, is given life and thought by what it replaces and what it returns to.[13]

Simpson's conception of displacement is informed by Louis Althusser's notions of ideology and Pierre Macherey's theories of literary production, whereby the task of materialist analysis is to study literary works 'not from the standpoint of their unity which is illusory and false' but with an eye for 'signs of contradictions (historically determined) which produced them and which appear as unevenly resolved conflicts in the text'.[14] Consciously invoking Freud's strategy for interpreting the dream-text, Macherey argued that it was the function of a scientific criticism to expose the operations of condensation, contradiction and displacement in literary texts through which the artefact is produced. Simpson's strategy is akin to that of McGann, although he argues convincingly that McGann presents us with a more assured and successful Romantic displacement of the world than was really ever achieved, replacing one totalizing and unifying model with another. In an extended discussion of Wordsworth's 'Gipsies' from *Poems, in Two Volumes* (1807) Simpson traces a host of displaced anxieties resulting from Wordsworth's position as a poet, exempt from labour due to his dependency on the Calvert legacy and the patronage of Sir George Beaumont, explaining the poet's hostility to the gypsies of the poem by his own insecurities. For Simpson, Wordsworth's bourgeois criticism of the gypsies for their idleness is countered by the peasant poet John Clare's more sympathetic treatment in a series of poems. Philip Martin's essay in this volume itself takes issue with Simpson's strategy of placing Clare at the margins in an effort to unmask the social blind spots of the canonical poet Wordsworth, and Tim Fulford's essay examines Simpson's idea of the 'displacement', of the political and social in Wordsworth, whose landscape poem 'The Haunted Tree' he finds to be replete with social and political meanings rather than with absences or denials.

Most troubling to many critics of the new historicist school is the concern with the decorum of the connections made between the poems and a series of contexts themselves absent from the poem. Perhaps the critic most associated with this kind of writing in Romantic circles is Majorie Levinson. Levinson has explored what she sees as absences, gaps and *aporias* in the Romantic text. Her *Wordsworth's great period poems* (1986) re-read four of the poet's most admired poems against the grain of their critical history, finding them to be poems of negation rather than of affirmation. Levinson regarded the poems as 'negative allegory', works which speak 'of one thing' because they 'cannot articulate another', presenting 'a sort of allegory by absence, where the signified is indicated by an identifiably absented signifier'. The function of the critic is thus to restore 'the contours of that repressed material'.[15] Notoriously, Levinson argued that Wordsworth's 'Tintern Abbey' repressed the industrial details of the topography of the Wye Valley, effacing the signs of economic dislocation and distress occasioned by the industrial process and the Revolutionary Wars, as well as the public significance of the dates 1793 and 1798 which Wordsworth subsumed into a purely autobiographical context.

The most thorough and sustained criticism of this kind was Alan Liu's *Wordsworth: The Sense of History* (1989) which argued that Wordsworth's work constituted a denial of history. Liu expressed the wish to go beyond the studies of literary displacement in McGann, Simpson, and Levinson. In a formulation that, once again, drew on Macherey's theories of literary production and its silences, Liu claimed that,

> the literary text is not just the displacement but the overdetermined and agonic *denial* of historical reference. Like the negations that fracture and so impose interpretive structure over historical context, the differentiating denials that compose literature are arbitrary; but they are also positively determined – indeed, overdetermined – in the substantive senses of the term: they are all material because they participate in the principle of structure creating the positivity of all context; they subsume the traditional notions of causation and reference; and they are limited by their historical context to place, time, and manifestation.[16]

For Liu, Wordsworth's poetry represents denial and he argues that what is required to uncover the objects of such denial is not the positivism of 'old' historicism but 'a deflected or denied positivism able to discriminate absence'.[17] As an exemplar of his critical practice he begins *Wordsworth: The Sense of History* with an analysis of the Simplon passage sections of Book VI of *The Prelude* which sifts the layers of textual meanings in the poetry in order to locate the denied historical referent, in this case the material historical presence of Napoleon's political and military progress. Although for Liu, history in itself is constructed from a fugitive and unreliable set of traces, there are nevertheless degrees of certainty that may be posited in establishing this concept. Liu argues that the 'description of the 1790 tour in Book VI, read in its own context, is a sustained effort to deny history by asserting nature as the separating mark constitutive of the egotistical self'. Nature is a as mirror which reflects the self's image, preventing it from looking through it to the underlying history.[18] The apostrophe to imagination, arising 'like an unfather'd vapour' to usurp the world of sense (*Prelude* 6.525-48) thus becomes a deflected reference to the 'usurper' Bonaparte, whose political and military imagination allowed his republican troops to cross the Alps on his progress to the battle of Marengo in 1800. Liu argues that 'in the context of 1804, any imagination of an Alpine pass would remember the military "genius" of Bonaparte'.[19]

It is not the purpose of the present Introduction to survey the extensive debates occasioned by new historicists' arguments for a criticism informed by notions of displacement, alienation, absence and denial. But it is clear that the essays collected in this volume are all, in one sense or another, *after* new historicism, informed by that critical moment of the 1980s, even when they are most resistant to it. Paul D. Sheats's 'Cultivating Margaret's Garden: Wordsworthian "Nature" and the Quest for Historical "Difference"', which begins this collection, takes on the central problem raised in new historicist criticism, that is, the recognition or construction of historical difference. The historical field is flattened so that historian can recognize the difference of past and present only with difficulty and, indeed, new historicists have argued that the sense of difference is only a reading back into the past of the concerns of the academy.[20] Sheats takes issue with McGann's notion that the loss of 'difference' is occasioned by the modern critic's assimilation of the 'Romantic Ideology' itself and his attempt to restore a 'differential' that prevents the uncritical repetition of the past. Sheats, taking McGann's reading of 'The Ruined Cottage' as a case in point, argues that the new historicist fetishism of 'difference' constitutes itself a privileging of the term which affects the reconstruction of the historical object. Sheats criticizes McGann for deducing 'from a single textual feature, a pattern of "displacement"' not only 'Wordsworth's view of nature, but also a history of his political opinions' (below, p. 21). Behind this is the assumption that any movement from the economic, social and particular to the pastoral and domestic, is *de facto* an act of apostasy which all will recognize as such. All turns from economic and social realities are therefore to be characterized as 'evasions'. McGann thus excludes from consideration Wordsworth's other poetry and his many letters, essays and other documents that indicate his humanitarian, social and political concerns in the period of the composition of 'The Ruined Cottage'. McGann's method is to define by exclusion. Sheats, instead, in a sensitive and careful close-reading of the poem, draws our attention to the ways in which Wordsworth's natural detail functions not as a transcendental sublimation but, rather, as a register of 'precise sympathetic inference', mapping both human and natural processes. McGann is thus blind to the synecdochic power of the Wordsworthian imagination where the domestic and intimate can also indicate the social. Rather than an example of 'false consciousness' Wordsworth's nature serves as a critique of an arrogant and abstract rationalism in a similar manner to Marx's 1845 critique of an abstract and totalizing 'German Ideology' which informs McGann's own critical praxis.

In a similar manner Tim Fulford's 'Wordsworth's "The Haunted Tree" and the Sexual Politics of Landscape' takes a less familiar Wordsworth poem and demonstates how political referents are not evaded or displaced but are, instead, present in the poem as meanings available for a contemporary reader. Wordsworth's poem thus constitutes an oblique contribution to the social and political debates of Regency Britain. Fulford is responding to Simpson's notion of 'displacement' whereby the social and political is not absent or evaded but present in a controlled form. As Fulford points out, in the nineteenth century the politics of landscape were also parliamentary politics and cannot thus be seen as a displacement of the political. To write about landscape was, in part, a political activity and images of the landscape were extremely familiar elements in political rhetoric. Fulford concentrates on the iconography of trees in political discourse.[21] In doing so he reconstructs a political context for 'The Haunted Tree' not immediately obvious to contemporary readers, finding in an oblique intervention in the poem against the Orientalist fashions of Regency Britain and the poetic, political and moral corruption Wordsworth believed it to signify. Employing the kind of close-reading sensitive to poetic form and language, also found in Sheats, Fulford argues that the poem is a part of an eighteenth-century tradition of political discourse, whereby the politics of nature was not an evasion of national politics but one of its essential components.

Philip Martin's 'John Clare's Gypsies: Problems of Placement and Displacement in Romantic Critical Practice' similarly adopts Simpson's notion of 'displacement' as a starting point but shifts its focus from Wordsworth to Clare. Simpson uses Clare, almost formulaically, to unmask Wordsworthian blind social spots. Martin is sympathetic to Simpson's critical method. However he points to the effects that such a method of criticism has, which centres the poet who does not see (Wordsworth) by marginalizing the poet who does see (Clare). This 'placing' of Clare at the margins of Romantic poetry is not simply a new historicist trait, but one shared with the major trends of Romantic Criticism. Most recent critics have tended to 'place' Clare in terms of class relations, validating his authenticity in representing agrarian experience. Martin, in a complex and sophisticated close-reading of Clare's gypsy poems, locates this authenticity as a textual effect of Clare's subject-positioning within the poems, both belonging and not belonging to the gypsy world.

In another Wordsworthian essay, Lucy Newlyn's 'How Wordsworth Keeps his Audience Fit', Wordsworth's own anxieties about the publication of his work and how these impinge on the general issue of the changing relations between author and reader in the Romantic period become central. Although work has been done on the material process of the production and consumption of literary text and Romantic conceptions of the reader, Newlyn argues that the rise of criticism and the consequences of expanding literacy meant that the burden of the future itself actually weighed much more heavily than the pressures of the past. Romantic writers thus experienced less of a Bloomian anxiety of influence resulting from the agonistic struggle with strong precursor poets but rather struggled with what Newlyn terms an 'anxiety of reception' whereby the poet, alarmed at the empowerment of critics, attempts to circumscribe the power that a future reader may have over his work. This is demonstrated in Wordsworth's notion that the great artist will '*create* the taste by which he is to be enjoyed' (*WW*, pp. 657-8). Wordsworth's poetry and its accompanying prefaces thus contain within them a strategy for constituting the model of an ideal reader.

The concern with the with the loco-descriptive subject positioning of the Romantic period writer, which featured in Philip Martin's essay, is taken up again in Michael Scrivener's 'Jacobin Romanticism: John Thelwall's "Wye" Essay and "Pedestrian Excursion" (1797-1801)' which places the literary essays of the radical poet and lecturer at the centre of Romantic period concerns. Scrivener, like many of the other contributors to this volume, does not see the turn to Romantic or picturesque nature writing as an evasion, denial or displacement of the political, but rather shows how this apparent retreat is marked everywhere by political hope and anxiety. The landscape that Thelwall constructs is primarily used as a site for sociological, cultural, and political reflection. By taking Thelwall's essays seriously Scrivener expands the canon of Romantic writing, enriching the social and political meanings contained within the notion of Romantic nature. Allowing Thelwall into the Romantic conversation about nature and politics provides another model contrasting with the paradigmatic disillusionment syndrome of Abrams's 'natural supernaturalism', and the equally paradigmatic new historicist sublimation of radical politics into imagination. Scrivener carefully places Thelwall as an Enlightenment rationalist, opposing both the traditions of popular and aristocratic cultures in the name of a universalizing Reason. The blindness resulting from this positioning is fortunate and constitutes the very distinctiveness that makes Thelwall's writing worthy of analysis; 'Letting Thelwall into the canon does not displace Wordsworth and Coleridge but expands and complicates the overall literary conversation' (below, p. 84).

Also concerned with the issue of 'placing' in the canonical sense is Lynda Pratt's 'Patriot Poetics and the Romantic National Epic: Placing and Displacing Southey's *Joan of Arc*' which provides a detailed and scholarly textual analysis of the several versions of Southey's *Joan of Arc* and speculates on its proper place both with in the Romantic canon and within the period sub-genre of the national epic. *Joan of Arc* usually figures at the margins of canonical Romantic writing, consulted only for a few hundred lines composed by Coleridge and then cut to make his 'Visions of the Maid of Orleans'. Pratt takes Southey's work and re-situates in its proper context, the history of the national epic in the 1790s. In so doing she claims that Southey was attempting to write a new and radical type of national epic, an epic which displaced national concerns from England to France. Re-situating Southey's *Joan* into the context of the national epics obliges us to look again at how our concern with Romantic aesthetics has distorted our understanding of the actual literary communities and how they functioned.

Philip Shaw's 'Re-placing Waterloo: Southey's Vision of Command' also deals with Southey's ideas about the national epic and features the poet's verse romance, *The Poet's Pilgrimage to Waterloo*. Shaw's discussion picks up a number of the central issues posed by the essays in this collection. The 'place' here is that of the Battle of Waterloo, or in Southey's preferred nomenclature, *Belle Alliance* (also Blucher's preference). The prospect of the Battle becomes a contested site between the Wellington who fought it, and the writers and travellers who visited it and commented upon its meanings. Southey's dispute with Wellington as to the name and meaning of the battle touches on an important series of questions relating to property, authority and identity. His interest in contemporary events reflects his own desire to make himself a power in English culture, transforming a geo-political reality into an abstracted space of literature over which the Poet Laureate has command. Images of Waterloo were not just the preserve of the poet, however, the battle was consumed by the public in a variety of modes: narratives, guide books, maps, and panorama. By placing Southey's perspectives alongside those of the popular commercial panorama, Shaw demonstrates how both media attempt to control the viewing subject's vistas, framing them within a politics of deference neither can command.

Michael Charlesworth's 'Subverting the Command of Place: Panorama and the Romantics' also deals with the visual dynamics of perspective in the Romantic period, a period which coincides with the sustained colonial and imperial development of British power. For Charlesworth, the loss of control over the panoramic view is the necessary precondition for a subversive view of empire, and it is the subversive view, which is closer to that of the Romantic. Charlesworth points out how panoramic representation was closely connected with military surveillance, functioning as a form of intelligence gathering. As the Hanoverian dynasty's possessions extended over the world, the commercial panorama became the chief means of their symbolic consumption by the populace. The point of view depicted by the panorama, as Shaw demonstrated, was, of course, that of the ruler, encouraging a sense of identity between viewer and political authority and excluding an identification with the marginalized and subjugated. Charlesworth finds in certain Romantic period texts, both visual and literary, challenges to the panoramic perspective of power. It is in the vertical, as opposed to the panoramic horizontal, dimension that Romanticism developed its enabling space for the imagination.

The misrepresentation that can occur when we extract Romantic ideas from the literary contexts in which they functioned is the subject of John Williams's 'Displacing Romanticism: Anna Seward, Joseph Weston, and the Unschooled Sons of Genius'. Williams takes issue with the still-familiar view that Wordsworth's and Coleridge's *Lyrical Ballads* of 1798 constituted a radical departure from other late eighteenth-century literary activity. He locates the contemporary debates relating to *Lyrical Ballads* within earlier literary controversies, in particular, the forgotten controversy between Joseph Weston and Anna Seward, that took place in the pages of the *Gentleman's Magazine* in 1789, over the relative merits of Dryden and Pope as classicists. By setting the debate over the *Ballads* within this template, we are left with a much more problematic view of opposing literary communities in which Wordsworth can appear as reactionary rather than progressive, displaced by the onset of modernity and saved for radicalism only by the French Revolution and its valorization of simplicity and the common.

John Keats's resistance to social and political readings is the subject of two essays in this collection. Michael O'Neill's 'Keats and the "Poetical Character"' questions how congenial Keats, the poet of 'Negative Capability', is to recent criticism of this kind. O'Neill argues that the application of historical and theoretical perspectives to Keats's poetry has resulted in both gain and loss. A sense of Keats's ambivalent engagements with history is gained at the risk of losing or denying the aesthetic power of the poetry. Marjorie Levinson recently argued that Keats's characteristically sensuous and luxurious style was a response to his social position as aspirant to the middle class. His poetry is thus the aesthetic solution to an ideological problem.[22] O'Neill instead champions a criticism sensitive to Keats's own ironic and ambivalent response to the 'aesthetic'. O'Neill shows how Keats's poetic sensibility is less concerned with an aspirant stylistic bravado than with a subtle and playful attempt to work with aesthetic contradictions. In a series of sensitive close-readings of Keats's writing, O'Neill shows how the poetry is self-conscious and aware of its own processes. This concern with the aesthetic and the formal is also present in Thomas McFarland's 'Masking in Keats', which focuses on issues of creativity and creation. 'Masking' for McFarland is a creative activity by which the artist transmutes his old self into a new being. McFarland sees in Keats's work the playing of two masks, the Mask of Hellas and the Mask of Camelot: the Hellenic and the medieval. Keats's art was so congenial to this strategy of masking because the poet was able to obliterate his subjective self, a thing that Wordsworth was never able to do successfully. In this powerful and sensitive piece, McFarland pleads for a criticism that is empathetic with its subject, that becomes an advocate for the brave and tragic poet, not the abstract and distant critique of a subject embroiled in social and psychic double binds of new historicist writing.

The notion of place as location and as utterance is the subject of Angela Esterhammer's 'Locationary Acts: Blake's *Jersusalem* and Holderlin's *Patmos*' which discusses two Romantic texts that create 'place' through the performative usages of language. In Blake and Holderlin language, or utterance, creates place. The archetype of the creative speech act is, of course, God's creation of the world through utterance, an act which foreshadows the Romantic concern with performative utterance. Taking Blake and Holderlin as cases, Esterhammer shows how the poets' imagined places, Jerusalem and Patmos, occupy spaces between the seer and the vision and between the speaker and the audience. For Esterhammer, the Romantic poet does not, God-like, create a world through an authoritative utterance but, rather, creates a relationship between the self and the world through discursive utterance.

Mary Anne Perkins's 'The Romantics: Cosmopolitan or Nationalist' deals with the place of nationalism in Romantic thought and the placing of Romantic philosophy itself. Like Esterhammer, her focus is comparative, as she views Romanticism as a European phenomenon rather than one localized to particular cultures. She confronts the issue of Romanticism's alleged prefiguring of twentieth-century nationalist ideologies, problematizing such notions by returning our gaze to the contemporary ideas themselves. Tracking the idea of nation through the writings of Luther, Herder, Coleridge and Fichte, Perkins shows how the concept of nationhood became identified with truth and essence. The Romantic linking of linguistic development with national moral character that we see in Herder, Fichte and Coleridge is clearly in evidence, nevertheless, Perkins counsels that we should also be prepared to appreciate the Romantic concern with distinction in unity. The Romantic concern with particularity and uniqueness should not thus automatically be associated with chauvinism and exclusivity. The work of Herder, William von Humboldt and Schleiermacher struggles to reconcile ideas of nationhood with a belief in a universal cosmopolitan ideal. A criticism which ignores the cosmopolitan and humanitarian ideals of many of the nationalist writers is flawed. Nevertheless, Perkins is sensitive to the dangerous tendencies within their writings which claim a cultural, moral and intellectual superiority. Perkins's essay pleas for the necessity of a self-critical examination of the history of nationhood, one which recognizes how this idea has shaped our own consciousness and experience.

Finally my own 'Romantic Displacements: Representing Cannibalism' explores the notions of place and displacement in Romantic period writing about cannibalism. The essay attempts to show how, in a period of sustained colonial expansion, allegations of cannibalism were used to create a distinction between the central imperial self and the marginalized colonial subject, a distinction that was possible only when earlier early modern and Enlightenment views of cannibalism were displaced by a notion of human difference based on race and degeneration. The developing notion that cannibalism was a sign of moral and physical degeneration gained currency in the early nineteenth century, gradually displacing the Enlightenment explanation of scarcity and need. Ironically the European fascination with, and demonization of, cannibalism, was coincident with a developed domestic discourse on the subject in gothic narratives and shipwreck narratives. Ultimately the West displaced its own fears and anxieties about the practice onto other races as a strategy for conquest, as well as a mechanism for defence. The essay looks at a series of Romantic period utterances on the subject and attempts to place them within the debates between Enlightenment and Romantic views of difference.

Overall the essays in this volume take forward the issues of place and displacement raised in recent critical writing about Romanticism. They show a desire to return to the complexity of the texts and the contexts in which they were written. They argue that Romantic texts are, themselves, self conscious and self-reflexive, often pre-empting later critical stances. These texts and contexts are revisited with fresh insights, demonstrating that, despite claims of evasion, Romantic texts are replete with explicit and implicit contributions to the political and social debates of their time. Combining the virtues of a new critical close analysis with an awareness of political and social meanings, the essays in this volume encourage a fresh critical stance of engaged formalist writing. Although in some sense *after* the moment of new historicism, they show, to some extent, how that moment has deeply influenced Romantic criticism and encouraged a host of exciting and engaged responses to its tenets.

Notes

1   René Wellek, 'The Concept of Romanticism in Literary History', in *Concepts of Criticism* (New Haven: Yale University Press, 1963). See also A. O. Lovejoy 'On the Discriminations of Romanticisms', in *English Romantic Poets*, ed. M. H. Abrams (New York and London; Oxford University Press, 1960: second edition, 1975), p. 3-12; David Perkins, 'The Construction of "The Romantic Movement" as a Literary Classification', *Nineteenth-Century Literature*, 45 (1990), pp. 130-9; David Simpson, 'Romanticism, Criticism and Theory', in *The Cambridge Companion to British*

Romanticism, ed. Stuart Curran (Cambridge: Cambridge University Press, 1993), pp. 1-24; Jerome J. McGann, 'Rethinking Romanticism', *ELH*, 59 (1992), pp. 735-54.

2   McGann, 'Rethinking Romanticism'.

3   Andrew Bennett, *Keats, Narrative and Audience: The Posthumous Life of Writing* (Cambridge: Cambridge University Press, 1994). See also his *Romantic Poets and the Culture of Posterity* (Cambridge: Cambridge University Press, 1999).

4   See Sukhdev Sandhu and David Dabydeen, ed. *Black Writers*. Vol. 1. *Slavery, Abolition and Emancipation: Writings in the British Romantic Period*, ed. Peter J. Kitson and Debbie Lee (Pickering and Chatto, 1999); Alan Richardson and Sonia Hofkosh, ed. *Romanticism, Race, and Imperial Culture, 1780-1834* (Bloomington; Indiana University Press, 1996); Tim Fulford and Peter J. Kitson, ed. *Romamticism and Colonialism* (Cambridge; Cambridge University Press, 1998); Alan Bewell, *Romanticism and Colonial Disease* (Baltimore and London: John Hopkins University Press, 1999).

5   M. H. Abrams, *Natural Supernaturalism: Tradition and Revolution in Romantic Literature* (New York: Oxford University Press, 1971).

6   Raymond Williams, *Marxism and Literature* (1977); *Culture and Society, 1780-1950* (London: Chatto and Windus, 1958); *The Country and the City* (London: Chatto and Windus, 1973).

7   Sigmund Freud, *The Interpretation of Dreams* (London: George Allen and Unwin, 1913 [1951]), pp. 294-96.

8   Williams, *Marxism and Literature*, p. 104.

9   Franco Moretti, *Signs Taken for Wonders: Essays in the Sociology of Literary Forms*, trans. Susan Fischer, David Forgacs and David Miller (London and New York: Verso, 1983), p. 105.

10   The most sustained and detailed reading of this kind is David Glover's *Bram Stoker and the Politics of Popular Fiction* (Durham and London: Duke University Press, 1996). For a recent collection demonstrating this point see Glenis Byron, *Dracula* (Basingstoke: Macmillan, 1999).

11   David Simpson, *Wordsworth's Historical Imagination: The Poetry of Displacement* (London: Methuen, 1987), pp. 1-2.

12   Simpson, *Wordsworth's Historical Imagination*, p. 3.

13   Simpson, *Wordsworth's Historical Imagination*, p. 8.

14   Etienne Balibar and Pierre Macherey, 'On Literature as an Ideological Form' (1974), in *Marxist Literary Theory*, ed. Terry Eagleton and Drew Milne (London; Blackwell, 1996), pp. 275-95 (p. 283). Pierre Macherey, *A Theory of Literary Production*, trans. Geoffrey Wall (London: Routledge and Kegan Paul, 1978).

15   Marjorie Levinson, *Wordsworth's great period poems* (Cambridge: Cambridge University Press, 1986), pp. 8-11.

16   Alan Liu, *Wordsworth: The Sense of History* (Stanford: Stanford University Press, 1989), p. 47.

17   Liu, *Wordsworth*, p. 24.

18   Liu, *Wordsworth*, p. 13, 45.

19   Liu, *Wordsworth*, pp. 23-31.

20   See, for instance, David Simpson, 'Introduction; The Moment of Materialism' in *Subject to History: Ideology, Class, Gender*, ed. David Simpson (Ithaca and London: Cornell University Press, 1991), pp. 1-33 (pp. 16-18).

21   These ideas are more fully explored in Fulford's, *Coleridge's Figurative Language* (Cambridge: Cambridge University Press, 1991).

22   Marjorie Levinson, *Keats's Life of Allegory* (Oxford: Blackwell, 1988), pp.1-28.

2 Cultivating Margaret's Garden: Wordsworthian 'Nature' and the Quest for Historical 'Difference'

PAUL D. SHEATS

'When me they fly, I am the wings'
Ralph Waldo Emerson, 'Brahma'.

Although the 'new' literary history displays a keen sense of the precariousness of its own procedures, that sense itself is not new. In Wordsworth's *Prelude*, for example, we find a critique of historical method that offers a useful perspective on postmodern concerns with the legitimacy of literary history, in terms that do not seem unfamiliar today. In a famous extended simile that interrupts the retrospective narrative of Book Four, Wordsworth likens the historian to a passenger in a 'slow-moving boat' that floats on 'the surface of past time' (*Prelude* [1805], 4.248, 263). Looking down into this 'still water' he sees a confusing medley of images. Reflections of sunshine, hills, and 'his own image' mingle with refractions of what is truly 'there' beneath the surface, in past time. He is 'perplexed' because he cannot tell the difference,

> cannot part
> The shadow from the substance, rocks and sky,
> Mountains and clouds, from that which is indeed
> The region, and the things which there abide
> In their true dwelling (*Prelude*, 4.254-58).

The analogy extends to the temporal dimension the scepticism Wordsworth recalled in his note to the 'Immortality Ode', where what was lost in the 'abyss of idealism' was not Nature's imagery, which remained perfectly accessible, but the status of that imagery as external to the mind, its 'outness'. Here it is the 'pastness' of the object of knowledge that is in question, its existence ('substance') in a 'region' that is history. The

16

historian's problem is not that he cannot know the past, but that he lacks a reliable touchstone for historicity. To shift to a modern idiom, the historical field is flattened, and the historian can recognize and represent historical 'difference' only with difficulty. We should not exaggerate the Romantic speaker's perplexity: there is no trace here of the awesome and frightening loss exacted by the 'abyss' of the Ode.[1] Indeed, Wordsworth goes out of his way to exorcize anxiety from the scrutiny of the past, which he renders as a kind of pastoral aestheticism bent on descrying 'beauteous sights' (*Prelude*, 4.252). Methodological 'impediments', he concludes, merely make his 'task more sweet' (*Prelude*, 4.261), and he gets on with the story of the past.

Today such negative capability is hard to find. 'No issue', according to Clifford Siskin, 'is more central to today's Romanticists than clarifying their historical relation to their subject matter'.[2] Although metaphors vary widely, the flattening of the historical field that Wordsworth's passage exemplifies is widely recognized and variously explained, as, for example, a lingering formalism endemic to the new historicism, or, in Jon Klancher's phrase, as a 'transhistorical echo' of the political agenda of the present.[3] Or the loss of 'difference' is traced to the co-optation of modern critics by historical ideologies transmitted through works of art. Influentially applied to English Romanticism by Jerome McGann, this last diagnosis remains convincing to materialist critics, who seek like him to restore a 'differential' that will prevent the uncritical 'repetition' of the past.[4] And yet, as Siskin has shown of McGann, such attempts often seem to mime the Romanticism they seek to escape.[5] It is possible, for example, to see the postmodern concern with historical difference as itself a 'repetition' of the problem Wordsworth identifies in the passage above. Such repetitions, which depend partly on prior constructions of 'Romanticism', seem potentially endless, and, depending on the circumstances of a particular critical practice, it may be the quest for 'difference' that constitutes them. Like Emerson's Brahma, the Romantic past may be implicit in the present's attempts to disengage from it.

My hope here is that by looking briefly at a single case, an attempt to reconstruct a particular historical object, we might see more clearly what 'difference' actually means in practice, and to what extent the decision to privilege it determines the outcome of that reconstruction. As a heuristic 'object' I propose Wordsworth's conception of 'Nature', which over the past half-century has provided a sensitive index to the constitutive effects of *a priori* commitments. The particular case I propose to examine reconstructs that naturalism at an important moment in Wordsworth's early career: Jerome McGann's brief but exemplary reading, in the eighth chapter of *The Romantic Ideology*, of 'The Ruined Cottage'.

I

As the first of three poetic exhibits that in McGann's view describe Wordsworth's retreat into 'the Romantic Ideology', 'The Ruined Cottage' also provides a first test of a critical method designed to expose that Ideology, and to end the 'uncritical absorption' of modern criticism in 'Romanticism's own self-representations' (*McGann*, p. 1). The 'obligation' of this defensive protocol is 'to resist incorporation' by using the 'weapon' of 'analysis' (*McGann*, p.2), and it offers a striking example of a quest for 'difference' that is urgent and highly self-conscious. By 'isolating and historicizing the originary forms of thought, by placing an intellectual gulf between the present and the past' (*McGann*, p.13), it will reconstruct the 'distance', 'differences', or 'differential' (*McGann*, pp. 30, 2, 3), that has been abolished by the illusions of modern criticism. It will thus restore historical Romanticism as an authentic cognitive object, revealing the 'human face' of the past (*McGann*, p. 66), the 'concrete, human particulars' that have been obscured by modern criticism (*McGann*, p. 11).

This dramatic account of a 'critical' act of reading is inflected morally by McGann's passionate individualism, which defines 'ideology' as the imposition of collective power ('a coherent or loosely organized set of ideas which is the expression of the special interests of some class or social group' [*McGann*, p. 5]), and consistently affirms the unique, specific, and particular against collectives of all kinds. 'Specificity' in McGann's usage often seems synonymous with 'difference': works of art can speak across time 'to alien cultures because they are so completely true to themselves, because they are time and place specific, because they are – from our point of view – *different*' (*McGann*, p. 2: emphasis McGann's). At the same time, as Frances Ferguson has shown, he concedes immense constitutive power to ideology: if it does not determine all we see, like Blake's 'metaphysics', ideology determines what we look at, our structures of attention.[6] And yet, by gaining a '*critical* vantage' McGann's protocol will 'necessarily' expose ideology as 'false consciousness' (*McGann*, p. 12; McGann's emphasis). Transmitted by 'forms [or structures] of feeling' within particular works of art, ideologies can 'reify' into modern culture with pernicious effect, if not prevented (*McGann*, p. 13). Although he urges his polemic with high feeling, McGann therefore approaches 'Romantic' emotion with caution, as if affective distance were productive of historical distance. This critical protocol is thus at once rhetorical and historical: on one hand it seeks an end best described as ideological prophylaxis, and on the other it claims to rewrite history, to restore the past to what Wordsworth calls its 'true dwelling'.

II

It is clear that the rhetorical form of McGann's reading responds to these mechanisms of ideological coöptation. As he approaches 'The Ruined Cottage' his prose undergoes a sea-change, becoming self-consciously difficult, impersonal, and (even as it calls for specificity) abstract: 'We begin by forcing the critical act to attend to the specific referential patterns which appear in specific poems' (*McGann*, p. 82). The critic forcibly reconceives the text as a structure of particular claims on the reader's attention, claims he subjects to formal analysis as expressions of false consciousness. Instead of looking *at* the object represented by the text – the pathetic figure of Margaret, for example – McGann observes a second-order 'pattern' that seeks to transfer attention to her and her cottage landscape, and away from a focus he characterizes as historically 'particular' (McGann, p. 83) – a twenty-seven-line description, early in the Pedlar's narrative, of the failure of the rural weaving industry as a result of foreign war and poor harvests. This transfer of attention becomes for McGann the diagnostic feature of the Romantic Ideology, a 'transcendental displacement of human desires' (*McGann*, p. 26) that is both escapist and reactionary, and that he finds in later works by Wordsworth, in other works of English Romanticism, and in the modern critical establishment. As he demonstrates its existence in the text of 'The Ruined Cottage', he describes this feature in ways that suggest either its textuality ('pattern' 'displacement', 'fact'), or its motive ('evasion', 'elide', 'occlude and disguise'). First characterized as reflexive, something a 'work' does to itself, it quickly becomes an 'act of evasion' (*McGann*, p. 82) and ultimately an act with personal agency: it is Wordsworth who 'is precisely interested in preventing – in actively countering' a focus of the reader's attention on the historical particular (*McGann*, p.84). The Romantic Ideology is thus identified with a particular transfer of attention, which McGann not only refuses to endorse but actively opposes in the formal strategies of his reading. He returns the reader's attention to the weavers' passage, for example, characterizing it as the poem's 'focus' (McGann, pp. 82, 84) and featuring it in his only quotation from the Pedlar's narrative, the rest of which he ignores or briefly paraphrases.

As he disputes the text's claim to the reader's attention, McGann also disables its power to evoke and direct feeling – a respect in which, judging from the testimony of many readers, 'The Ruined Cottage' provides a worthy adversary. Its designs on the reader's feelings are transparent and insistent: the epigraph from Burns that begins the version of early 1798 claims power to 'touch the heart' – a phrase pencilled a second time in Wordsworth's hand on the same manuscript page (*Butler*, p. 135).[7] Throughout the poem the Pedlar exhorts and models sympathetic response, his own ('It moved my very heart' [l. 146]) or that of his audience ('It would have grieved / Your very soul to see her' [ll. 414-415]). In the poem's earliest fragments a still-undifferentiated narrator characterizes a ruined cottage as 'a melancholy thing to any man who has a heart to feel' (*Butler*, p. 83) – a phrase that specifies sympathetic feeling as essential to a valid interpretation of external objects, and simultaneously defines the poem's audience, threatening exclusion of those whose hearts, as the Pedlar puts it during his lament for Margaret, 'are dry as summer dust' (l. 151).

McGann neutralizes such appeals for sympathetic openness with astringent paraphrase. He summarizes the poem's action, for example, in a single sentence: 'Robert disappears in the gulf of war while his wife and child are left to the beautiful slow-motion narrative of their painfully slow-motion demise' (*McGann*, p. 83). If we attend to its form and diction, this sentence renders Robert a central figure, while Margaret recedes (and one of her two children disappears entirely). Syntactic symmetries and the idiom of cinematic suspension ('slow-motion') freeze and stylize her 'demise'. Pathos is noted ('painfully') but distanced by a counterpoised aestheticism ('beautiful') – an antithesis that neatly yokes and pins two principal modern targets of McGann's critical polemic. Elsewhere a single adjective acknowledges a reigning critical consensus ('a great poem' [*McGann*, p. 82], 'this pitiful story' [*McGann*, p. 83]), a consensus he tacitly subverts by going on to imply, often in the same sentence, that this 'great' poem betrays humanity. On occasion the word 'pathos' itself becomes his target: twice its forms are lowered to the colloquial sense of 'hopeless', and transported from their obvious site in the text, human suffering, to Robert's enlistment (a 'pathetically incompetent . . . effort') and to Wordsworth's political apostasy (which dismisses social action as 'pathetic incompetence' [*McGann*, p. 83]). Yet a few pages later McGann vigorously appropriates pathos on behalf of his own project, describing Wordsworth's disappearance into the gulf of ideology as 'piteous' (*McGann*, p. 88) and 'tragic' (*McGann*, p. 90), displacing pathos from poem to poet without apparent irony. Considered as a defense against ideological 'incorporation', this reading artfully deploys the formal and rhetorical apparatus of displacement, evasion, occlusion, and sympathy that McGann simultaneously attributes to the ideologically active Romantic text. He combats ideology, as it were, with its own poetic weapons. To do otherwise – to risk a sustained, sympathetic look at the imagery of Margaret's decline – would presumably invite coöptation and sacrifice historical difference.

Such modes of ideological prophylaxis are essentially rhetorical: they intervene on behalf of a modern audience to decontaminate and defamilarize a dangerous text. But is this equivalent to writing history? From a single textual feature, a pattern of 'displacement', McGann deduces not only Wordsworth's view of nature but also a history of his political opinions, asserting that by 1797-98 he had abandoned all hope and interest in social and political reform. What begins as textual analysis ends as historical predication, a shift that produces no corresponding adjustment of evidentiary procedure. Our only historical evidence for Wordsworth's apostasy remains the 'pattern' in the text, a transfer of attention from an 'A' McGann characterizes variously as particular, economic, social, and historical, to a 'B' that is pathetic, natural, spiritual, and transcendent. McGann perceives this 'turn' as an attempt to conceal 'A', an 'evasion' he attributes, as we have seen, to the motives of the historical subject, Wordsworth. But the evidence for this 'evasion' remains self-evidence; it depends on the assumption that any reasonable observer will find an analogous transfer of attention, from an 'A' that is economic and political to a 'B' that is pastoral and domestic, to be evasive. Such a response is by no means unusual, as the history of pastoral exegesis would suggest; many readers before McGann have found a pastoral surface intrinsically unworthy of attention, and have looked beneath it for some sort of evasive political or urban subtext, like Virgil's compliment to Caesar in the first Eclogue. But in the absence of independent evidence (as is available for Virgil) such judgments simply report the critic's own commitments. Unaided intuitions of the motive behind a particular textual 'turn' will always be potentially reciprocal; it may be that McGann, a dedicated cultural materialist, overdetermines 'historical particulars' and so reads all turns away from them as 'evasions'. Our only recourse, as Hume said of reported miracles, is to compare relative probabilities. Unless it can be correlated with evidence that is both extrinsic and historical, in other words, the argument from textual displacement can tell us little about Wordsworth's view of Nature or politics in 1797-98.

But extrinsic evidence is just what is excluded by McGann's unrelenting focus on the formal 'pattern' in this text. One of the continuing ironies of his reading is the stark contrast between a materialism that exuberantly privileges the historical particular and a critical practice that silently excludes from consideration all historical particulars that are relevant to the historicity of the claim being made. It is not difficult to name documents contemporary to 'The Ruined Cottage', for example, in which Wordsworth or his correspondents seem to contradict McGann's claim that by 1797-98 he had abandoned 'the Party of Humanity' (*McGann*, p. 84), letters, essays, or poems that describe his purposes as humanitarian, social, and political.[8] None of these is mentioned. Nor does McGann attempt to test his claims by determining whether an analogous 'transcendental displacement' takes place in poems written within weeks of 'The Ruined Cottage', rhymed ballads such as 'Goody Blake' or 'The Last of the Flock', or didactic blank verse like 'The Old Cumberland Beggar'. Nor is any competing reading of 'The Ruined Cottage' recognized or answered. McGann's protocol is in fact remarkably solitary: it defines itself by exclusion. I cite these limitations not to make my own case for the historical 'facts' of Wordsworth's apostasy – a charge that has been around a long time – but rather to show that McGann's method entails a massive occlusion of discursive evidence, and that it does so, remarkably, in the name of an historiography that is 'critical'.[9]

McGann's protocol offers a straightforward reconstruction of Wordsworthian 'Nature': 'Margaret's cottage is gradually overgrown and 'ruined' when 'Nature' invades its neglected precincts' (*McGann*, p. 83). Although his syntax hesitates between passive and active, McGann regards Wordsworthian 'Nature' as an agent in the action of the poem: it 'invades' Margaret's space. This 'process', he argues, comes to stand in the poem as 'an emblem of Nature's care and ceaseless governance, just as it glances obliquely at the pathetic incompetence of individual, cultural, and institutional efforts to give stability to human affairs' (*McGann*, p. 83). To conceive of Nature as offering 'care and ceaseless governance' is, for McGann, equivalent to abandoning human agency and human hope: it tells us, in short, that the radical of 1793 has sold out. But this formulation of Wordsworth's naturalism draws less on 'The Ruined Cottage' than on McGann's earlier dictum that 'in moments of crisis the Romantic will turn to Nature . . . as his place of last resort' (*McGann*, p. 67). That generalization is exemplified by a passage from *Childe Harold* III, where the speaker turns with relief from an analysis of Napoleonic ambition to a 'Nature' that is explicitly 'Maternal':

> Away with these! true Wisdom's world will be
> Within its own creation, or in thine,
> Maternal Nature! for who teems like thee,

Thus on the banks of thy majestic Rhine? (*Childe Harold*, III, 46.1-4: *BCPW*, III, 93).

An older Wordsworth found this kind of thing derivative and ersatz, '*assumed* rather than natural', but McGann seems unaware of any difference between Byron's Rhine and Wordsworth's Dorset (Wordsworth's emphasis: *LY*, I, 237). The landscape of 'The Ruined Cottage' he dismisses as 'a gathering mass of sensory, and chiefly vegetable, details', a 'sensational surface' that hypnotizes all onlookers (*McGann*, p. 83), and focuses instead on a much-admired speech that concludes the 1799 version of the poem, where the Pedlar recalls an image of rain-silvered speargrass that witnessed the power of 'meditation' over the 'grief / The passing shews of being leave behind' (D. 521-24). McGann regards this as a transparent attempt to transfer the reader's 'attention and commitments' from 'the Party of Humanity' to a 'secret spiritual replacement' in the landscape (*McGann*, p. 84). Attention to 'Nature' thus becomes equivalent to Romantic sublimation, escapism, and political reaction; in ideological terms the natural landscape functions as a more or less vacant screen, a residue of displacement significant not for itself but for the apostasy it enacts and conceals. The possibility that other conceptions of 'Nature' might have been available to the historical Wordsworth is not considered.

In many respects, then, McGann's reading of 'The Ruined Cottage' constitutes a remarkable rhetorical and polemic achievement. It silently opposes ideological displacements perceived in the text with its own preemptive displacements of attention. It disables a historical discourse of sensibility, and yet appropriates sympathetic feeling on behalf of its own modern polemic, casting the poet as a pathetic victim of ideological error. All evidence beyond the single self-evident instance of 'displacement' is silently removed from view. Such strong interventions are implicitly justified by the moral urgency of the occasion, which puts to the test the critic's power to block the transmission of a pernicious ideology. For all its rhetorical power, however, this critique becomes remarkably self-indulgent when it seeks to represent the past.

III

What such a protocol conceals is as important as what it reveals, and it is worth returning, in a less defensive mode, to the narrative that McGann selectively screens from view. If directness risks coöptation, it also affords an opportunity to compare McGann's representations of the text with a few passages from that text, and to explore lines of historical inference his method forecloses.[10] To speak of *the* text is of course misleading: Wordsworth left a sequence of versions, none of which he saw fit to publish separately, which represent stages in the transformation of 'The Ruined Cottage' of June 1797, a spare, literal narrative, into a longer vehicle for the articulation of a philosophic naturalism suitable to *The Recluse*.[11] If we seek to represent Wordsworth's construction of 'Nature' in 1797-98, we are aiming at a rapidly moving target; the passage McGann cites as evidence of Romantic sublimation does not appear, for example, in the version transcribed by early March, 1798. Although probably composed a few weeks later, its present role in the poem was not fixed until sometime in 1799, perhaps as late as December.[12] It is clearly part of Wordsworth's attempt to transform the earlier version into the philosophical *Recluse*, and McGann's characterization of it should be tested against the decorum and the socio-political aims of that poem, as far as they are available. Here, however, I want to consider that part of 'The Ruined Cottage' that seems most likely to predate *The Recluse,* the Pedlar's narrative.

Perhaps the most striking contrast between McGann's account of this narrative and Wordsworth's text has to do with the latter's particularity. The landscape McGann describes drily as 'a gathering mass . . . of chiefly vegetable details' resolves, when we attend to it, into a pattern of highly specific images, presented in a diction that is exact and circumstantial: plants discriminated by species, hairs on a door-jamb, a staff by an idle loom. Since F. W. Bateson called attention to the way such 'significant' detail 'illustrates or symbolizes the central meaning of the poem', readers have noted the hermeneutic character of these domestic particulars, which function not only as sites of feeling but as a system of signs that shows, among other things, how 'poverty and grief' are approaching Margaret in space as in time.[13]

It is on his second visit, six months after he first hears of Robert's departure, that the Pedlar is most attentive to such 'details'. He begins by noting that Margaret's cottage:

> . . . in its outward look appeared
> As chearful as before; in any shew
> Of neatness little changed, but that I thought
> The honeysuckle crowded round the door
> And from the wall hung down in heavier tufts (lines, 363-67).

Such images do not qualify as 'particulars' in McGann's reading, which regards their collective ideological function as escapist and reactionary. What this brief sequence registers with great delicacy, however, is rather the movement and quality of human attention. The Pedlar's choice of objects implies a prior expectation of visible change as a consequence of Robert's departure, an expectation that a sympathetic reader, who has already seen the 'matted weeds' and 'cold bare wall' of the poem's present time (lines, 117, 161), will share. But the Pedlar begins by denying such change, at least at the general and 'outward' level of the 'cottage' ('as chearful as before'). He immediately qualifies himself, however, conceding a 'little' change with respect to 'neatness', an abstract category that provides a visual index of Margaret's decline throughout the narrative. He then qualifies himself again ('but that I thought'), as his attention constricts to a single visual detail, the point at which a linear border – a door-frame – has since his last visit been 'crowded' by the honeysuckle. Evidence of change, that is, is admitted serially and incrementally, as if resisted by the sympathetic and hopeful speaker, even as the object of attention itself – a slight change in the position of the honeysuckle – implies the onset of a process that points to Margaret's decline and death. When the Pedlar enters her garden, a few lines later, any remaining resistance is abruptly abandoned by a flat monosyllabic predication: 'It was changed' (line, 371). What these lines enact, on a small scale, is not Romantic escapism but the discipline of hope by empirical experience. This chastened empiricism becomes an explicit theme of Margaret's story, but here it is implicit, available only to a direct and sympathetic reading that endorses the text's own hermeneutic.

Particular images function in this passage not as 'transcendental' symbols but as sites of precise sympathetic inference. As he looks into Margaret's garden, the Pedlar notes that

> The border tufts–
> Daisy, and thrift, and lowly camomile,
> And thyme–had straggled out into the paths
> Which they were used to deck (lines, 375-78).

These 'particulars' map two forces, natural and human, which exhibit roughly opposite physical vectors, centripetal and centrifugal with respect to the cottage. Their resultant is measured by the Pedlar's eye in terms of motion: the advance of a daisy beyond its appointed border registers not only its continued vitality, but the failure of the force that had opposed it, a force we are encouraged to read simultaneously as Margaret's hand, 'busy' with her 'garden tools' (line, 342), her labour, and finally the moral and psychological causes of that labour, her love for her cottage, her family, and herself. On later visits these particulars are replaced by the abstractions they come to embody, but their vectors remain the same:

> Once again
> I turned towards the garden-gate and saw
> More plainly still that poverty and grief
> Were now come *nearer* to her (lines, 450-453: my emphasis).

In the poem's final passage these forces, now unopposed, drive to a centre that is at once architectural, somatic, and psychological, a hearth and a heart:

> And so she sate
> Through the long winter, reckless and alone,
> Till this reft house by frost, and thaw, and rain
> Was sapped; and when she slept the nightly damps
> Did chill her breast, and in the stormy day
> Her tattered clothes were ruffled by the wind
> Even at the side of her own fire (lines, 516-522).

If this text specifies 'a heart to feel' as a precondition of hermeneutic success, it ends by asking for a far more complex response that incorporates sensation, feeling, and thought. This ability to 'read / The forms of things' (MS D lines, 510-11) becomes the explicit subject-matter of later philosophical additions, but the rhetorical apparatus that educes it is evident in the first passages to be composed, in the spring of 1797.

Now it is remarkable, given McGann's insistence on the importance of the particular, that he does not acknowledge the degree to which the Wordsworthian text does the same thing. He may not regard these pastoral and domestic images as legitimate 'particulars', of course, because in his view they evade the 'social and economic' causes an 'Enlightenment mind' (McGann, p. 84) would tease out of Margaret's story. But does this hermeneutic apparatus in fact turn us away from 'the Party of Humanity' toward ends that are escapist and reactionary? Does it enforce a 'transcendental displacement of desire'? A strong case can be made, I think, that we are invited to 'read' particular images in terms that resist any sacrifice of materiality, terms that insist most obviously on the value and dignity of human labour.[14] Margaret's domestic history is indeed quite strictly 'economic' in that term's root sense of 'household management', a sense McGann clearly does not intend. And yet what these particulars make visible is the decay of her 'economy', whether it is implied by an epithet (the 'unprofitable' bindweed [line, 372]) or figured, as the narrative ends, as a perverse displacement of labour from the material to the ideal:

> for evermore
> Her eye was busy in the distance, shaping things
> That made her heart beat quick (lines, 491-93).

'Profitable' labour and its substantial products are displaced by the 'busy' production of illusive objects of desire. Just before Margaret's story ends, the energy of productive labour comes briefly alive in the quickened rhythms and muscular consonants of the blank verse line:

> for he was gone whose hand,
> At the first nippings of October frost,
> Closed up each chink and with fresh bands of straw
> Chequered the green-grown thatch (lines, 513-16).

The prosodic elements of verse rise, as it were, to impersonate the absent husband, intensifying an image of a working 'hand' that is not a transcendental but an immanent and particular object of desire.[15]

McGann's protocol excludes prosodic evidence, of course, as being irrelevant to social and economic causation, but it is clearly not irrelevant to the representation of what he calls 'desire'. Nor does he acknowledge the synecdochic power of Wordsworth's imagery. The psychological effects of poverty and its moral and emotional causes are situated within a domestic institution, the Household, that in the 1790s offered a common synecdoche for society, as it does today. William Blake could read the ruin of the nation in a starving dog at a gate, and if a social synecdoche is not explicit in the early version of 'The Ruined Cottage' it could have become so in *The Recluse*, which (as Coleridge reminded Wordsworth in 1799) sought to reawaken a general hope for 'the amelioration of mankind' (*CL*, I, p. 257).[16]

McGann does not see such 'social and economic' options, perhaps, because he disables the hermeneutic that reveals them. He may not 'see' these particulars, however, in a more literal sense. To describe this landscape as 'a gathering mass of sensory, and chiefly vegetable, details' (McGann, p. 83) is to stress not the 'details' but their ongoing incorporation within an amorphous and growing 'mass' that has no recognizable counterpart in the narrative. Here, I think, we catch the strong critic in the act of intuiting the self-evidence that is his case – a vision of Ideology absorbing and incorporating its particulate victims. Equally creative is McGann's statement that 'Nature' invades Margaret's cottage, where his quotation marks seem to attribute the personification to Wordsworth (McGann, p. 83). But the personifying imagination is McGann's: 'Nature' is not named within the narrative proper, and although the noun appears twice in the philosophical additions of early 1798 it never acts as the subject of a verb that has material effects.[17] Such casual personification may typify the Byronic Wordsworthianism McGann regards as exemplary, but it violates the epistemological decorum of Wordsworth's poem, which insists on representing physical effects in terms of physical causes, and consistently avoids confusing the literal and the figurative. 'Nature' is not the material cause of Margaret's death, for example, but 'frost' and 'thaw' and 'rain'. Nor does 'Nature' seem the efficient cause of her death, which, as we have seen, results from a failure of parity between two forms of power, natural vitality and its reciprocal, human domestic labour. One of these powers defaults, allowing the other to prevail. Despite the pathos of her situation, Margaret is shown not as the pitiful victim of an invasive 'Nature', but as a 'reckless' agent of her own destruction, who refuses to surrender the 'one torturing hope' (line 525) that shields her from despair. A few years later Wordsworth would famously celebrate a hope that can never die, but here it is hope that kills.

If this alternative account is at all accurate, any attempt to generalize about 'natural' agents in the poem's landscape must be largely content with negatives. Taken collectively, these natural particulars manifest an active power that remains unqualified except for its continuity, an austere presence that can be described as a provider of 'care and governance' only by sentimentalizing the naturalism of 1797-98. Like the sea of Yeats's poem, this landscape murders innocently, to efface a mind that rejects the empirical world, a 'rebellious heart' that 'to its own will / Fashions the laws of nature', as a related fragment of 1797 puts it.[18]

In this respect the early version of 'The Ruined Cottage' resembles Wordsworth's contemporary tragedy, *The Borderers*. There an accused but innocent character is exposed to a tribunal of the natural elements, which are invited to rule on what the audience knows is a systematic and totalizing perversion of moral and historical reality, a type, that is, of what would come to be called 'false consciousness'. There too Wordsworth refuses to sentimentalize the natural world: the indifferent justice of natural law takes the form of a 'solitary crow' rising from a 'spot' in a field, where the innocent victim's body lies unseen but not unimagined.[19] This outcome resists an anthropomorphic reading, whether as judicial verdict or pledge of 'care and governance'. As in 'The Ruined Cottage', the value of Nature in *The Borderers* resides in its ontological persistence, 'beyond' totalizing systems of human thought – to use the preposition Wordsworth applied to this period in *The Prelude*.[20] In neither work does 'Nature' appear to offer a 'transcendental displacement of human desire' that evades or cancels out Wordsworth's earlier commitment to the 'Party of Humanity'. It functions rather as a touchstone of false consciousness, as an agent, in other words, of values that inform McGann's own 'critical' method. That this should be so is not surprising, given the resemblances between Wordsworth's critique in 1797-98 of an arrogant and abstract rationalism and McGann's theoretical model, Marx's critique in 1845 of an abstract, totalizing, and self-deceptive 'German Ideology'.

A more open approach to Margaret's story can thus recall a phase in Wordsworth's early career during which he constructed 'Nature' in terms of its opposition to a sick and contaminated human subjectivity. After March, 1798, in the meditative blank verse McGann takes as the epitome of an escapist naturalism, Wordsworth began to dramatize not the purgation of subjective error but the saving interpenetration of mind and Nature, the 'One Life' central to M.H. Abrams' conception of Romanticism. In still later work he would resolve the equivocations of British empiricism in other directions or transpose them into the categories of Anglican theology. In the base text of 'The Ruined Cottage', however, the epistemological and moral authority of the natural world appears to derive from its ontological independence of the human mind.

McGann's ruling assumption of ideological displacement requires, however, that Wordsworthian 'Nature' be read as a screen for the radical political agenda he, McGann, seeks to proselytize in present time. The effect is similar in M. H. Abrams' classic reading of Romantic 'Nature' as a ground for attitudes and emotions displaced by the failure of the French Revolution.[21] McGann may reverse the story's moral, deploring the sublimation of politics that Abrams seems to celebrate, but both accounts offer the same choice between a sentimentalized and sublimating naturalism on the one hand and a radical social agenda on the other. Such a division of the historical field effaces other options available to Wordsworth in 1797-98, one of them being a realist construction of 'Nature' as an autonomous power capable of effects that can be described today as 'political'.[22]

IV

On the one hand McGann's critical method erects a rhetorical barrier against ideological contamination from the past, and on the other it claims privileged knowledge of that past. This case study asks, among other things, whether these two purposes are mutually exclusive. McGann's concession of virtually unlimited constitutive power to ideology justifies a 'strong' defensive critique that is equally constitutive, pre-empting (and mirroring) the techniques and assumptions it opposes in the Romantic text.

In the case of 'The Ruined Cottage', however, this strategy demands the rejection of a Romantic protocol of reading that makes its own urgent 'truth' claims. An instrument as well as an object of historical knowledge, that protocol seeks (among other things) to install a concerned and sympathetic attention as a precondition of knowledge. By rejecting it McGann alters the object he seeks to know, the object that provides his only historical evidence; he idealizes the poem's construction of 'Nature', transforming it into an epiphenomenon of ideology, and fails to see crucial resemblances between Wordsworth's project and his own. If such artifacts are generated by the urgency with which he seeks 'difference', they are protected from critical scrutiny by his exclusion of discursive historical evidence, which becomes irrelevant to the end of blocking the transmission of a pernicious ideology. What is at stake here is not the value of McGann's modern critical or political agenda, but whether that agenda can legitimately require the sacrifice of an evidentiary procedure that is relatively open and comprehensive.

Such critiques as this may of course be dismissed as evidence of the coöptation McGann successfully resists, or as further proof of the truism that all historical discourse is in some degree constitutive. If so, his example points even more forcefully to the critical value of methods capable of dialectical self-correction, methods reluctant to exclude the evidence that threatens to contradict them. The struggle to avoid 'repetition' at any cost would seem, on the other hand, to be self-defeating. In the absence of some kind of repetition 'difference' becomes unrecognizable, and it would seem more useful to accept certain forms of repetition as methodologically unavoidable, appropriate, and even fruitful, and to try to minimize those that are not. Because of his urgent commitment to 'difference', McGann cannot see how closely Wordsworth's project in 1797-98 resembles his own. But that two individuals separated by two centuries should resist totalizing systems of thought, and should urgently seek a 'vantage' that guarantees personal identity as well as intellectual freedom – this hardly seems a 'repetition' we should deplore.

Notes

1   I'm grateful to Lucy Newlyn and Tom Furniss for helping me see this difference.
2   Clifford Siskin, *The Historicity of Romantic Discourse*, (New York: Oxford University Press, 1988), p. 5.
3   Jon Klancher, 'English Romanticism and Cultural Production', in *The New Historicism*, ed. H. Aram Veeser (New York and London: Routledge, 1989), p. 77.

4   See also Carolyn Porter, 'Are We Being Historical Yet?', *South Atlantic Quarterly*, 87 (1988), pp. 743-786; Richard Lehan, 'The Theoretical Limits of the New Historicism', *New Literary History*, 21 (1989) pp. 533-53; and Alan Liu, 'The Power of Formalism: The New Historicism', *ELH*, 56 (1989), pp. 721-71.

5   Siskin shows, for example, that McGann privileges feeling as 'a form of deep truth' (p. 59), and that he reproduces 'the Romantic distinction between the creative and the critical' (p. 61).

6   Frances Ferguson, 'On the Numbers of Romanticisms', *ELH*, 58 (1991), pp. 476-79.

7   *Butler*, p. 135. Unless otherwise indicated all references are to the Reading Text of MS. B.

8   Such evidence was gathered, for example, by Z. S. Fink, 'Wordsworth and the English Republican Tradition' *Journal of English and Germanic Philology*, 47 (1948), pp. 107-26; E. P. Thompson 'Disenchantment or Default? A Lay Sermon', in *Power & Consciousness*, ed. Conor Cruise O'Brien and William Dean Vanech (London: University of London Press, 1969), pp. 149-81; and Carl Woodring *Politics in English Romantic Poetry* (Cambridge, Mass.: Harvard University Press, 1970). For detailed historical accounts that reply to McGann see Nicholas Roe's *Wordsworth and Coleridge: The Radical Years* (Oxford: Clarendon Press, 1988) and *The Politics of Nature: Wordsworth and Some Contemporaries* (New York: St. Martin's Press, 1992). See also Alan Grob's 'Afterword: Wordsworth and the Politics of Consciousness', in *Critical Essays on William Wordsworth*, ed. George H. Gilpin (Boston: G.K. Hall, 1990), pp. 339-56.

9   McGann exemplifies the 'tendency to press the moment of political disenchantment further and further back' that E. P. Thompson noted in 1969, 'Disenchantment or Default', p. 149.

10 It may be unnecessary to point out that the close attention given particular images in the following paragraphs should not imply a veiled formalism, as will I hope become clear. Although the iconic character of these images can seem to reinstall New Critical procedures, as Alan Liu points out, the attempt to understand the function of the 'image' has an important and well-known eighteenth-century history (*Wordsworth: The Sense of History* [Stanford: Stanford University Press, 1989] pp. 311 ff.).

11 The poem's manuscript history in 1797-99 is described in *Butler*, 7-24. For its relation to *The Recluse*, see *Butler*, pp. 15-16 and Kenneth R. Johnston, *Wordsworth and The Recluse* (New Haven: Yale University Press, 1984), pp. 5-6.

12 According to Butler, MS. D was transcribed between February and December, 1799, (p. 23). The 'spear-grass' passage was first conceived not as a conclusion but as an interpolated reply by the Pedlar to his own lament; see my discussion in *The Making of Wordsworth's Poetry; 1798-1798* (Cambridge, Mass.: Harvard University Press, 1973), pp. 177-180.

13 F. W. Bateson, *Wordsworth: A Re-interpretation* (London: Longman, 1954), p. 126. Many readers have seconded Bateson's remarks, and the following account is especially indebted to Jonathan Wordsworth's close reading in *The Music of Humanity: A Critical Study of Wordsworth's* Ruined Cottage (London: Thomas Nelson, 1969). I have also profited from Diane C. Macdonnell's systematic account of the sign systems of the poem, 'The Place of the Device of Expectation, or 'Seeing Through a Medium', in Book I of *The Excursion*', *SiR*, 18 (1979), pp. 427-51, as well as Alan Liu's discussion of its imagery, cited above. I draw as well on my discussion in *The Making of Wordsworth's Poetry*.

14 For Alan Liu the poem's humanism is invested in the imagery of manual labour, but it is rejected by the Pedlar's 'vision of humanity as Nature' (*Sense of History*, p. 320). My point is that the poem's semiotic apparatus presents such imagery an 'object of desire'

that is by no means 'transcendental'. David Simpson notes the acute analysis of the psychological effects of unemployment in the description of Robert, *Wordsworth's Historical Imagination: The Poetry of Displacement* (New York: Methuen, 1987), pp. 192-3.

15   This imaginative emphasis on the agency of productive labour may heighten the response that Jonathan Barron and Kenneth Johnston christen 'literalist or "Anti-Jacobin,"' namely the sense that 'somebody should or could have done something for Margaret' ('"Power to Virtue Friendly": The Pedlar's Guilt in Wordsworth's "Ruined Cottage"' in *Romantic Revisions*, ed. Robert Brinkley and Keith Hanley (Cambridge: Cambridge University Press, 1992), p. 66. Such a response exemplifies the problem pointed out by Alan Liu, of historicizing the relation between 'representation' and 'action' (*Sense of History*, p. 580).

16   My point here, that Wordsworth's poem does not exhibit the 'ideological' characteristics McGann attributes to it, may be compared with Karen Swann's argument that the poem engages history, but in the sense of a response to the contemporary literary marketplace ('Suffering and Sensation in *The Ruined Cottage*', *PMLA*, 106 [1991] 84-00). A complementary account is given by David Perkins, who shows that the historical site of the attitudes and beliefs that McGann gathers under the name of 'Romantic Ideology' was the late nineteenth century (*Is Literary History Possible?* [Baltimore and London: Johns Hopkins University Press, 1992], p. 104).

17   'Nature' is named once in the Pedlar's biography (78) and once in the transition passage that separates the two parts of the narrative (256).

18   *Butler*, p. 463. See Yeats's 'A Prayer for My Daughter', line 16.

19   *The Borderers*, ed. Robert Osborn (Ithaca: Cornell University Press, 1982). V, ii, pp. 70-71 (version of 1797-99).

20   'The laws of things which lie / Beyond the reach of human will or power' (I, 97-98).

21   M.H. Abrams, 'English Romanticism: The Spirit of the Age', in *Romanticism Reconsidered: Selected Papers from the English Institute*, ed. Northrop Frye (New York: Columbia University Press, 1963), pp. 26-72.

22   'The historical force of nature' as understood by Wordsworth has been persuasively demonstrated by Nicholas Roe (*Politics of Nature*, p. 3). In *Romantic Ecology: Wordsworth and the Environmental Tradition* (London and New York: Routledge, 1991), Jonathan Bate argues forcefully for a realist interpretation of Romantic 'nature'.

3 Wordsworth's 'The Haunted Tree' and the Sexual Politics of Landscape

TIM FULFORD

In 1819 Wordsworth began to write a short poem that he published in 1820. He called it 'The Haunted Tree'. Unusual within his corpus in that it is fancifully mythological and playfully erotic, this poem is nevertheless an evocation of a particular oak-tree in the familiar landscape of Rydal Park Grasmere (although the park is not named within the poem). Wordsworth dwells upon the tree in a manner that links the poem to 'The Thorn' and to the poems on the naming of places. It is part of a kind of arboreal sub-genre within Wordsworth's landscape poetry and continues the modification of the eighteenth-century georgic he had previously made in 'Yew-Trees' and *The Excursion*:

> Those silver clouds collected round the sun
> His mid-day warmth abate not, seeming less
> To overshade than multiply his beams
> By soft reflection – grateful to the sky,
> To rocks, fields, woods. Nor doth our human sense
> Ask, for its pleasure, screen or canopy
> More ample than the time-dismantled Oak
> Spreads o'er this tuft of heath, which now, attired
> In the whole fulness of its bloom, affords
> Couch beautiful as e'er for earthly use   10
> Was fashioned; whether by the hand of Art,
> That eastern Sultan, amid flowers enwrought
> On silken tissue, might diffuse his limbs
> In languor; or, by Nature, for repose
> Of panting Wood-nymph, wearied with the chase.
> O Lady! fairer in thy Poet's sight
> Than fairest spiritual creature of the groves,
> Approach; - and, thus invited, crown with rest
> The noon-tide hour: though truly some there are
> Whose footsteps superstitiously avoid   20
> This venerable Tree; for, when the wind

Blows keenly, it sends forth a creaking sound
(Above the general roar of woods and crags)
Distinctly heard from far - a doleful note!
As if (so Grecian shepherds would have deemed)
The Hamadryad, pent within, bewailed
Some bitter wrong. Nor it is unbelieved,
By ruder fancy, that a troubled ghost
Haunts the old trunk; lamenting deeds of which
The flowery ground is conscious. But no wind   30
Sweeps now along this elevated ridge;
Not even a zephyr stirs; – the obnoxious Tree
Is mute; and, in his silence, would look down,
O lovely Wanderer of the trackless hills,
On thy reclining form with more delight
Than his coevals in the sheltered vale
Seem to participate, the while they view
Their own far-stretching arms and leafy heads
Vividly pictured in some glassy pool,
That, for a brief space, checks the hurrying stream!   40
                    (*WPW*, II, p. 291).

That 'The Haunted Tree' has been unjustly neglected by critics is surprising, since it alludes to a number of poems that have been regarded as icons of high Romanticism – poems by Coleridge as well as by Wordsworth himself. It continues the debate about nature, the feminine, love and inspiration begun in 'Dejection' and the 'Immortality' ode. And it introduces into that debate quiet topical reference to some of the most fundamental social issues and fashionable literary trends of Regency Britain. In this essay I shall try to rectify critical neglect of the poem by examining it in detail, arguing that we need to read it – and much of Wordsworth's later poetry – as an intelligent and witty, if oblique, contribution to contemporary political and social debate, a contribution more and not less pertinent in its choice of a mythologized English nature as its setting.

A number of North American critics have suggested that Wordsworth's nature poetry is a flight from political issues into the sublime area of his own subjectivity – that it reveals a loss of faith in political and social argument. For Marjorie Levinson it is an 'evasion', for Alan Liu a 'denial', of history.[1] The concept of 'displacement' – originally Raymond Williams's but revived by David Simpson[2] – is more subtle but still, I shall argue, not wholly adequate as a formulation of Wordsworth's poetic relationship with the political and social issues of the early nineteenth century since it presumes that landscape functions as a secondary stage on which issues that arose elsewhere can be depicted in controlled form. Such a presumption, however, ignores the fact that in Wordsworth's Britain ownership of land was still a fundamental political issue: the gentry's and nobility's possession of it was used to justify their domination of parliament, whilst labourers' (and women's) lack of it was used to explain their poverty and disenfranchisement. The politics of landscape, in other words, were parliamentary politics too. They were also sexual politics: for Burkeian traditionalists it was the duty of those given authority by landownership to shelter vulnerable women. And for Mary Wollstonecraft women would not escape the appearance of natural inferiority (and the fact of social inferiority) to men unless they could acquire independence through property-ownership.[3]

'The Haunted Tree' updates the (sexual) politics of landscape found in Burke and in the eighteenth-century tradition in which political arguments were advanced by use of nature imagery – in particular by the iconographical use of trees. At the same time it intervenes in the debate (stimulated by Burke) about gender and sexual roles that reached fever pitch in 1819-20. That debate was fuelled by Byron's Orientalist poetry, in particular, the newly published *Don Juan*, and by the attack upon him made by Wordsworth's friend the Poet Laureate, Robert Southey. The debate was accompanied by a political crisis, with revolution widely expected, when George IV caused Lord Liverpool's administration to have his wife, Caroline, 'tried' before the House of Lords in an attempt to show that she was unfit, on the grounds of her sexual immorality, to become Queen.

I begin by examining the use made of landscape-imagery in political argument. Both radical opponents and conservative defenders of Britain's unreformed constitution employed nature imagery to render their arguments appealing. Trees figured prominently in that imagery after John Locke had used the oak to illustrate the notion of organic unity.[4] Oaks' longevity, rootedness and strength made them suitable emblems for writers who portrayed an ancient constitution secured in the heritable property of land and capable of gradual change as a growth of English soil.[5] Edmund Burke depicted Britain's form of government as tree-like, of ancient growth: it 'moves on through the varied tenor of perpetual decay, fall, renovation and progression' in 'the method of nature'.[6] The people were 'great cattle reposed beneath the shadow of the British oak'.[7] Burke was opposed by Thomas Paine and other radicals who employed the political iconography of the French Revolution, in which the Liberty tree was an emblem of the new growth possible once ancient injustices had been uprooted.[8] Like an oak Burke's constitution was rooted in the land, time-honoured, slow to change and grow, protective of the subjects who sheltered beneath it. Wordsworth characterized Burke himself as a tree, acknowledging the power of his symbolic oak as an anti-revolutionary naturalization of conservative politics:

> I see him, - old, but vigorous in age,
> Stand like an oak whose stag-horn branches start
> Out of its leafy crown, the more to awe
> The younger brethren of the grove . . .
> While he forewarns, denounces, launches forth,
> Against all systems built on abstract rights,
> Keen ridicule; the majesty proclaims
> Of Institutes and Laws, hallowed by time;
> Declares the vital power of social ties
> Endeared by Custom; and with high disdain,
> Exploding upstart Theory, insists
> Upon the allegiance to which men are born
> (*Prelude* [1850] 7.519-22; 523-30).

Wordsworth wrote this tribute when a political supporter of his patron, the Tory landowner and political magnate Lord Lowther.

Landowners and conservative moralists exploited the political symbolism of trees in an attempt to show liberty to be more truly rooted in the British constitution than in the French Revolution. Uvedale Price, the Whig squire and theorist of the picturesque, put such ideas into practice. He designed his estate at Foxley as a display of paternalism. Cottagers were not cleared from his park but included within it, their rustic dwellings sheltered by the oak and ash woods which Price spent much of his time and income maintaining and planting.[9] His tenants were visibly under his protection in a symbolic ordering of the real landscape which emphasized that order and liberty depended upon the mutual duties owed by rich and poor. Wordsworth corresponded with Price and visited Foxley, without entirely approving of the landscape park (*MY*, I, p. 505).

Price's fellow theorist Richard Payne Knight, also a Herefordshire Whig squire, both planted oaks and poeticized about their political significance. He portrayed the oak tree as a symbol of a constitutional British monarch paternally sheltering lesser trees grouped around it: 'Then Britain's genius to thy aid invoke / And spread around the rich, high-clustering oak: / King of the woods!' The cedar by contrast was shown to be 'like some great eastern king', destroying everything in its shade, 'Secure and shelter'd, every subject lies; / But, robb'd of moisture, sickens, droops, and dies'.[10]

Wordsworth's 'The Haunted Tree' depicts the oak in a similar way. His tree is an image of the English gentry's authority, rooted, paternalist, like Burke's tree-like constitution. Like Knight, Wordsworth opposes his English tree to an Oriental monarch – to a Sultan – a standard figure of political and sexual despotism:

> Nor doth our human sense
> Ask, for its pleasure, screen or canopy
> More ample than the time-dismantled Oak
> Spreads o'er this tuft of heath, which now, attired
> In the whole fulness of its bloom, affords
> Couch beautiful as e'er for earthly use
> Was fashioned; whether by the hand of Art,
> That eastern Sultan, amid flowers enwrought
> On silken tissue, might diffuse his limbs
> In languor; or, by Nature, for repose
> Of panting Wood-nymph, wearied with the chase (lines 1-15).

The phrase 'time-dismantled oak' alludes to Cowper's poem 'Yardley Oak' in which the aged tree is made a symbol of Britain's ancient constitution, a constitution so deeply rooted in the past that, like the landed gentry on whose estates oaks grew, it should offer stability (*PWC*, III, pp. 77-83).[11] Wordsworth had borrowed from Cowper's poem before, in 'Yew-Trees' and *The Excursion*:[12] there as here Wordsworth's oaks, like Cowper's, are not just English trees but trees of Englishness – or rather icons of a conservative and anti-revolutionary identification of national unity with the landed gentry and the 1688 constitutional settlement. Similarly Southey, admirer of Burke and editor of Cowper, claimed the order of the nation to depend on men 'whose names and families are older in the country than the old oaks upon their estates'.[13]

The politics of 'The Haunted Tree' are more complex than are Southey's Tory polemics. Wordsworth examines, when Southey does not, the power relations implicit in the Burkeian model of authority. He shows these power relations to be constructed upon sexual oppositions. His oak is a sublime male sheltering a beautiful female, whose presence tempers and mollifies his masculine authority: it 'affords / Couch beautiful' for the Lady of the poem. Burke had understood political authority in these terms: Caesar, in Burke's discussion of the sublime, had achieved political power by combining the awe-inspiring masculinity of the warrior with attractive feminine qualities.[14] The man of sublime authority had, furthermore, a duty to protect the vulnerable and weak.[15] Wordsworth's poem sexualizes nature in similar terms: masculinity is awe-inspiring and sublime, femininity tender and beautiful. It places this gendering of power, adapted from Burke, against a potentially aggressive masculinity whose power is that of unsocialized self-assertion, threatening rape. Burkeian paternal masculinity, tempered by the feminine, confronts the Oriental Sultan, a figure of eastern political and sexual despotism. The paternal authority that the Burkeian oak symbolizes is 'dismantled' by age and tempered by the beautiful. It is protective rather than subordinative, traditional and rooted rather than aggressive and despotic.

There was a political context for the poem, not immediately apparent today. In July 1819 the first two cantos of Byron's *Don Juan* were published. To Wordsworth their licentious wit and sexual theme were dangerously corrupting. In a letter of January 1820 he called *Don Juan* 'that infamous publication' and referred to the 'despicable quality of the powers requisite for [its] production', adding 'I am persuaded that Don Juan will do more harm to the English character, than anything of our time; not so much as a Book; – But thousands who would be afraid to have it in that shape, will batten upon choice bits of it in the shape of Extracts'. He bemoaned the fact that the close association of its editor with Byron had prevented the *Quarterly Review* from defending the threatened 'English character': 'every true-born Englishman will regard the pretension of the Review to the character of a faithful defender of the Institutions of the country, as *hollow*' (*MY*, II, p. 579).

In *Don Juan*, as in the earlier *Bride of Abydos*, Byron was widely thought to have poeticized his own sexual history. He used Oriental figures to image himself as one who preferred sexual conquest to Wordsworthian solitude-in-nature: 'By solitude I mean a Sultan's (not / A Hermit's), with a haram for a grot' (*Don Juan*, Canto I, stanza 87: *BCPW*, V). He had also portrayed Orientalism as 'the only poetical policy'[16] guaranteed to achieve commercial success, as an undemanding literary trend:

> Oh that I had the art of easy writing
>   What should be easy reading! could I scale
> Parnassus, where the Muses sit inditing
>   Those pretty poems never known to fail,
> How quickly would I print (the world delighting)
>   A Grecian, Syrian or Assyrian tale;
> And sell you, mix'd with western sentimentalism,
> Some samples of the finest Orientalism!
>   (*Beppo*, stanza 51: *BCPW*, IV, p.145).

Byron's Orientalist poetry portrayed English character and institutions as repressive and tame; similarly, the publication of his verses on his own failed marriage suggested that he saw poetry as a means of publicly declaring his own personal refusal to be bound by such restrictions. Wordsworth was disgusted by their publication as he was by *Don Juan* not only because their sexual theme threatened his conservative vision of character and society but because they corrupted poetry's rôle as the defender of true-born Englishness.

The second canto of *Don Juan* contains an Orientalist erotic fantasy in which the young Juan, washed ashore on an island governed by a pirate, meets the pirate's daughter Haidée 'the greatest heiress of the Eastern Isles' 'and like a lovely tree' (II, line 128). Dressed by Haidée in Turkish clothes, Juan becomes the object of her desire and, when her father leaves the island on a voyage:

> Then came her freedom, for she had no mother,
>   So that, her father being at sea, she was
> Free as a married woman, or such other
>   Female, as where she likes may freely pass,
> Without even the encumbrance of a brother,
>   The freest she that ever gazed on glass:
> I speak of Christian lands in this comparison,
> Where wives, at least, are seldom kept in garrison
>   (*Don Juan*, II, 175: *BCPW*, V, p. 143).

Byron mixed cynical wit about the sexual codes and marital practices of Christian countries with a vision of Juan's and Haidée's sexual encounter as an exotic and erotic escape from all paternal and social authority, an escape in which Haidée was also able, as Christian wives were not, openly to admit and act upon her sexual desires:

> They feared no eyes nor ears on that lone beach,
>   They felt no terrors from the night, they were
> All in all to each other: though their speech
>   Was broken words, they *thought* a language there, –
> And all the burning tongues the Passions teach
>   Found in one sigh the best interpreter
> Of Nature's oracle – first love, – that all
> Which Eve has left her daughters since her fall
>   (*Don Juan*, II, 189: *BCPW*, V, p. 148).

Byron also, in the first canto of *Don Juan*, attacked Wordsworth in person as 'crazed beyond all hope' (I, 205: *BCPW*, I, p. 74) and parodied his 'unintelligible' nature poetry (I, 90: *BCPW*, I, p. 37). In addition, in the dedication verses, which were left unpublished (save as a broadside sold in the streets) Wordsworth was attacked along with Southey as a hireling of the aristocracy. Byron depicted Wordsworth as tedious and reactionary and the Laureate as sexually and poetically impotent, as a harem slave of George and his eunuch ministers – one who would 'adore a sultan' and 'obey / The intellectual eunuch Castlereagh' (Dedication, 11: *BCPW*, I, p. 6). Southey's knowledge of this Orientalist satire on his poetic and political manhood was probably responsible for his 1821 attack upon Byron's 'Satanic School' of poetry in the Preface to his funeral ode for George III, the 'Vision of Judgement'.

Wordsworth, like his friend and fellow object of Byron's satire, felt the need to resist Byron's specific attacks and the general example of his Orientalist poetry. For both 'Lake Poets' Byron's popularity epitomized a worrying tendency in the nation to prefer sensual extravagance over obedience to proper (and usually paternal) authorities and to the poetry that defended them (including their own which continued to be far less popular than Byron's). In 1819 and 1820 this worrying tendency was more than usually evident in the very father of the nation, the monarch. The Prince Regent, who succeeded George III in 1820, had been notoriously extravagant, both sexually and financially, since 1795. In 1816 Wordsworth had declared that 'the blame of unnecessary expenditure . . . rests with the Prince Regent' (*MY*, II, p. 334). In 1818 Wordsworth was worried that the Regent's request to Parliament for extra allowances for the other Princes would make it hard for the candidates of the Lowther family to be returned in the election.

The Regent's extravagance seemed truly Oriental: he spent £155,000 on improvements to Brighton Pavilion by which pagodas, minarets, onion shaped domes and Indian columns were added. Thousands more were spent on interior decoration which made the place resemble a seraglio. Rather than display the paternal restraint of his father the Prince accrued debts of £335,000 and entertained a succession of mistresses, whilst his estranged wife, Caroline, toured Europe, dressed in fashionable Oriental costumes, having numerous affairs. She returned to England in 1820, and Lord Liverpool's Tory Ministry, acting at the King's instigation, had her 'tried' before the House of Lords, attempting to produce enough evidence of her sexual misdemeanours to enable it to deny her the title of 'Queen' and the accompanying rights and privileges. The trial caused widespread fears of revolution and occasioned street protests – a crowd gathered outside the house of the Duke of York viewed Caroline as a victim of George's 'Oriental' despotism, shouting 'We like princes who show themselves; we don't like Grand Turks who shut themselves up in their seraglio'.[17] Radical and labouring-class protest was accompanied by opposition from middle-class women, who clearly understood that the affair had implications for the sexual politics of the nation: an address to the Queen from the 'Ladies of Edinburgh', printed in *The Times* on 4th September, noted

> As your majesty has justly observed, the principles and doctrines now advanced by your accusers do not apply to your case alone, but, if made part of the law of this land, may hereafter be applied as a precedent by every careless and dissipated husband to rid himself of his wife, however good and innocent she may be; and to render his family, however, amiable, illegitimate; thereby destroying the sacred bond of matrimony, and rendering all domestic felicity very uncertain.[18]

Cartoonists portrayed the threat George's actions posed to the family and to the principle of heredity by turning George's penchant for Oriental decoration against him: one depicted him as a Chinese potentate surrounded by his concubines (his mistresses Lady Hertford, Lady Conyngham and Mrs. Quentin).[19] The affair discredited Lord Liverpool's ministry, which was shown to have prostituted parliament's independence rather than lose office: they had bribed witnesses against Caroline. Wordsworth attended the last day of the trial in November, having expressed some of the sympathy for her that was widely felt in the country.

In those contexts *The Haunted Tree* can be seen as an oblique answer to the Orientalist fashion, and the poetic, political and moral corruption which, for Wordsworth, that fashion manifested at the heart of Regency Britain. It revives and revises a rural rather than metropolitan, Burkeian rather than Byronic understanding of gender, sexuality and power. It attempts to govern desire by defining masculinity as a benevolent paternalism properly protecting women in particular and the land in general. It implicitly rejects Byron's depiction of the 'Lake Poets' as worshippers of the Sultan's eunuchs, whilst seeking to provide a more stable (and ostensibly native) model of masculine power than that provided by the 'Sultans' George IV and Byron himself.

Having outlined the political and aesthetic debates which 'The Haunted Tree' addresses I turn now to a detailed close reading of the poem. In the opening lines the threats that characterize the sublime are evoked as possibilities, but are soon banished by the actual scene:

> Those silver clouds collected round the sun
> His mid-day warmth abate not, seeming less
> To overshade than multiply his beams
> By soft reflection – grateful to the sky,
> To rocks, fields, woods. Nor doth our human sense
> Ask, for its pleasure, screen or canopy

More ample than the time-dismantled Oak
Spreads o'er this tuft of heath, which now, attired
In the whole fulness of its bloom, affords
Couch beautiful as e'er for earthly use
Was fashioned; whether by the hand of Art,
That eastern Sultan, amid flowers enwrought
On silken tissue, might diffuse his limbs
In languor; or, by Nature, for repose
Of panting Wood-nymph, wearied with the chase
(lines 1-15: WPW, II, p. 291).

The clouds multiply the sunbeams rather than 'overshade' them, and even time's dismantling of the oak serves only to make it less powerful, more delightful in its provision of just shade enough for one. The 'Couch beautiful' is rendered both exotic and erotic by the image of the Sultan diffusing 'his limbs / In languor', an eroticism continued in the more 'natural' (or rather Ovidian) image of the 'panting Wood-nymph'. Such eroticism is unusual for Wordsworth. And it is an eroticism based upon what Wordsworth claims to be the masculinity of English nature – and the nature of English masculinity: an oak-like strength that creates a safe sensual playground. It is contrasted with the predatory sexual violence upon which Greek nature is founded – Apollo's pursuit of Daphne caused her to be turned into a tree. And it is capable of lulling the figure of Oriental despotism (political and sexual), the Sultan (a figure to whom the King had been compared often enough in 1819-20). Here, for Wordsworth, a soft and sensual feminine 'heath' lulls the threat of unrestrained monarchical power, itself protected by the shading oak (a tree of English masculinity, traditional, restrained, protective for Burke, Cowper, and Wordsworth in *The Prelude*).

The poem attacks the sexual politics of the Regent then, in that a Burkeian masculine sublime, an English sheltering tree defined against the possibly violent masculinity of Greek and Turk, makes a space for a feminine and erotic beautiful which can then flower under its protection, both softening it (as Burke said the beautiful should soften the sublime)[20] and allowing it an erotic satisfaction defined as *looking*. The feminine is still governed by and defined for the satisfaction of the masculine, but in an affectionate yet formal address: the narrator can offer the tree to the Lady as a place of peace and show himself doing so, subsuming troubling intimations in social generosity:

O Lady! fairer in thy Poet's sight
Than fairest spiritual creature of the groves,

Approach; – and, thus invited, crown with rest
The noon-tide hour: though truly some there are
Whose footsteps superstitiously avoid
This venerable Tree; for, when the wind
Blows keenly, it sends forth a creaking sound
(Above the general roar of woods and crags)
Distinctly heard from far – a doleful note!
As if (so Grecian shepherds would have deemed)
The Hamadryad, pent within, bewailed
Some bitter wrong. Nor it is unbelieved,
By ruder fancy, that a troubled ghost
Haunts the old trunk; lamenting deeds of which
The flowery ground is conscious. But no wind
Sweeps now along this elevated ridge;
Not even a zephyr stirs; – the obnoxious Tree
Is mute; and, in his silence, would look down,
O lovely Wanderer of the trackless hills,
On thy reclining form with more delight
Than his coevals in the sheltered vale
Seem to participate, the while they view
Their own far-stretching arms and leafy heads
Vividly pictured in some glassy pool,
That, for a brief space, checks the hurrying stream!
(lines 16-40: WPW, II, p. 291).

Yet those troubling intimations are present: the Burkeian tree is haunted by the temptations attendant upon the equation of sublimity, masculinity, and political authority. These are the temptations of masculine self-assertion – the violent rapes committed by Greek gods. But the rootedness of the tree allows these temptations to remain as ghosts, laid to rest or at least confined within the tree by the poet-narrator, like Sycorax by Prospero. Wordsworth raises and then confines the ghosts. He lays the demons of male power by aligning that power (including his own as a male poet) with the stable and safe ground of a known and little-changing English landscape/landscape of Englishness. He does so by a carefully self-cancelling syntax: the phrase 'Nor is it unbelieved' establishes a disturbingly unattributed half-belief in ghosts which taints the beautiful – as is indicated by the lines 'lamenting deeds of which / The flowery ground is conscious'. Yet the phrase 'no wind / Sweeps now along' then counters this. The repeated negative forms a positive, cancelling the dangerous negative forces of lament and thereby restoring the flowery ground for the Lady to approach. Or, to put it another way, the poem raises the possibility of the defloration of the ground (and of the Lady), only to allay fears by confidently asserting that such violence is absent for the moment. It is a spot (and a poetry) won back from sublime threat, from an intimation of the threatening violence of male desire, in favour of an erotic but also decorous beautiful. Desire will be expressed not as rape but by an entreaty to the Lady which seeks her confidence by preparing the (peaceful) ground. Desire will be satisfied by the voyeurism of the tree watching her 'reclining form' and of the narrator imagining them both. Since the whole scene is imagined *for* the Lady it acts, at the same time, as a gift to her in which hopes for a more direct and intimate relationship are encoded, an encodement which, if understood, might lead to actual acceptance by her.

The difficulty of containing the violence traditionally inherent in the masculine authority categorized as sublime is apparent in the word 'obnoxious'. Meaning principally 'vulnerable to harm', 'subject to authority', the word also meant, then though more commonly now, 'harmful'.[21] The vulnerable 'time-dismantled' tree remains haunted then by intimations of harm and violence: it may be 'mute' but a silent ambiguity remains. What also remain, although the poem works hard to contain them, are allusions to other poems which trouble the serenity that the poem seeks. The ancient and lone tree on 'this elevated ridge' and the 'Wanderer of the trackless hills' recall the bleak and disturbing pairing in 'The Thorn' of the tree and the lone woman in a landscape haunted by violent death. Working against such allusions, however, are others which show that disturbance can lead to a greater harmony: 'it sends forth a creaking sound / (Above the general roar of woods and crags) / Distinctly heard from far – a doleful note' echoes Coleridge's 'This Lime-Tree Bower My Prison', in which the senses 'keep the heart / Awake to Love and Beauty' and the 'last rook' 'flew creaking o'er thy head, and had a charm / For thee, my gentle-hearted Charles, to whom / No sound is dissonant which tells of Life' (lines 63-4, 74-6: *CPW*, I, p. 181). Further echoes, of *Home at Grasmere*'s 'sheltered vale' and of Coleridge's 'Dejection: an Ode', in which solitary melancholy is overcome by appealing and dedicating the verse to a Lady, also help to incorporate disruptive intimations within a harmonious social community in nature. It is an allusive strategy designed to temper the visionary power of the solitary sublime, which Wordsworth had explored in 1802 in the 'Immortality' ode in reaction and contradistinction to Coleridge's 'Dejection', with 'Dejection's' beautiful appeal to feminine sympathy.

The last eight lines of the poem replace the troubling sounds of the tree with the loving look of a male unbending his solitary uprightness, as Burke had declared he should, because entranced and completed by the female that he shelters in her appealingly available beauty: 'in his silence, would look down . . .'. This scene complements, rather than rejects, Coleridge's less paternal and more desperate appeal to female sympathy in

'Dejection'. This scene is more delightful for the male tree than are – in the poem's very last lines – their own reflections for the 'coeval' trees in the sheltered vale. Yet viewing those reflections is itself a powerful act, since it allows a momentary self-knowledge 'vividly pictured' out of the flux of 'the hurrying stream' of time and space:

> while they view
> Their own far-stretching arms and leafy heads
> Vividly pictured in some glassy pool,
> That, for a brief space, checks the hurrying stream! (lines 37-40).

Powerful though it is, however, the privileged picture that these waterside trees together gain of themselves is potentially narcissistic (and Narcissus was changed into a waterside plant). It is less permanent than the reconciliation of sublime and beautiful, of male and female available to the poetic tree and Lady.

The narrator lays his sole and potentially violent possession of masculine authority to rest in a sexualized nature, making of the object world a mythical place in which the sublime violence of rape and metamorphosis is replaced by a beautiful viewing. This viewing completes and delights the independent male and offers the female secure sensual pleasure (no apples to pluck). She is, of course, in a subordinate position as were all women and most men in the oak-like paternalist constitution that Burke and Wordsworth supported.

The landscape of 'The Haunted Tree' is not an evasion or denial of political and social issues. It is not a displacement of such issues into some secondary area of nature. On the contrary, it is a modification of an eighteenth-century tradition in which the landscape was treated as a testing ground for the moral and social health of the nation, as the place upon which proper authority could be measured. That tradition was itself founded on the fact that the politics of local landscapes were also national politics: it was the ownership of land which gave the nobility and gentry political power and which defined their duties in the state. The politics of nature in Regency Britain were not substitutes for some more fundamental level of politics but were vital in a nation in which reform of a parliament still dominated by the landed gentry was the most important issue. Burke, Cowper and Price had redefined and reasserted the authority of the gentry in their iconography of landscape. To this Wordsworth added an anti-Byronic anti-Regent redefinition of the sexual politics of the Burkeian sublime. In doing so he countered Orientalist fashions and the corruption they revealed in the contemporary aristocracy.

'The Haunted Tree' achieves what I think it is appropriate to call a mythologization of nature. Like Greek myth it places issues of power and desire at the heart of the national landscape. In a critique of Greek myth, however, it founds English nature not on rape and metamorphosis, but sensual playfulness (including the playful language of the poem itself) – on a looking but not touching. This playfulness flourishes when the ghosts of male violence that haunt the scene have been confined within the oak of masculine self-restraining strength. Narrator and Lady, poet and reader can then meet in a land safe for loving play (or at least for voyeuristic looking). It is a poetic land in which one encounters the human as if it were natural and the natural as if it were human – a dreamy and languorous land of representation poised between self and other, subject and object, power and love, violence and peace, sight and sound. It is a land, Wordsworth suggests, in which poetry must make men live lest the solitary man, like a despotic ruler or usurping poet, hear in all things only his own violent desire, see only his own beloved self.

Notes

1   See Marjorie Levinson, *Wordsworth's great period poems* (Cambridge: Cambridge University Press, 1986); Alan Liu, *Wordsworth: The Sense of History* (Stanford: University of California Press, 1989) and *McGann*, p. 91.

2   See Raymond Williams, *Marxism and Literature* (Oxford: Oxford University Press, 1977); David Simpson, *Wordsworth's Historical Imagination* (New York and London: Methuen, 1987), pp. 15-20.

3   Mary Wollstonecraft, *A Vindication of the Rights of Woman* (London, 1985), pp. 259-63.

4   Locke's discussion appears in Book II, Chapter 27 of *An Essay Concerning Human Understanding*, ed. Peter H. Nidditch (Oxford: Oxford University Press, 1975), pp. 330-1.

5   Simon Schama discusses this political tree-symbolism in *Landscape and Memory* (London: HarperCollins, 1995), pp. 53-74.

6   Edmund Burke, *Reflections on the Revolution in France*, ed. Conor Cruise O'Brien, (Harmondsworth: Penguin, 1982), p. 120.

7   Ibid., p. 181.

8   See William Ruddick, 'Liberty trees and loyal oaks: emblematic presences in some English poems of the French Revolutionary period', in Alison Yarrington and Kelvin Everest, ed. *Reflections of Revolution: Images of Romanticism* (London and New York: Routledge, 1993), pp. 59-67.

9   See Stephen Daniels and Charles Watkins, 'Picturesque Landscaping', in Stephen Copley and Peter Garside, ed. *The Politics of the Picturesque* (Cambridge: Cambridge University Press, 1994), pp. 13-41 and Stephen Daniels, 'The Political Iconography of Woodland in Later Georgian England', in Denis Cosgrove and Stephen Daniels, ed. *The Iconography of Landscape* (Cambridge: Cambridge University Press, 1980), pp. 43-82 (p. 61, 79).

10   Richard Payne Knight, *The Landscape*, 2nd edn. (1795), Book V, lines 61-63; Book V, lines 111-20 (pp. 72-5).

11   Wordsworth's line echoes lines 50-2, 103-4. See my discussion in 'Cowper, Wordsworth, Clare: the Politics of Trees', *The John Clare Society Journal*. 14 (1995), pp. 47-59.

12   See my essays 'Wordsworth's "Yew-Trees": Politics, Ecology and Imagination', *Romanticism*, 1 (1995), pp. 272-88 and 'Wordsworth, Cowper and the Language of Eighteenth-Century Politics', in Thomas Woodman, ed. *Early Romanticism: Perspectives in British Poetry from Pope to Wordsworth* (London: Macmillan, 1999, pp. 117-33.

13   Robert Southey, *Essays, Moral and Political*. 2 vols (London, 1832), I, pp. 11-12.

14   See Edmund Burke, *A Philosophical Enquiry into the Origin of Our Ideas of the Sublime and the Beautiful*, ed. James T. Boulton (Oxford: Blackwell, 1987), p. 111.

15   Burke, *Reflections*, pp. 170-71.

16   *Letters and Journals of Lord Byron*, ed. Leslie Marchand. 12 vols (London: John Murray, 1973-82), II, p. 68.

17   Letter of 21st June 1820, from Princess Lieven to Prince Metternich, quoted in E. A. Smith, *A Queen on Trial: The Affair of Queen Caroline* (Stroud: Sutton, 1993), p. 40.

18   Quoted in Smith, *Queen on Trial*, p. 106.

19   'The bill thrown out, but the pains and penalties inflicted' (15th November 1820); reproduced in Smith, *Queen on Trial*, p. 142.

20   See Burke, *Sublime and the Beautiful*, pp. 111, 157.

21   The word appears in *Paradise Lost*, where its ambiguity reveals the fallen Satan's vulnerability and his harmfulness as he enters Eden ready to tempt Eve: 'Who aspires must down as low / As high he soared, obnoxious first or last / To basest things' (IX, 169-71). Wordsworth's use of the word here makes his tree possibly Satanic, possibly one vulnerable to an occupation by the evil spirit of Satanic desire. But in the poem as a whole the temptation to know good and evil and the sexual fall that ensues is refused. There is no serpentine rape of Eve, no sublime pursuit of knowledge and power by the male narrator to its independent but bitter end.

4   John Clare's Gypsies: Problems of Placement and Displacement in Romantic Critical Practice

PHILIP W. MARTIN

In his remarkable exploration of displacement in Wordsworth's 'Gipsies', David Simpson passes some incidental commentary on John Clare, in which he situates Clare's depiction of gypsies as relatively 'complex'. This complexity he attributes to Clare's personal acquaintance with gypsies and his 'alternative political perception of the nature of civil society'. The argument about Clare is not at all central to Simpson's point about Wordsworth, but it is repeated, without further detail, towards the end of the chapter, where Clare's understanding becomes a way of defining Wordsworth's social blind spots.[1]

In one very important sense, Simpson's commentary is typical of the habits of a prevalent Romantic critical discourse which is fascinated by what certain major canonical poets do not see, or by what they choose to leave out of their poems. Among others, Jonathan Bate has complained about this fetishization of 'absence', and is, quite bluntly at times, dismissive of the relevance and point of the criticism of displacement.[2] 'Bluntly' because an argument such as Simpson's *is* sensitive to the difficulties; his object is to show Wordsworth as a 'subject in transit' troubled by middle class insecurities,[3] and his analysis, far from demonstrating what has been left out of the poetry, is crammed with the repletion of what it contains. My concern is not to quarrel with the method of such criticism, but to note, and then attempt to counteract, its effects. In the instance of *Wordsworth's Historical Imagination,* the consequence is ironic: Simpson's commentary centers the poet who does not see by marginalizing the poet who sees. Here Clare's marginality is contiguous to his complexity, while Wordsworth's relative 'simplicity' of view yields the complex criticism. Simultaneously this keeps Wordsworth at the centre of Romantic critical debate and Clare on the outside. Of course it is not only the criticism of displacement that maintains this state of things: Bate's

Romantic Ecology produced a similar effect by placing Wordsworth at the centre of Romantic ecology rather than Clare even though Clare's work is more obviously ecological. Bate's most recent work recognizes this, but his 'placing' of Wordsworth in 1991 and Simpson's 'displacing' operated in canonical harmony nevertheless.[4]

This essay takes issue with the displacements that are continuously likely to place Clare on the margins of Romanticism even while gesturing to his greater perception in broad claims for authenticity. At the same time I want to address the difficulties that attend an opposing critical approach which claims for Clare an authenticity that grants him a special place. Clare's representation of gypsies acts as a focus for this discussion. Although this is not a region of his writing that has received extensive critical attention, critics have been attracted to these representations because of the resonances that move so well between a marginal poet and a marginal social group: the implication may be – quite simply – that there is some kind of identification or natural sympathy here. In such readings Clare is a very different poet to those troubled subjects, Goldsmith and Wordsworth, with which Simpson opens his sophisticated discussion of the poetry of displacement, subjects constituted in the paradoxes of labour and leisure, work and poetry-writing, subjectivity and inter-subjectivity. Simpson rightly identifies Wordsworth's awkward poem about gypsies as a place in which we can observe the complex making of a series of poetical statements about the poet's relation to the social order, and indeed, social otherness. He is also right to note how complex Clare's poems about gypsies may be.

While I am intrigued by the critical practices which place Clare variously as central, complex, or marginal because complex, and while, necessarily, I need to site my own contribution in relation to others, the main purpose of this essay will be to address the nature of Clare's representations of gypsies in a series of poems that multiply perceptions of home, homeliness and homelessness; labour and indolence; property, use and utility; and – however remotely – civic and social relations. Part of the purpose will be to acknowledge the status of the tropological in Clare's writings, and to discuss the sources and kinds of rhetoric through which he engages with 'the real'. At the same time, my purpose will be to resist the collapsing of these engagements into mere textuality, and this will constitute the other part of my essay. The attitudes to gypsies apparently implied in Clare's representations of them, I concede, derive partly from the identifiable and available discourses which figure vagrancy and gypsies in specific ways, in turn, these are resisted, accepted or modified in his writings. At the same time I will argue that Simpson's incidental remark about Clare's authenticity (Clare actually knew gypsies) is a remark of real consequence. Figuring authenticity, inside the poem – or indeed outside, as it were, by the author's signature (with all its 'rustic credibility') – will be the object of some attention here. My *placing* of gypsies in Clare's writing, precisely because of the claims made for authenticity by Clare and on his behalf, will therefore also involve a critical reconfiguration; the placing and displacing of the critical methods through which authority, authenticity, and canonical status are sustained.

If a broadly canonical criticism has this predictable effect of displacing Clare from the centre to the margins in its sophisticated concern to provide complexity for that which is relatively straightforward, then how does Clare criticism operate within these terms? In answering this question I will refer to two recent essays which deal with Clare's poems about gypsies: James C. McKusick's 'Beyond the Visionary Company: John Clare's resistance to Romanticism' and 'John Clare: the trespasser' by John Goodridge and Kelsey Thornton.[5] McKusick's essay is highly conscious of the criticism of displacement, and works both within and against its paradigms using Bakhtinian dialogics to accommodate counter-relations of vocabulary and politics. Contesting Harold Bloom's half-hearted legitimation of Clare as a Romantic by marking him out as a *failed* Romantic, McKusick's placing of Clare relies upon another kind of legitimation that has considerable currency in criticism of Clare: his interpellation as a 'peasant-poet', and the argument here is that the 'material base of class identity' yields very specific qualities in the verse itself. Further, the critical activity which attempts to place Clare in relation to 'established conceptions' (and the example before us is Bloom's attempt to see Clare as a Romantic) is in a way an 'historical repression' of class and regionality.[6] These elements of Clare's experience – his 'remaining true to his origins' – combine with the more formal demands of loco-descriptive traditions to produce a disruptive heteroglossia. In this argument, Clare's gypsy poems have a crucial role, for it is that strong sense of identification or sympathy with the marginalized or the outcast that pulls the poet towards a vocabulary or style at odds with the formal demands of poetic decorum:

> For Clare, however, who has come to know the gypsies through intimate personal acquaintance, there is a sense of class solidarity that exposes the inauthenticity of such effete poetic diction as 'Boreal' and 'sybil', conveying instead the desperate scarcity that pervades these 'short-sward pastures'.[7]

For Goodridge and Thornton, the overarching concern is to advance an understanding of Clare's poetry that recognizes more than the previous prevalent critical preoccupation with descriptive veracity. They suggest that Clare's poetry works through groupings of linked ideas, and ideas and images of trespass – both figural and literal – constitute one such grouping. Again, Clare's sympathetic interest in gypsies and the counter-culture they represent is a keystone for the argument. His close identification with the gypsies is stressed: 'gypsies were overwhelmingly the most important human trespassers in Clare's writing, apart from the poet himself. They were his natural allies (unlike the static, alien breed of Wordsworth's 'Gypsies')'.[8] So, as users of common land, outsiders, songsters and country folk with an intimate knowledge of all things rural in Clare's characterisation of them, gypsies are seen here as 'natural trespassers' in the landscape.

Simpson and the critics of Clare that I have brought forward here share a common concern with remarking upon Clare's first-hand acquaintance with gypsies, and underlining thereby the claims made for 'complexity' (Simpson), 'stark candour' (McKusick) or 'an honest documentary approach' (Goodridge and Thornton).[9] *Placing* Clare is evidently a practice caught up with notions of authenticity, and in the special placing that attends peasants and lunatics, this practice is never neutralized within a non-evaluative taxonomy. Placing Clare is evaluative and allusive, the evaluation alluding to an appeal (rarely accepted in our common critical practice) to authenticity and the validation of real experience transformed into poetry. This is not to parody the critics to whom I have referred by representing them as disciples of social realism, but to suggest that it is Clare's case that justly forces a reconsideration of authenticity. Similar arguments of course, surround other writers subject to canonical or colonial repression, for whom the questions of origin, identity and lived experience are vital political oppositions to a prevalent post-structuralist anxiety about the status of original, subjective experience. My point is not to disqualify this method of authentication (although I am worried by it), but to note how placing Clare is often a matter of placing in terms of class relations, and that this, in turn, sets up a region of critical practice in which a broad liberalism finds itself approving of Clare's disruption of tropological orthodoxy in the name of a better truth.

While McKusick's focussed argument about Clare's heteroglossia is a compelling and cogent one, the more general allusion to Clare's authenticity or 'honest documentary approach' needs further qualification. It is not that Clare's critics show no consciousness of this need. On the contrary, Goodridge and Thornton freely acknowledge that Clare 'figures' gypsies within the conventions of the picturesque, explaining this as a cautious strategy adopted in the face of authoritarian patrons and power.

Even so, they argue that the prose passages on gypsies in the *Autobiographical Writings,* and the passage on gypsies in *The Village Minstrel* offer the honest documentary approach because 'no overt emotional appeal is needed to mitigate the fact that gypsies trespass and steal firewood, when we learn that need drives them to eat diseased sheep carcasses, or "any nauceaous thing their frowning fates provide"'. This engenders a new way of seeing gypsies 'as fellow mortals ... vulnerable to the hardship of rural life'.[10] Yet it is precisely the features identified by these critics in their arguments for Clare's documentary approach that loom large in Cowper's famous passage on gypsies in Book One of *The Task.:*

> A kettle, slung
> Between two poles upon a stick transverse,
> Receives the morsel; flesh obscene of dog,
> Or vermin, or at best, of cock purloin'd
> From his accustom'd perch. Hard-faring race!
> They pick their fuel out of ev'ry hedge,
> Which kindled with dry leaves, just saves unquench'd
> The spark of life (*PWC*, II, p. 131).

Both the vocabulary and the figures of Cowper's passage reappear in Clare's writings on gypsies (the tawny or vellum skin, the eating of vermin, the stealing of sticks, the exposure of palmistry). Further, the ambivalent representation of gypsies in one of Clare's most interesting poems, 'The Gypsy Camp', where they are figured as 'A quiet, pilfering, unprotected race'[11] might also be seen to derive broadly from Cowper. This derivation consists not in the detail of the phrase, which Clare's critical admirers rightly see as singular, but in the apparent mixing of attitudes which suggests approval and disapproval. In Cowper's poem, for all the obvious enlightenment moralizing which condemns the gypsies as anti-social and useless, there is a readiness also to extol them as emblems of nature's innocence and simplicity, untouched by the corruption of luxury:

> Such health and gaiety of heart enjoy
> The houseless rovers of the sylvan world;
> And breathing wholesome air, and wand'ring much,
> Need other physic none to heal th'effects
> Of loathsome diet, penury, and cold
>   (*The Task*, I, lines 587-91: *PWC*, II, p. 132).

The ambivalence of Cowper's poem, in which the gypsies serve two emblematic functions as representations of idleness and innocence, perhaps derives from this tendency to use them not only as picturesque domesticized *banditti*, but as quasi-satiric dystopias or utopias, paradigms of social ordinance that antithetically or otherwise multiply *exempla* of civil society. Fielding used the gypsy episode in *Tom Jones* in this way for example, to present alternative models of justice and judgement in a rational world. Cowper's apparent ambivalence only remains as a paradox so long as we see it as representative of 'an attitude' towards (real) gypsies. If, however, we regard the representation of gypsies as serving the desire to hypothesize an improved society, or indeed castigate a corrupt one, then this 'ambivalence' is entirely consistent, controlled and determined by the enlightenment values of utility, simplicity, civic duty, honest labour and frugality.

This use of the gypsy people as devices through which civic society can be defined is politicized in Thelwall's *The Peripatetic* (1793). Here again, the gypsies stand not as one consistent representation, but as many, as Thelwall's mobile irony moves the dialogue of his two pedestrians to present gypsies as emblems of a conservative, introspective society, unchanging and reactionary, as just recipients of charity (and therefore as representatives of the poor), as subjects for discussions on labour and prejudice (during which Ambulator remarks that he 'cannot detest these poor vagrants with all that Christian fervor with which, considering them as *infidels* and *sans culottes, I* may be, perhaps in duty bound') and finally, as objects perceived in a landscape which figures *both* the picturesque and the social prejudice which reads their 'expedition of discovery' as a voyage of 'pillage and devastation'.[12]

By the time that Clare writes his poems about gypsies, there is an established habit of representation that does not allow us to read his figures as original and remarkable because of the documentary details they contain, but might encourage us to see that representations of gypsies were used for the purposes of socio-political satire. This, however, is not a sufficient basis on which to throw out the notion of authenticity altogether. I wish to contribute to the evolution of that notion within some of the poems themselves and not as a biographical fact. It is Clare's language of knowing, together with his self-authenticating rustic style, I suggest, that textualizes authenticity, by a subtle figuration of the writer writing, or the rustic seeing. The representation of the identity of the perceiving self is all-important here (and that question of identity is a preoccupation running throughout Clare's poetry).[13] In this respect, Simpson's comparison between Wordsworth and Clare can be usefully extended and modified. For Simpson's discovery of Wordsworth's depiction of gypsies through Milton allows us to read the poem as a self-conscious literary production, even if the associations of that literariness (the identification of the narrator with

Satan and thereby, the envious eye, or indeed the allusion to innocent bliss) are regarded as subliminal elements in the poem's composition. Clare's poems, although they use certain familiar tropes, construct no consistent allusive references, and moreover, they place the perceiving eye in a series of different positions which variously situate the poet within, rather than above or beyond the scene. In certain of his poems Clare engages yet diminishes what might be called that anthropological othering which is of so much consequence in Wordsworth, Cowper, or even Thelwall.

In the poem known as 'The Gypseys Camp' ('How oft on Sundays when Id time to tramp') for example, there is a complex placing of the speaker's voice in relation both to his habits and the objects of his description:

> How oft on Sundays when Id time to tramp
> My rambles led me to a gypseys camp
> Where the real effigies of midnight hags
> Wi tawney smoaked flesh & tatterd rags . . .[14]

The lines might be read as infelicitous in one sense, since the opening phrase (a construction commonly used by Clare in his prose) suggests a habitual and familiar practice while the clichéd 'my rambles led me' suggests a chance encounter. Clare adapts the slightly whimsical mode of the pedestrian poetry of encounter to accommodate such paradoxes within a broad characterization of the pedestrian as a person of leisure and habit or familiarity. Simultaneously this characterization is qualified by the insertion of the conditional phrase, 'when Id time to tramp', which indicates the freedoms enjoyed on Sundays, but also implies the constraints of circumstance, the duties of the Sabbath, or the demands of the labourer's life. Either way, the leisure which permits pedestrianism is evoked in the poem as a privilege, or something stolen away from a more pressing duty, and in this way Clare avoids the kind of conflict between the poet's 'labour' and the poet's leisure time that Simpson sees as the source of the fissures in Wordsworth's poem. The mode of perceiving therefore, sits somewhere between that of the conventional leisured wanderer and the subject of an undeclared but circumscribed circumstance. At the same time the oxymoronic phrase 'real effigies' evokes, exaggerates and disqualifies the gypsy stereotype all at once: here it is not the poem which explicitly mediates 'reality', but mediation itself which is the poem's subject. The material encounter with the gypsies which the poem represents is mediated through an expectation based on an artificial representation – the gypsy women are 'real effigies of midnight hags' – representations not of themselves but of literary tropes in the light of this ironic perception.

This is just one of the ways in which the poem avoids the conventional mode of the loco-descriptive specular poem. The gypsies here are not perceived as a scene set in a landscape, the subject of the educated picturesque gaze, so much as encountered in their activities, including the setting up of shelters in the lee of the wind which Clare describes in such detail. And at the centre of the poem there is an uncanny sense of belonging but not belonging, of participation and alienation:

> How oft Ive bent me oer their fire & smoak
> To hear their gibberish tale so quaintly spoke

The fireside tale, that powerful emblem of a civil community joined together by custom and a common story is a well-used motif in Clare's poetry. It has a special place for him as a signifier of shared experience and the common ownership of a specific history, often potently suggested in the image of the aged story-teller narrating tales to the young, or, more simply, by the repetition of the familiar tale (Jack the Giant-Killer for example) wherein the common history becomes the common culture. This poem uses that motif, but recasts it too by emphasizing the *romanes* (the language of the gypsies) to produce the idea of the attentive listener who does not comprehend, yet is a fireside listener still. At the poem's centre there is therefore an image that is a powerful resonating analogue of the writer's relation to the community. He is at home and not at home there, a part of, and apart from this social group. That notion is continued as this strange poem shifts into the quasi-satiric mode of its final section, where Clare both participates in, and derides, the ritual of fortune-telling. Here he presents himself as a willing participant, confirming the stereotype of him projected by the gypsies, before then repudiating this role in the self-deprecating humorous ending.

It is in these unprecedented ways that this poem negotiates a position for its act of looking that avoids the anthropological othering of the gypsies and simultaneously rejects the alternative presumption of identification. So we discover a new kind of placing here, a new parallax which effectively displaces the rhetoric of the picturesque observer, tourist, or rustic pedestrian. The perceiving eye as the centre of knowledge or co-ordinator of a perspective allotting status to the constituent elements of the picture – a perceiving eye such as Cowper's for example – is thus relocated by this parallax that intimates Clare's 'placing' within the gypsy camp as well as his placing of the gypsy camp. It is precisely this that makes the claim for authenticity. The poem textualizes this double placing within the ambiguity of belonging and not belonging.

This is not always the case in Clare's gypsy poems. 'The Gipsies Evening Blaze' consciously employs the language of conventional aesthetics to frame its view. Thus the opening offers a dramatic tableau:

> To me, how wildly pleasing is that scene
> Which does present in evenings dusky hour
> A group of gypsies, center'd on the green ...[15]

And although the vocabulary to which James McKusick has alerted us counters the language of the picturesque, our understanding of the poem's dialogics would have to include its point of closure, which is an entirely conventional appeal:

> When this I view the all attentive mind
> Will oft exclaim so strong the scene prevades
> 'Grant me this life thou spirit of the shades!'

It is also an appeal which consciously makes an artifice out of the biographical fact of Clare's occasional dwelling with gypsies. In this respect the poem uses conventions to de-authenticate the real by displacing what may have been Clare's desire to stay with the gypsies into the realm of a very specific kind of poetic decorum, even if it does this alongside the series of counter-relations to which McKusick has justly drawn our attention.[16]

'The Gipsy Camp' (High Beech, 1840-41) operates in a similar way. Its arrangement derives from its presentation of a scene which has a distinct pictorial quality, and the poem freely draws on the motifs to be found in the literary representation of gypsies. Interestingly, and perhaps rather in the manner of the line in 'The Gypseys Camp' which consciously uses a convention as a means of representing or mediating the real ('the real effigies of midnight hags'), the poem seems as set on a de-authentication of its perception as an authentication of it. Of moment here is the way in which we read the penultimate line:

> 'Tis thus they live – a picture to the place [17]

The force of the preposition suggests that the gypsies are to be seen as an aesthetic attribute of the environment, a supplementary and picturesque complement to the place itself. In the *Autobiographical Writings*, Clare makes a remark of similar import, when he writes that he thought 'the gypseys camp by the green woodside a picturesque and adorning object to nature'. Here there is none of the enabling irony of Thelwall's *Peripatetic,* wherein the narrator remarks:

> tell me, do you not feel that if these idle wanderers were exterminated, the landscape painter would be robbed of one of his most agreeable sources of embellishment, and the poet of an object well-calculated to give variety to his descriptions?[18]

Yet there is another way to read the line whereby the making of the picture is not to be seen as a reduction, so much as a conflation of the aesthetics of representation and the life that the gypsies lead: both clauses in the penultimate line are given equal weight in such a reading, which makes a naive claim for an unproblematized mimesis, a claim expanded upon in Clare's staunch defence of Peter de Wint's paintings in his 'Essay on Landscape'.[19]

Conscious of his position in the commodified poetry market of his day, Clare would have been aware of the expectation that his poetry should register his standing as a peasant-poet, that impossible paradox. Signs of the naive or the authentic in the uneducated rural gaze needed to be simultaneously accompanied by some form of poetic legitimation: the acknowledgement of the pictorial or the picturesque, or the employment of a series of motifs that might invoke, as here, the tradition of Cowper. In *The Shepherd's Calendar,* a poem which also concerns itself with the representation of gypsies, the literary conventions of representing a homogeneous and viable rural economy operating through itinerate rural wanderers who work their way around the country, in this example repairing chairs, selling bullrushes, or playing the fiddle, are in full play. The poem presents the knowing rural eye of the peasant as its reader's access to a rural England which, no doubt, they wish to preserve, one undivided by conflict, hardship or opposing interests, epitomized in the festivals of a merry England:

> The gypsey fiddler jogs away
> To village feast and holiday
> Scraping in public house to trye
> What beer his music will supply . . . [20]

The poem inscribes the two kinds of authenticity that the paradox of the peasant-poet demands: it includes ruralisms and dialect words which worried Clare's publisher, Taylor, and it also includes the legitimation of writing itself in the employment of pastoral and georgic conventions, for this is Clare's means of authenticating himself as a writer. To be an authentic writer is not to be an authentic observer in this instance.

The examples of Clare's poems about gypsies discussed here are therefore founded on paradoxes, but these are markedly different in kind to that conflict which Simpson discovers in Wordsworth's poem. The act of observation in Clare is distinct because of the continuous concern with the documentation, however lightly sketched, of a regimen or way of life that centres on subsistence. Whereas Wordsworth discovered a rift between his labour as a poet and the gypsies' apparent idleness which generates notions of utility and social responsibility (what Hazlitt wittily called his 'Sunday-school philosophising'), the passage between Clare's poetic labour and the object of his attention is less troubled and largely bereft of anxiety. Clare's gypsies are displaced certainly: they are consciously engaged as an alternative to civil society, a group whose social arrangements are clearly distinct. They do not serve as a satiric foil with a contemporary reference, and neither do they constitute utopian or dystopian models. Clare's vignettes offer too few details in these respects, and are therefore inimical to analyses of this kind. They are, however, remarkable in their representation of gypsy homeliness: as 'vagrant dwellers in the houseless woods' (to borrow Wordsworth's reverberative phrase from 'Tintern Abbey') the paradoxical condition of dwelling in a homeless place is powerfully re-iterated in Clare's poetry, which desists, on all occasions, from the approving rhetoric of utility that attends almost all other examples of representations of gypsies in this period. Clare's poetry grants the gypsies a legitimate home in the landscape, and it is that sense of home, or more correctly, of dwelling, that does not permit them to be alienated on account of barbarism, brutality or idleness. They are instead an alternative civil society held together by bonds of subsistence, domestic harmony and togetherness, whose place in the landscape is confirmed not by the rights of property or ownership, but by the peasant-poet's sympathetic and radical perception of their right to dwell.[21]

Notes

1   David Simpson, *Wordsworth's Historical Imagination: the Poetry of Displacement* (London: Methuen, 1987), pp. 45, 54.
2   Jonathan Bate, *Romantic Ecology* (London and New York: Routledge, 1991). See pp. 15-16.
3   Simpson, *Wordsworth's Historical Imagination.* p. 55.
4   Bate's recent article on Clare ('The Rights of Nature', *The John Clare Society Journal*, 14 [July 1995], pp. 7-15) produces an interesting reading of Clare's ecology in a continuation of this critic's battle with a new historicism which, he argues, fails

to read the complexity of Romantic rural politics by reducing it continually to a shying away from political activism. In justice to Bate, this argument implicitly pushes Clare into a more central position. For a more thorough-going exploration of Clare's ecology see the important article by James McKusick, "'A language that is ever green": the Ecological Vision of John Clare', *University of Toronto Quarterly*, 61 (1991-2), pp. 226-49.

5   Both essays are to be found in Hugh Haughton, Adam Phillips and Geoffrey Summerfield, ed., *John Clare in Context* (Cambridge University Press: Cambridge, 1994).

6   Haughton, *et al.*, *Clare in Context*, p. 222.

7   Haughton, *et al.*, *Clare in Context*, p. 227.

8   Haughton, *et al.*, *Clare in Context*, p. 103.

9   Simpson, *Wordsworth's Historical Imagination*, p. 45. Haughton *et al.*, *Clare in Context*, p. 223, p. 108.

10   Haughton *et al.*, *Clare in Context*, p.108.

11   *The Later Poetry of John Clare*, ed. Eric Robinson and David Powell, 2 vols (Oxford: Clarendon Press, 1984), I, p. 29.

12   *The Peripatetic; or Sketches of the Heart, of Nature and Society; in a series of politico-sentimental Journals, in Verse and Prose, of the Eccentric Excursions of Sylvanus Theophrastus, supposed to have been written by himself,* 3 vols (London, 1793). See 'The Gypsies', II, 41-8. The quotations here are from pp. 47-8.

13   Of particular relevance to the question of identity in Clare's poetry is John Barrell's essay, 'Being is perceiving: James Thomson and John Clare' in John Barrell, *Poetry, Language and Politics* (Manchester: Manchester University Press, 1988).

14   *The Early Poems of John Clare, 1804-22,* ed. Eric Robinson and David Powell, 2 vols (Oxford: Clarendon Press, 1989), II, p. 119.

15   *Early Poems*, I, p. 33.

16   McKusick's understanding of the dialogic process of the making of Clare's poetry, combining with his insightful reading of Clare's vocabularies make his argument a particularly strong one. Alongside it, however, I think we have to acknowledge the relatively restricted range of motifs used by Clare in his gypsy poems, and indeed, the fact that some of the motifs are derivative. Many of these motifs (the picturesque camp, the expression of fondness in the act of viewing, wrongful accusation of theft, the stolen food, the hard fare, the 'gibberish', the discovery of gypsies on a Sunday walk) can be found in the gypsy episode in *The Village Minstrel*, pp. 113-14.

17   *Later Poems*, I, p. 29.

18   *The Peripatetic*, II, pp. 47-8.

19   *The Prose of John Clare*, ed. J.W. and Anne Tibble (London, Routledge and Kegan Paul, 1970), pp.211-15.

20   *The Shepherd's Calendar*, ed. Eric Robinson and Geoffrey Summerfield (London: Oxford University Press, 1964), p.76.

21   In the preparation of this article I am indebted to two articles from which I have not quoted: Angus M. Fraser, 'John Clare's Gypsies', *Northamptonshire Past and Present*, 4.v (1970-71), pp. 259-267; Claire Lamont, 'John Clare and the Gipsies', *The John Clare Society Journal*, 13 (July, 1994), pp. 19-31. I am also indebted to the advice of John Goodridge and Yvonne Jayne.

5 How Wordsworth Keeps His Audience Fit

LUCY NEWLYN

I

'There is little need to advise me against publishing; it is a thing which I dread almost as much as death itself'. So Wordsworth wrote to James Tobin in March 1798, when he had begun seriously to conceive of himself as a professional poet' (*EY*, p. 211). His comment betrays the sense that there is a deep implicit connection between emergence into the public sphere and loss of personal identity – a connection felt so strongly that it resembles the threat of extinction. One thinks ahead, to the moment in *Prelude* Book Eight when imaginative closure is revealingly likened to a 'written book', lying open, 'exposed and lifeless', to the gaze of passers by.[1]

I want in this essay to pursue the implications of this link between death and publication, in the light of changing power relations between author and reader at the end of the eighteenth century. From two different perspectives, the period has been seen to undergo an upheaval in assumptions about what readers are. Jon Klancher, Alan Richardson, and, most recently, Kathryn Sunderland have looked at audiences as a materialist phenomenon, tracing advances in literacy, the growth and diversification of the reading-public, and the extraordinary proliferation of reading-matter.[2] On the other side of the sociological/hermeneutic divide, Tilottama Rajan has considered constructions of 'the reader' in the light of Romantic theory and its later developments.[3] Little attention, however, has so far been paid to the increased pressures inevitably experienced by authors, as a consequence of expanding literacy on the one hand, and the rise of criticism on the other. My own research would suggest that under these pressures the burden of the future weighed more heavily than the burden of the past; and that the Romantics laboured under what might be called an 'anxiety of reception'.[4]

A study has yet to be produced in which materialist and idealist approaches to the reader are adequately combined: only then will it be possible to understand the anxiety of reception as, simultaneously, a

60

psychic defence, an historical phenomenon, and a hermeneutic event. In the meantime, I want to try out a number of hypotheses: firstly, that if literary identity is as much a question of negotiating misreaders as of displacing precursors, then pre-emptive defence-mechanisms will be just as telling as Bloom's 'revisionary ratios'. Secondly, that in the period in question, the recent experience of revolution may have accentuated an awareness that revision breeds revision – and that authority, under such conditions, can only be provisional. Thirdly, that as a consequence of this awareness there were divided allegiances in the writing-reading subject: while welcoming the increased freedom of readers, Romantic writers attempted to place constraints on their power, so as to stabilise their own authority as writers. They also evinced uncertainties about the direction in which to move their theories of interpretation.

Coleridge, for instance, to whom indiscriminate reviewers and a lazy reading-public were proof of the nation's spiritual degeneracy, saw it as his mission to turn passive into reflective readers. But there were limitations to the amount of power he wished the reader to possess; and the sublime aesthetic which underpins his reading-theory leads him to favour the reader's submission, along Burkean lines, to mystery and authority.[5] Paradoxically, then, his apparently liberal engagement of active reader-response has conservative undercurrents. These surface more evidently in sweeping comments about degenerating intellectual standards. 'The misgrowth of our luxuriant activity: a READING PUBLIC' (*The Statesman's Manual*: *LS*, p. 36), carries a heavy political inflection, when it is seen how frequently the emergent power of the reader – and especially the female reader – is apprehended as a fearful and proliferating by-product of the French Revolution.[6] Nor is Coleridge's position atypical. The status of the written text, as bearer of authoritative meaning, was increasingly being brought under question; and an implicit binary logic began to associate the empowerment of reading with the demise of authority. It is astonishing how literally, urgently, and personally Romantic writers appear to have anticipated Roland Barthes' claim, that 'the birth of the reader must be at the cost of the death of the author'.[7]

In Wordsworth's case, especially, the 'anxiety of reception' takes a subject-centred form, betraying an almost paranoid fear that authors are at the mercy, not just of anonymous reviewers and the reading-public at large, but of uncooperative individual acts of interpretation. A more fearless revisionary poet than Coleridge, Wordsworth was presumably subject to graver doubts about his own stability as a writing-subject; and, having no overarching system of authority on which to rely, saw that the provisionality of literary tradition made his work vulnerable to strong misreaders. While sharing Coleridge's assumptions about the damaging effects of passive reading, he did not believe that the Bible provided a model for reflective understanding. Nor did he place so much faith in hermeneutic principles of sympathy and community as the means whereby taste might be transformed. His less theorized, more improvisatory position appears by comparison beleaguered. For him, the question of how to 'create the taste by which he is to be enjoyed' ('Essay Supplementary to the Preface [1815]'): *WW*, pp. 657-8) is one of eliciting the reader's trust and co-operation in his literary endeavour – or, as he puts it in 1815, of 'establishing that dominion over the spirits of Readers by which they are to be humbled and humanised, in order that they may be purified and exalted' (*WW*, p. 658). In this position of maximum dependency disguised as maximum power, the continuity and coherence of poetic self are all that can be relied on to ensure survival.

For this reason Wordsworth's negotiations with his audience show a mixture of tough-minded pragmatism and vulnerability. Throughout his career, the hope that he might ensure his correct reception involves him in the careful oversight of how his volumes are produced, advertised and marketed, as well as in a more theoretical attempt to direct the public's expectations. It is not until the hostile reception of *Poems in Two Volumes* (1807) that he has any genuine cause to feel aggrieved, yet as early as 1800 the pre-emptive direction of his authorial strategies is visible. The production of *Lyrical Ballads* must be warily supervised if identity is to be made secure. Letters to Joseph Cottle dictating the shape of the volumes and the appearance of the type-face show his concern with the minutiae of presentation;[8] while the Preface attempts to frame the volume's critical reception in a semi-apologetic series of directives to the reader. He intervenes in both production and reception as a defensive measure.

Defence-mechanisms are, however, notorious for eliciting the responses they are designed to pre-empt. Lamb wished the Preface had appeared separately, because it made the ballads look as if they were 'experiments on the public taste' (*Marrs*, I, pp. 266-7) – so provoking Jeffrey's labelling of the Lake poets as a new sect, to which Wordsworth violently objected.[9] There is no doubt that by presenting himself as both theorist and practitioner Wordsworth made himself more vulnerable to attack – a position further weakened when his exalted claims for the poet appeared in 1802. But this was not how he himself saw the matter. Indeed, the earnestness with which he packaged himself for public consumption increased as a result of attacks on *Poems in Two Volumes*, which he had risked submitting to the public with no theoretical framework. 'It is impossible that any expectations can be lower than mine concerning the effect of these poems upon what is called the public', he had claimed in a letter of May 1807 (To Lady Beaumont, May 1807: *MY*, I, p. 41). Yet when they were lambasted by Francis Jeffrey his reaction had been one of wounded horror. The lesson he chose to learn from this was that the public could be relied on not at all; and that the reception of future volumes must be more tightly controlled than ever.

If hostile reviewers were to discard some of his output as trivial, it was Wordsworth's prerogative to show that underlying principles connected all his works according to a predetermined plan: hence his Preface to *The Excursion*. When both Jeffrey and Hazlitt proved resistant to these unifying claims, he retaliated with more. *Poems* (1815) has both a directive Preface, explaining his categorization of poetic faculties; and an 'Essay Supplementary' proclaiming his immunity to hostile reception. Subsequent volumes are even more monolithic, showing an increasing preoccupation with the coherence of his poetic identity. Revising each poem for its new appearance, Wordsworth places what Stephen Gill has called 'an inordinate demand' on his readers, who must check every poem for its revisions to keep track of the growth of the poet's mind.[10] Nowhere since Milton's *Defences* had self-image, or the illusion of a seamless continuity between public and private identities, been so carefully cultivated.[11]

Nor does the parallel with Milton stop there. Wordsworth's abiding concern was with finding a worthy audience; and increasingly the label 'fit though few' has an appropriate resonance, given his expectations of and disappointment with the public at large'.[12] As early as 1800 in the Preface to *Lyrical Ballads* he establishes the imaginative poverty of professional critics by referring to them as 'numerous'(*WW*, p. 601). Worthy readers are by inference at once enlightened and singular. Such exclusiveness afforded him little compensation, however, for failing to reach his wider audience. Even less convincing, as a defensive measure, is his slanted account of literary history in the 'Essay Supplementary' of 1815. Tracing the unreliability of critical taste through the eighteenth century, he uses the 'slow progress of [Milton's] fame' and the public's 'unremitting hostility' to his own works as 'pledges and tokens' that 'the products of [hisl industry will endure' (*WW*, pp. 649, 657). It is a case of special pleading, made more transparent by his wish to distinguish 'the people' from 'the public' and so to keep open the possibility of becoming a popular poet' (*WW*, p. 661). Sounding increasingly like Coleridge, whose pronouncements on the reading-public are notorious for their stentorian moral tone, Wordsworth comes eventually to an awareness that he must look to posterity for lasting fame. 'If it be of God – it must stand' has a quiet self-justifying confidence that is again reminiscent of Milton (To Catherine Clarkson, 31 Dec. 1814: *MY*, II, p. 81).

II

But, if the public failed him, who were the 'few' on whose fitness Wordsworth could depend? A generous critic has recently suggested that 'while he had little time for the professional reviewer, Wordsworth was responsive to constructive criticism from other creative writers',[13] and were it not for both poets' inherent competitiveness, one might take the dialogue with Coleridge as paradigmatic of such healthy egalitarian exchange.[14] Yet Wordsworth also showed a lifelong dependence on coterie audiences, not all of whom wrote themselves, or were considered to be on his intellectual level. W. J. Fox told Henry Crabb Robinson that his response to Wordsworth's poetry was less than whole-hearted because 'he was not initiated or fraternised';[15] while Coleridge's sarcastic description of a poet 'living almost wholly among devotees' suggests his reliance for self-esteem on an intimate circle of adoring family and friends (To Tom Poole, 14 Oct. 1803: *CL*, I, p. 1013) Fraternity in its unfamiliar sense is not part of the picture.

The animus behind Coleridge's remark is assuredly his growing sense of exclusion from the Wordsworth household, but there is much more to their different ideas of an audience than that. Coleridge saw the bond of sympathy between author and reader in terms of a communitarian spirit, whose cohesiveness had its roots in Christianity. The models for his reading-circles can be traced back, as Elinor Shaffer has shown, to pantisocracy and its seventeenth-century analogues;[16] as can the principle of 'friendship', which underwrites both his literary dialogues and publishing ventures including *The Friend* itself. Wordsworth's relations with his readers are both more exclusive and more quarrelsome, depending as they do on loyalty and co-operation. When Southey reviewed *Lyrical Ballads* in 1798, Wordsworth complained to Cottle: 'If he could not conscientiously have spoken differently of the volume, he ought to have declined the task of reviewing it' (24 June 1799: *EY*, p. 64). Southey had clearly overstepped the mark, by allowing his professional role to obscure his private allegiance.

Small interpretative communities are frequently organized during this period in such a way that they define and constrain the activity of reading.[17] The circulation of manuscripts among family and friends was, for instance, a practice observed by Wordsworth throughout his life; and as early as

1793 Dorothy records that she and Christopher 'amused themselves by analysing every line and sending a very bulky criticism . . . to transmit to William' (To Jane Pollard, 16 Feb. 1793: *EY*, p. 89). Dorothy came as near as anyone to being his ideal reader, but on the whole 'bulky criticism' was not what Wordsworth expected. Of Lamb's response to 'The White Doe' he wrote to Coleridge: 'Let Lamb learn to be ashamed of himself in not taking some pleasure in the contemplation of this picture' (19 April 1808: *MY*, I, pp. 222-3). The tone of this remark would have greatly amused Lamb, who in 1801 had received 'a long letter of four sweating pages' telling him why Wordsworth 'was compelled to wish that his range of sensibility was more extended' (*Marrs*, I, p. 272) Lamb had merely indicated his personal preferences among the *Lyrical Ballads*.

When Sara Hutchinson complained that 'The Leechgatherer' was tedious, Wordsworth's outraged rejoinder – 'everything is tedious when one does not read with the feelings of the author' (*EY*, p. 367) – suggests the expectation of absolute empathy from his readers. Nothing less is required than that 'A person [should read] this poem with feelings like mine' (*EY*, p. 366). Similarly, replying to an otherwise unqualified letter of homage from John Wilson, also in 1802, Wordsworth rebukes him for not responding with the poet's own exquisite delight to 'The Idiot Boy' (*EY*, p. 355). On such occasions, Wordsworth's directives to members of a coterie audience shade into the tones of solemn persuasiveness adopted in his Prefaces. Somewhere in-between are instructions of the kind issued to Charles James Fox, about how to read 'The Brothers' and 'Michael'. In its optimistic reliance on exemplary individuals and reflective reading as a means for political change, this letter comes as near as Wordsworth ever does to Coleridge's endeavours to induce a clerisy (14 Jan. 1801: *EY*, p. 312-5).

But always the key to his bond with readers is his power to persuade and their willingness to be persuaded, rather than (as in Coleridge's case) the mutual observance of a religious aesthetic, whose rules have been established by long tradition.[18] It is this that gives Wordsworth's engagement with the reader its querulous egotism,[19] making the transition between 'private' and 'public' audiences problematic. The purpose of his poetry is to extend the range of his audience's feelings; yet, to do this, he depends absolutely on his readers' willingness to enter his own emotional world. John Wilson's resistance to the poetic representation of idiocy, or Sara Hutchinson's to the 'naked simplicity' of 'The Leechgatherer' (*EY*, p. 366), represent for Wordsworth the breakdown of that implicit trust between author and reader on which his poetic project is founded. That he should go ahead, after receiving Sara's letter, and revise 'The

Leechgatherer' in the direction he did, is a measure of the transparency with which his demand for obedience masks his need for approval.[20]

III

The problem Wordsworth encounters in his dealings with readers is described in Schleiermacher's *Hermeneutics* as the precondition for all acts of understanding: 'One must already know a man in order to understand what he says, and yet one first becomes acquainted with him by what he says'.[21] In other words, to know an author you have to understand him, but to understand him you have already to know him. Understanding presupposes a dialectic between self and other. Yet, without the readiness to enter the other's imaginative world, no genuine act of understanding can take place; and this entry involves relinquishing one's separateness (and thus difference) from the other.[22]

Such is the extent of Wordsworth's need for empathy on the part of his readers that it can lead to an erasure of difference; and frequently this appears to be something striven-for rather than accidentally achieved. In his critical prose, for instance, trust has to be carefully established by rhetorical strategies, rather than either relied on as an emotional given or assumed as a contractual undertaking. Hence the deployment of defensive manoeuvres such as apology and the anticipation of objections, alongside tones ranging from the diplomatically appeasing, 'I hope therefore the Reader will not censure me' (*WW*, p. 596), to the coercive, 'there are few persons of good sense who would not allow' (*WW*, p. 607). This latter, as it turns out is his favoured method for appealing to his readers as though they are already members of the elect.

Wordsworth's aim is thus to transform an anonymous public into a sympathetic readership, whose credentials for understanding him are as sound as his family's and friends'. But rhetorically, as well as conceptually, an impasse is produced in the process. 'The understanding of the being to whom we address ourselves, if he be in a healthful state of association, must necessarily be in some degree enlightened' (*WW*, p. 598); so Wordsworth claims in the 1802 Preface, without appearing to notice that his capacity to improve his readers' health must therefore depend upon their being already healthy. One wonders whether city-dwellers, readers of newspapers and novels, or any of the other examples he gives of people addicted to 'gross and violent stimulants' (*WW*, p. 599) are included in the fitness programme he is proposing?

Jon Klancher has argued that Wordsworth saw the middle class audience as 'consumers of a brutalised popular culture fashioned for urban readers', and that 'he sought to reverse that consumption into a form of reception'.[23] Whereas 'consumption' suggests an activity that is appetitive and mindless, 'reception' is tacitly passive but reflective. Wordsworth's task, then, was to demonstrate that the 'craving for extraordinary incident' and the 'degrading thirst after outrageous stimulation' (*WW*, p. 599) could evolve into a reflective awareness that action is transitory, and that the capacity for deep feeling may be awakened by 'gentle shock[s] of mild surprize'.[24] But how was subtlety to be appreciated, except by the subtle?

In negotiating the circularity of his own argument, Wordsworth draws the circle ever more tightly; for the model of reading proposed in the Preface does not in fact separate 'reception' from its sensationalist opposite; rather, it proposes what might be called an erotics of reading, in which receptivity is measured in terms of the extent of pleasure received. 'The end of Poetry', Wordsworth says in the Preface to *Lyrical Ballads* (1802), 'is to produce excitement in co-existence with an over-balance of pleasure' (*WW*, p. 609); the poet's words must 'raise the Reader to a height of desirable excitement' (*WW*, p. 610); and again: 'the poet must take care, that whatever passions he communicates to his Reader, those passions, *if his Reader's mind he sound and vigorous*, should always be accompanied with an overbalance of pleasure' (*WW*, p. 611). None of this makes it clear just *how* the pleasure produced by poetry is distinct from the pleasure of reading a frantic novel or a sickly and stupid German tragedy, except (implicitly) in the manliness with which it is administered. Nor does Wordsworth suggest how the reader's 'soundness' and 'vigour' are to be tested, other than through their capacity to be excited 'without the application of gross and violent stimulants' (*WW*, p. 599). The poet is left giving pleasure only where pleasure is already due, to those fit and few enough to be properly receptive.

The same circularity is shown when discussing the 'endless fluctuations and arbitrary associations' (*WW*, p. 660) to which language is subject, in the 'Essay Supplementary' of 1815. Wordsworth claims that 'the genius of the Poet melts these down for his purpose; but they retain their shape and quality to him who is not capable of exerting, within his own mind, a corresponding energy' (*WW*, p. 660). The capacity for 'energy' is therefore a pre-requisite for healthy reader-response, but it must 'correspond' to the poet's own; and this correspondence depends implicitly on being in a 'healthful state of association'.

Operating from within a circular hermeneutics of identification, Wordsworth betrays a consequent confusion about the extent to which readers must be active or passive, if they are truly to understand. He claims, for instance, that 'without the exertion of a co-operating *power* in the mind of the Reader', there can be no sympathy with pathos or sublimity: indeed, 'without this auxiliary impulse elevated or profound passion cannot exist' (*WW*, p. 659). And yet readers are only nominally exerting themselves, in an interchange where power is seen as auxiliary and co-operative. In much the same way, his rhetorical question –'Is it to be supposed that the Reader can make progress . . . like an Indian Prince or General – stretched on his Palanquin, and borne by his Slaves?' – implicitly rebukes his readers for their lack of exercise: 'No . . . he cannot proceed in quiescence, he cannot be carried like a dead weight' (*WW*, pp. 659-60). Such enthusiasm for the reader's activity does not however amount to a claim for equality. Wordsworth suggests, rather, that the 'advance made by the soul of a poet' over his readers is akin to a 'conquest', and that the great and original genius is 'in the condition of Hannibal among the Alps' (*WW*, p. 658). Such militaristic metaphors take one back to the idea of sublime invulnerability with which he protects his authorial status – ruling out the possibility of dialogue, at least in the critical prose.

IV

If one is looking at Wordsworthian epistemology as a kind of blueprint for creative reciprocity, then the poems suggest a more egalitarian analogue for writer-reader relations than anything in the prose. Indeed, the 'interchangeable supremacy' of mind and nature posited in 'The Prelude' comes as near as possible to genuine dialectic. For this reason, it has provided the material for all those accounts of Wordsworth's hermeneutics which seek to maximize his generosity to the reader – accounts ranging from the poetics of indeterminacy teased out by Geoffrey Hartman, through Susan Meisenhelder's more bland application of Wolfgang Iser's reader-response theory, and on into Tilottama Rajan's proposal that the poems encourage the reader to practice a 'negative hermeneutic'.[25] Equally, it is in the poetry that the bond (or perhaps bondage) of identification between author and reader is acknowledged by Wordsworth to be inadequate protection against the anxiety of reception.

His handling of dialogues between human subjects shows that when self constitutes the other as its own reflex communication has effectively broken down. One thinks, not just of 'Anecdote for Fathers' or 'We are Seven', where communication-problems are considered as aspects of educational theory; but of poems such as 'Old Man Travelling', 'The

Discharged Soldier' and 'The Leechgatherer', where the potential mismatch between subjectivities is accepted as an epistemological given. In these dialogue and encounter poems, Wordsworth exposes the over interpreting tendencies of narrators whom he closely identifies with his poetic self. The problem of misunderstanding is presented as a problem of mis-*reading*, but writers are implicitly akin to readers in their acts of appropriation.

Even more interesting, as reflections on the interchange between author and reader, are poems in which misunderstanding is explicitly perceived to work both ways – as an authorial imposition and as a readerly resistance. In 'There was a Boy', the child mocking the owls is mocked in turn by their refusal to play his game; and in the silence of non-reception he learns to be himself receptive rather than coercive.[26] In 'To Joanna', the poet-persona's 'ravishment' at Nature's beauty is mocked by Joanna's laughter; but her derision comes back to admonish her in an uncanny echo.[27] If one were reading these as allegories of the anxiety of reception, one might say that in the first poem the object of Wordsworth's fear is non-co-operation on the part of his readers, whereas in the second it is their insensitivity; and that in both the threat of mockery is anticipated, only to be replayed and thus defused. But Wordsworth's handling of subject-object positions refuses so comfortable an alignment of author-reader roles. If these are allegories at all, they work in two directions at once, turning an implicit rebuke to readers for failing to respond into an admonishment of poets for attempting to predetermine response. In this respect, they closely resemble 'Nutting', where the poet's injunction to 'move along these shades / In gentleness of heart', applies both to his own writing, which threatens to invade or colonize what is other, and also to reading, which replicates this threat in respect of the texts it seeks to master.[28]

In these poems, Wordsworth explores the potential for reciprocity between poet and reader in terms of a movement to and fro between self and other which is constitutive of hermeneutic consciousness.[29] But by showing how readily this movement can turn into absorption or narcissistic reflection, he provides a semi-parodic critique of the impasse we have seen operating in his critical prose, where the expectation of readerly sympathy resembles the need for a reflex or echo of his authorial self.

These poems unsettle that authoritative bond between author and reader which Wordsworth asserts repeatedly, in his attempts to frame his public reception, in his relations with individual readers, and in his theory of reading; and they do so by acknowledging the dependencies and anxieties which the critical prose holds at bay. We might be tempted to conclude from this that (contrary to Hazlitt's belief) the language of prose naturally falls in with the language of power, whereas the language of poetry is democratic (*Howe*, IV, pp. 214-5). I suspect however that on closer inspection these binaries could be broken down, or at least shown to be operating across as well as between generic categories. It might be said with more truth that the authoritative voice of Wordsworth's criticism masks a deep uncertainty about the direction in which he wishes to move his theory of interpretation – towards the hermeticism on which he over-insists, or towards the hermeneutics of collaboration which implicitly contradicts it. Further, that while his poems more readily acknowledge a division of allegiances within the writing-reading subject, they do not relinquish the hope that a hiatus between 'creation' and 'reception' might be bridged, and the poet's authority thereby preserved.

It is in the construction of a 'model reader' closely akin to his own persona that Wordsworth could be said to carry the strategies of his prose over into his poetry, attempting to allay the fear that the reader is born only at the cost of the author's death. This model reader practices what Rajan has called a 'positive hermeneutic', undoing the shocking binary logic of Barthes' equation.[30] Like Dorothy at the end of 'Tintern Abbey' who goes on seeing for the poet, and as it were with his vision, after his own demise,[31] or like the traveller who enters the cave of Yordas in *The Prelude* (8.711-41) Wordsworth's model reader is a figure of continuity and recuperation, as well as of understanding. This figure provides reassurance that books are by no means 'exposed and lifeless' after publication, but are subject to a vivid continuing life in their readers' minds. The author dies, perhaps – but only perhaps, because a 'new quickening' soon succeeds.

Notes

1   See *Prelude* (1805), 8.711-41. For discussions of this passage in terms of Wordsworth's fear of textuality, see Jonathan Wordsworth, *William Wordsworth: The Borders of Vision* (Oxford: Clarendon Press, 1982), pp. 188-9; Mary Jacobus, *Romanticism. Writing and Sexual Difference* (Oxford: Clarendon Press, 1989), pp. 14-16; and Lucy Newlyn, '"Questionable Shape": The Aesthetics of Indeterminacy' in John Beer, ed., *Questioning Romanticism* (Baltimore and London: John Hopkins University Press, 1995), pp. 226-9.

2   Jon Klancher, *The Making of English Reading Audiences, 1790-1832* (Wisconsin: University of Wisconsin Press, 1978); Alan Richardson, *Literature, Education and Romanticism: Reading as Social Practice, 1780-1832* (Cambridge: Cambridge University Press, 1994); Kathryn Sunderland, '"Events have made us a World of Readers": Reader-Relations, 1780-1830' in *The Penguin History of The Romantic Period*, ed. David Pirie (Harmondsworth: Penguin, 1994), pp. 1-48.

3   Tilottama Rajan, *The Supplement of Reading: Figures of Understanding in Romantic Theory and Practice* (Ithaca and London: Cornell University Press, 1990).

4   See my article, 'Coleridge and the Anxiety of Reception', in *Romanticism*, 1 (1995), pp. 206-38.

5   Newlyn, 'Coleridge and the Anxiety of Reception', pp. 224-7.

6   Newlyn, 'Coleridge and the Anxiety of Reception', pp. 210-13.

7   Roland Barthes, 'The Death of the Author' in David Lodge, ed. *Modern Criticism and Theory: A Reader* (Harlow: Longman, 1988), p. 172. See also my '"Questionable Shape": The Aesthetics of Indeterminacy', pp. 213-15, pp. 229-33.

8   See Stephen Gill, *William Wordsworth: A Life* (Oxford: Clarendon, 1989), p. 185.

9   Gill, *William Wordsworth*, p. 367.

10   Gill, *William Wordsworth*, p. 367.

11   See Dustin Griffin, *Regaining Paradise: Milton and the Eighteenth Century* (Cambridge: Cambridge University Press, 1986), pp. 22-32; Lucy Newlyn, *Paradise Lost and the Romantic Reader* (Oxford: Clarendon Press, 1993), pp. 7-8.

12   See Milton's invocation to Urania, *Paradise Lost*, VIII lines 30-1; echoed by Wordsworth in his 'Prospectus' to *The Recluse*, which was incorporated into 'Home at Grasmere': see 11.970-72 (*WW*, p. 197.)

13   Gill, *William Wordsworth*, p. 81.

14   For the collaborative/competitive nature of Wordsworth's dialogue with Coleridge, see Thomas McFarland, 'The Symbiosis of Coleridge and Wordsworth' in *Romanticism and the Forms of Ruin: Wordsworth, Coleridge, and Modalities of Fragmentation* (Princeton, New Jersey: Princeton University Press, 1981), pp. 56-103; and Lucy Newlyn. *Coleridge, Wordsworth and the Language of Allusion* (Oxford: Clarendon Press, 1986).

15   *The Correspondence of Henry Crabb Robinson with the Wordsworth Circle*, ed. Edith J. Morley. 2 vols. (Oxford: Clarendon Press, 1927), I, p. 83.

16   See Elinor Shaffer, 'The Hermeneutic Community: Coleridge and Schleiermacher' in *Coleridge Connection*, ed. Richard Gravil and Molly Lefebure (Houndmills, Basingstoke: Macmillan, 1990), pp. 41-80.

17   For an account which argues that the persistence of small reading circles is a throwback to earlier, patronage models of readership, and that these should be set against the emergence of an anonymous reading public, see Klancher, *English Reading Audiences*, pp. 1-15.

18   See Newlyn, 'Coleridge and the Anxiety of Reception', pp. 216-27.

19   The phrase is Coleridge's: see *Poems on Various Subjects* (London: G.G. and J. Robinsons, and J. Cottle, 1796), p. A 3.

20   For the significance of Wordsworth's revisions to 'The Leechgatherer', all of which move the poem away from its ballad origins and matter-of-fact style, see Newlyn, *Coleridge, Wordsworth, and the Language of Allusion*, pp. 117-37.

21   *Hermeneutics: The Original Manuscripts*, ed. Heinz Kimmerle, trans. James Duke and Jack Forstman (Missoula, Montana: Scholars' Press, 1977), p. 99.

22   Schleiermacher discusses this ability to enter the other's imaginative world as 'divinatory' understanding: see Kimmerle, *Hermeneutics*, p. 150.

23   Klancher, *English Reading Audience*, p. 143.

24   I quote from 'There was a Boy' line 19. Wordsworth's theory of metre, like his theory of the sublime, works on the principle that our deepest feelings occur at moments when concentration, strained to the utmost, suddenly relaxes, making us acutely receptive.

25   For my discussion of Hartman's poetics, see my article, 'Reading After: The Anxiety of the Writing-subject', *SiR*, 35 (1996), pp. 609-31. For a less dialectical model of the reading process than Hartman's, see Susan Edwards Meisenhelder, *Wordsworth's Informed Reader: Structures of Experience in his Poetry* (Nashville:

Vanderbilt University Press, 1988). For Tilottama Rajan's definition of 'negative' hermeneutic, see *Supplement of Reading*, p. 5; and, for her understanding of Wordsworth's engagement with the reader, pp. 141-66.

26   See 'There was a Boy', lines 21-6.

27   See 'To Joanna', lines 52-76.

28   See 'Nutting', lines 52-5. The 'dearest maiden' is thus construed as a figure of the reader, whose sensitivity to the authorial spirit compensates for any lapses made by the poet. For a much fuller discussion of 'There was a Boy', 'Nutting' and 'To Joanna' in the light of Wordsworth's theory of reading, see my, 'Reading After: The Anxiety of the Writing -Subject'.

29   See Gadamer, *Philosophical Hermeneutics*, trans. and ed. David E. Linge (Berkeley, Los Angeles, London: University of California Press, 1976), p. 57.

30   Rajan, *Supplement of Reading*, pp. 25-6.

31   'Lines written a few miles above Tintern Abbey', lines 146-60.

6 Jacobin Romanticism: John Thelwall's 'Wye' Essay and 'Pedestrian Excursion' (1797-1801)

MICHAEL SCRIVENER

Thelwall's essays appeared appropriately in the *Monthly Magazine*, established in 1796 as, according to Jon Klancher, 'the first organ of a newly self-conscious English middle-class reading audience'.[1] The loco-descriptive and walking tour essays in the *Monthly Magazine* represent a 'nature' that is hardly a pastoral retreat from social strife but is rather marked everywhere by political hope and anxiety. Uniquely positioned as an intellectual with ties to both the plebeian and middle-class publics, Thelwall in the late 1790s negotiated a painful transition from radical political activism to middle-class professionalism, variously as farmer, poet, novelist, elocutionary expert and speech therapist, while at the same time sustaining a radical political position. Thelwall's retreat from political activism was strategic and temporary, not a repudiation of radicalism itself or even activism altogether, as he resumed an activist role in 1818.[2]

E. P. Thompson characterized John Thelwall's essay, the 'Pedestrian Excursion', as 'unremarkable', dismissing it as merely 'conventional rehearsals of the "romantic and picturesque"'.[3] I find this essay and Thelwall's essay on the Wye valley much more valuable than Thompson suggests.[4] How Thelwall represents nature in these essays is distinctive and should therefore be included in the Romantic conversation about nature and politics. 'The Phenomena of the Wye, during the Winter of 1797-98' is an essay interesting in its own right and for a contrast with how Wordsworth wrote about the Wye in 'Tintern Abbey'. Indeed, several months after this essay was published in May 1798, the Wordsworths made their historic visit to Tintern Abbey; shortly after that, in early August, accompanied this time by Coleridge, they visited Lyswen farm. The sociological reports on the living conditions of the poor in the 'Pedestrian Excursion' anticipate similar writings by William Cobbett. The land Thelwall traverses and the journey he constructs are sites for sociological, cultural, and political-

73

economic reflection. The aesthetic moments of picture-painting within the conventions of the guidebooks and the traditions of the picturesque and sublime are infrequent and somewhat unconventional.[5] Thompson's belief that Thelwall's writing is marred as well by class bias is something that must be taken seriously, but I find that when Thelwall's writing becomes contradictory it is usually traceable to his situation as a hunted radical, not snobbery. The most disturbing subtext of the essays is the fear of violence and the concomitant sense of powerlessness. Finally, if Thelwall's essays are taken seriously, an expanded canon of Romantic writing requires both a richer sense of the social meanings of Romantic nature and different models of intellectual development than the ones hinging on political disillusionment.

Thelwall was forced to retire from politics in the summer of 1797 because of the political repression and the violent attacks against him. As he would later explain it in the pages of the *Champion*: 'He never did desert the public – the public deserted him. He was left alone, as it were, in the field – abandoned by timid friends, and surrounded by sanguinary enemies. . . . [It was necessary to take] a temporary retreat to silence and obscurity' in order to save his life .[6] An alternative that Thelwall deemed unthinkable but one that was taken by a large number of 1790s radicals was political apostasy and anti-Jacobinism; such a move would have stopped the political repression and violent harassment and would have been an undoubtedly lucrative career move. As he began his walking tour from Derby, unable to work as a provincial journalist – he had just been fired after only two weeks as editor of the Derby *Courier* – he had to find a way to support his family because he could no longer lecture in public, having barely escaped with his life during a provincial lecture tour in 1796-97.[7] After a very happy ten-day visit with Coleridge and the Wordsworths, he stayed with several other friends in nearby Gloucestershire, then he rented a farm in Lyswen, Brecknockshire. His first choice for a residence had been Nether Stowey that, however, could not accommodate the most infamous 'acquitted felon' in Britain (William Windham's phrase for the 1794 treason trial suspects). Thelwall's letter to his wife and the blank verse poem 'Lines written at Bridgewater' express clearly how much Thelwall wanted to settle near the Coleridges and Wordsworths.[8] Meanwhile, government spies had taken notice of Coleridge's friends, and spies sent several reports to the Home Office.[9] Thelwall's presence, however brief, was so disruptive that, because of it, the Wordsworths lost their lease to the Alfoxden cottage.[10] Thelwall's renting the Welsh farm signified his inability to continue any longer as a political activist. Like the republican and regicide Henry Marten, who was imprisoned after the Restoration in

Chepstow Castle on the Wye, Thelwall at Lyswyn farm on the Wye in 1798 was also a monument to the failure of revolution, as Nicholas Roe has pointed out in relation to 'Tintern Abbey'.[11]

I

Broken up into ten separate pieces in the *Monthly Magazine*, and published between August 1799 and November 1801, the 'Pedestrian Excursion' makes no mention of Thelwall's experiences with repression, the violent encounters with anti-Jacobins, almost being kidnapped at Yarmouth by sailors, and the spies who shadowed him apparently wherever he went. The genre of the travel journal, especially at that time by that particular author, required a suppression of that very important context. Phillips the publisher and John Aikin the editor might not have published the essay if it had included yet another 'appeal' to the public by Thelwall on the repression that victimized him. The *Monthly Magazine*, formed in the wake of the repressive Two Acts, purchased its freedom to publish by practising rigorous self-censorship. Only at the very end of the essay does he become self-reflective but continues to refrain from providing specific complaints: '*Saturday* 15, my companion took his farewel of me, directing his course homeward in the Southampton stage; and shortly after I took my farewell of Bath, thenceforward to pursue my way with solitary step – far from each endearing intercourse – seeking from without for the happiness that was not within, and exclaiming, every time that the smoke of the lone cottage from some sequestered dingle chanced to rise upon my view – 'When – when shall I be the peaceful lord of such a mansion, and repose me again in obscurity!' (*MM*, 12 [November 1801], 308).

Thelwall dramatizes here a solitary pathos, some of which Coleridge seems to have borrowed in his 1802 'Dejection' ode (the lines 'seeking from without for the happiness that was not within' are too distinctive to be coincidental [*PWC*, I, p.3 65]). The 'Pedestrian Excursion' is, in the tradition of William Gilpin, public travel literature that excludes merely personal commentary, not the more privately inflected 'sentimental journey' after Sterne and Rousseau. Thelwall's earlier *Peripatetic* (1793) was a more Sternean lyrical 'journey' where the journalist's own thoughts and associations took precedence over external events.[12] Were the 'Pedestrian Excursion' to continue after the last paragraph, it would have to be modulated to the new lyrical, self-conscious inwardness. (The lyrical mode would also necessitate suppression of specific deeds of repression that victimized Thelwall.) The lyrical turn in the essay's conclusion disturbingly punctuates the whole previous essay, undermining its status as reportage. What he cannot discuss directly – the public violence against him, his sense of being abandoned – nevertheless affects the essay in numerous ways.

Prior to the abrupt and surprising conclusion of the essay, it conforms roughly to the generic expectations of a travel journal. Although parts of the essay do indeed rehearse the conventions of the picturesque genteel tour, as Thompson claims, Thelwall also works against those conventions in certain ways. The walking tour itself, although it became thoroughly respectable in the Victorian period, still had democratic associations, as the preferred means of travel was by coach and horseback.[13] When the essay describes some inns as more pleasant and generous than others, it is shifting the emphasis from the tourist sights themselves, always Gilpin's focus, to the walk itself.

A remarkable revision of picturesque conventions occurs when he is directed to a beautiful view not by Gilpin or Gray but by an old peasant near East Knoyle. The description and meditation, perhaps because of the unusually spontaneous circumstances of finding the view, show Thelwall at his descriptive best.

> From the summit, thus pointed out to us, we commanded one of the most pleasing views I had ever seen. Hills and vallies, rich, fertile, and variegated, were seen finely interspersed with woodlands and cottages, and here and there some prouder mansions; while other hills, dimly descried through the mists, bounded the prospect and mingled with the horizon. Beautiful slopes and dells and climes, cloathed with fern and coppice, formed the rough foreground of the picture; and the sky, cloudy, but rather wild and sublime than monotonous, formed a *sombre* but not unsuitable accompaniment; while a shower of rain gave additional freshness to all the nearer objects, and deepened the emerald tint of the short close turf we trod. Anon the moving curtains of the sky were rent, and the beams of the sun, breaking through the interstices of dark clouds, brightly illuminated the distant western hills, whose mitigated splendours, seen through the misty veil of an intervening shower, gave a finishing tho' transient beauty to the whole
>
> (*MM*, 11 [March 1801], p.104).

The description never moves inward or becomes allegorical, never emphasizes any special receptivity that Thelwall uniquely possesses, and escapes to some extent the static and painterly qualities of the picturesque tradition. Although he does indeed 'compose' a picturesque view with foreground and horizon, his language does not strain to get remarkable effects. The description pays more attention to general shapes and configurations than details. Thelwall does not pretend he can capture fully the beauty of the scene, but he accepts the more modest task of representation. Although he calls this 'the most pleasing view' he had ever seen in his life, he strikes here the same comfortable tone he adopts in his most successful blank-verse meditations, as his nature description partakes somewhat of the qualities of the Romantic genre, the conversation poem. It is difficult to imagine Wordsworth, Coleridge or Shelley letting an opportunity like this to slip by without making post-rhapsodic commentary on nature, imagination, theology, philosophy and so on. This restraint, which we find also in Dorothy Wordsworth's landscape descriptions, corresponds to Thelwall's overall treatment of landscape and aesthetics: picturesque beauty, however valuable and pleasurable, is never permitted to displace the social labour and political conflicts that also are part of the land's meaning; by not representing his private reactions to the beauty except in a general way, he suggests that receptivity to beauty is not an aristocratic privilege, deriving neither from birth nor from special spiritual election.

That the 'Pedestrian Excursion' does not have many 'views' like this is one of the essay's distinctive features. Although he does not attack the conventions of the picturesque tour directly, he nibbles away at some of its assumptions. Thelwall's response to the classical statuary in Wilton House is an even more clear example of his unconventional tourism, as he uses the occasion to evoke classical republicanism, defend tyrannicides like Brutus, and praise the uncompromising Socrates at the expense of the time-serving Seneca (9 [February 1800], p. 17).[14]

Although the essay has a minor aesthetic connoisseur dimension, the essay's most distinctive feature is its sociological focus. The sociological observations predate Cobbett's by several decades and in some respects are superior to Cobbett's: Thelwall dramatizes himself far less, generates far fewer simplistic myths about an imaginary past, provides more information about the lives of the rural poor, and does not scapegoat Jews and Quakers. Thelwall's evaluation of the overall quality of life is more reliable than Cobbett's quirky perceptions. Thelwall's writing has its own moments of blindness but they are not caused, as E. P. Thompson claims, by class prejudice. When Thelwall reaches a village, he records how well the labourers seem to be doing in the following categories: the fertility of the land on which they work, their physical appearance, the condition of the children, their wages, their dwellings, their work hours if they work in a factory, their degree of literary education, and their overall cultural state. He takes note of whether the poor have a cow or access to the commons. The overall effect of his reports is extraordinarily gloomy because for the most part the labourers seem to be ignorant, overworked, listless, in poor health, with their standard of living declining. Moreover, the children of the poor are exploited in factories and deprived of both an education and freedom to play. The recurrent theme of his sociological reports is that 'monopoly' is reducing the number of farmers, increasing the size of farms, and wrecking a previous rural economy that seemed to work well. Moreover, he notes with much concern the spread of the factory system that concentrates workers into unhealthy dwellings and that is especially harmful to children.

Indeed, he saves his most concentrated ire for child labour in factories. As someone who did not have much playtime in his own childhood, Thelwall sees child's play as one of the 'rights' of humanity. He applies the 'luxury' critique to explain the unequal distribution of leisure and labour: while squires frolic, children toil. At the Overton silk mill, for example, he reports that most of the workers are children, 'from 5 years of age to 14 or 15. They have 1s. per week during the first year they are employed, and an addition of 3d. per week every year that they continue at this employment. The hours are from 6 in the morning to 7 or 8 at night' (*MM,* 8 [November 1799], p. 784). He compares the factory to a prison that produces, finally, female prostitutes and male soldiers and sailors (8 *MM,* [November 1799], p. 785). At the Quidhampton woollen mill children start work as young as five when these children should instead be 'stretching their wanton limbs in noisy gambols over the green' (*MM,* 8 [January 1800], p. 967). At the Froome cloth mill the children work fourteen hours a day, earning between 1s 6d and 2s 6d per week (*MM,* 12 [October 1801], p. 199).

As an urban intellectual, Thelwall also pays attention to the literacy and cultural quality of each place he visits, noting the presence and more often absence of libraries, reading rooms, and book shops. His lament for the low cultural level of every place he visits is sometimes connected with a protest against the new stamp tax that discouraged popular literacy, but one cannot ignore Thelwall's tone of disappointment in the people's lack of intellectual initiative.

One disappointment Thelwall records is the meagre amount of conversation he was able to elicit from those he met. Cobbett's *Rural Rides* are spiced with narratives by labourers and farmers, using their own words and references, but there is very little of that dialogic dimension in Thelwall's essay. Militating against any frank interchange between Thelwall and the people he met would be his own identity as a notorious radical. Yet another factor would be the recent naval mutinies and the fear of invasion from France. It is not surprising that he found few labourers willing to talk to him extensively.

His meeting with one literate labourer ('he read *several* newspapers') is an occasion for lamenting the low cultural level of the poor who, even if educated, have very limited horizons. 'Unfortunately, however, we could no way turn his conversation into the channel we desired. He talked of nothing but Parker and the delegates, of war and of parties. In short, he was too full of liquor and *temporary politics*, to furnish any information on the subject of *political economy* . . '. (*MM*, 8 [September 1799], p. 619). If Thelwall identified himself, as one imagines he must have, then one has to recognize the reluctance to talk with this 'acquitted felon' shadowed by a variety of spies. The anxiety, fear, and anger Thelwall might have experienced at various times during his journey go unreported, but perhaps one can find something of his frustration displaced in his commenting on the invariably obtuse state in which he finds working people. Thelwall's distinction between temporary and more enduring politics is curious, because although he always, even at the peak of his political career as a radical orator, took a philosophical view of politics, he also had no trouble making meaningful the newsworthy minutiae and ephemera that comprised a good portion of political discourse. Thelwall, like most intellectuals, could not accept political and philosophical differences at face value from labourers who had to be seen as being culturally deprived, 'hopelessly surrounded by a sort of intellectual desert', 'driven into habits of intemperance to supply the deficiency of external stimuli' (*MM*, 8 [September 1799], p. 619). After all, Thelwall had paid a high price for being a 'tribune' for such people. Now that he was being forced to retire as tribune, he devalues the prose of politics while taking away with him, as compensation for a real loss, the poetry, the truly enduring ideas.

There is a detail in Thelwall's report on the worker that cannot be passed over and that is the reference to Parker and his 'delegates'. On the day after Thelwall began his journey Richard Parker (1767-97; *DNB*) was hanged for his leadership of the Nore mutiny, which had begun on May 10. Would there be anyone in Britain who would not have wanted to talk about this remarkable rebellion? Thelwall makes it seem that the labourer was interested in mere trivia. Unfortunately we have no account of the labourer's comments or Thelwall's response. In actual context, talking about 'political economy' would have been intellectually escapist. Something else might be at work here, namely Thelwall's own strenuous desire to separate himself from political activism, at least in writing. There was much speculation at the time about the mutineers' possible revolutionary motives, so that it would not have been entirely impossible for Thelwall to have got re-imprisoned on some imagined link between himself and the naval mutinies.[15] Additionally, in the final years of the

London Corresponding Society's existence, from 1797 to 1799 when it was outlawed altogether, the group moved toward plotting violence with the United Irishmen. What better way to illustrate how utterly free he was from anything resembling violent conspiracies against the government than to express boredom and lofty disdain for discussions with labourers about the naval mutinies?

Thelwall was impatient with other poor people he met. Near Murrel Green he meets an old thresher whose 'rustic humour' is amusing, but when Thelwall presses him for sociological information – wages, living conditions, and so on – he clams up. Thelwall then complains about the general English reluctance to discuss the most important issues that affect them, and he insists that this reluctance is a major obstacle to 'improving' overall conditions (*MM*, 8 [September 1799], p. 619). If anyone should understand the power of repression and social intimidation to affect one's willingness to speak frankly, it should have been Thelwall. At Fonthill, for example, when he calls the people 'immersed in the most stupid ignorance, and scarcely competent either to the answering or the comprehending of the most simple question' (*MM*, 11 [March 1801], p. 124), he is forgetting his more rational analyses of why people are so uncommunicative. His particular blindness, I believe, is not class prejudice, as Thompson thought, but self-deception: Thelwall cannot fully acknowledge the extent to which the government and what was then called the political nation have criminalized both him and his political ideas. Rather than face his own powerlessness, he blames the poor for being powerless.

Thelwall's travel essay, then, is a remarkable document, one of the finer achievements of English Jacobin prose, at least as energetic and intellectually rigorous as anything Cobbett wrote later. The principal limitation of the essay is its inability to reflect critically upon Thelwall's role as London intellectual. If ideological blindness exists in the essay, it exists here: Thelwall's 'truth' is the antithetical product of opposing both traditional popular culture and traditional aristocratic culture in the name of a 'reason' that is in fact derived from two contradictory sources, Enlightenment rationalism and traditional morality. Remove the rationalism and one gets Cobbett or the post-radical Southey; remove the traditional morality, and one gets James Mill and Bentham. The blindness, then, turns out to be fortunate and constitutes the very heart of what makes his writing distinctive.

II

The second essay, 'Phenomena of the Wye', is much shorter and has the concentrated effect of a prose poem. While paying homage to Gilpin in the first paragraph, and noting how 'an excursion on the Wye has become an essential part of the education, as it were, of all who aspire to the reputation of elegance, taste, and fashion' (*MM*, 5 [May 1798], 343), Thelwall proceeds to develop the unfamiliar aspects of the familiar: how the Wye's beauties at night, in winter, and during the spring floods provide a surprising allegorical narrative of natural and social meanings.

Here is Thelwall describing the Wye on an especially dark night when almost nothing can be seen:

> The night was dark and comfortless – no moon, no star in the firmament; and the atmosphere was so thick with vapours and descending showers, that even the course of the river was scarcely discernible. In short, nothing was visible but a sky of most sullen grey, and one vast sable mass of surrounding mountain, skirting on either side the sinuous valley, and prescribing in every direction the bounds of vision. Never before was I so deeply impressed with the power of mere outline. Here were no diversities of tint, no varied masses of light and shadows: the whole picture consisted of one bold, unbroken, but eternally diversifying line, and two broad masses of modified shade – 'No, light, but rather darkness visible;' and yet the eye was feasted, and the imagination was filled with mingled impressions of sublimity and beauty'
>
> (*MM*, 5 [May 1798], p.344).

If the Wye is beautiful even in winter, without vegetation, then it could be beautiful still at night; by logical extension, its beauties could be experienced mostly within the imagination, with only a few visual hints. The kind of picture he is painting here is remote from the picturesque views at the time. It is not something that could be captured in a Claude glass or within the parameters of a frame. Like the view from the hilltop offered by the peasant guide in the previous essay, this particular view requires the presence of the whole body situated in time; it is not an experience that can be captured fully in any aesthetic medium but rather writing can *represent* it to some extent.

As political allegory, the well known Milton line from *Paradise Lost* (1.63) leads us to the blinded Milton, blind but living on after a failed revolution, blind but with a lucid intelligence and imagination; we are also led to Satan, expelled and exiled, after having fought the good fight. This section of Thelwall's essay has none of the self-pity that he could have drawn from Milton. Within the darkness, visible Thelwall, the defeated rebel, gains strength and power from the elemental nature that ought to be but is not frightening, enfeebling, and symbolic of loss and death.

The essay also stresses the winter landscape. Thelwall portrays the naked beauty that the vegetation conceals, as he establishes both nakedness and underlying structure as allegorical elements. In James Thomson's 'Winter', for example, the poet tries to counter the overwhelmingly negative associations of that season with death, but Thelwall's affirmation of winter is even more unequivocal. 'To know how to cloath her [nature] to the best advantage, we must strip her naked' (p. 343). The French revolutionary style in clothing, which the English democrats imitated, was the more 'natural' style that followed the body's contours. The usually prudish Wordsworth uses the word 'naked' in his poetry to signify only the most emotionally intense moments. From the nakedness of nature Thelwall turns to abstract nakedness – 'nakedness itself is but beauty without a veil' – to human nakedness, 'the perfection of the human form', and 'the sublime of human nature' (p. 344). By humanizing the sublime of winter, by transforming the absence of vegetation into a metaphor for nakedness, Thelwall avoids making his aesthetic appreciation into just another pictorial commodity; his aesthetic values are attached ordinarily to social values. The winter landscape is in fact better than the lush summer's – 'more permanent' and with 'a superior charm' (p. 344).

Even the spring flood becomes a social allegory, as the extraordinarily harsh flood of 1795, which he himself did not witness but heard about, is described with its own 'sublimity' and 'terrors', as '[r]ails, land-marks, trees innumerable, and even sheep and cattle, were borne down by the rapid torrents from the mountains, or whirled away from the meadows and low lands by the infuriated course of the river; whole plantations were shattered, and several bridges were entirely swept away' (p. 345). The spring flood that he did not witness but is imagining is called a 'universal deluge'. Thelwall is representing natural violence with the same rhetoric used at the time for political violence (and used also in Milton's 'fiery deluge' in the darkness visible passage). Everything falls victim to the universal deluge and the overwhelming sublimity of a powerful force that sweeps all before it. The very geography becomes transformed as the familiar guideposts and human constructions within nature are swept away, forcing people to start over. The parallels here with social revolution as Thelwall and other intellectuals experienced the 1790s are too obvious to expatiate upon. Thelwall's angle on this destructiveness is not elegiac, as one might have expected, but just the opposite, affirmative, as the violent flood actually assists poor people in getting free firewood and fertilizing silt for their crops (p. 346). Indeed, 'the ravages they [the floods] commit are more than compensated by the good which they distribute' (p. 345). The 'nature' in this passage, according to Nicholas Roe, does not produce Romantic ideology but instead expresses purely 'revolutionary force that works to expose ... [social] misery and inequality'.[16]

The wintry nakedness provides an apt symbol for Thelwall's own ruined political efforts, for the 'fruitless' efforts of the revolutionaries. In this context, his defence of the underlying strength and beauty of nature, which he links to human nature, is a defence of his own philosophical assumptions concerning the overall rationality of nature and the improvability of humanity. That is, humans are not monsters; winter is not a graveyard; the absence of greenery does not mean the absence of meaning and purpose.

If one compares another treatment of the Wye written roughly at the same time in similar circumstances, one finds that the most remarkable thing about Wordsworth's 'Tintern Abbey' is the number and kind of similarities. One cannot discount Wordsworth's being influenced by Thelwall's essay that he almost certainly had to have read. In neither text is the static, pictorial view prominent. Except for the first verse paragraph, there is little word-painting in 'Tintern Abbey', and the word-painting in Thelwall is not in the picturesque tradition. In both texts there is an acute sense of loss and destruction but a concomitant sense of compensation. Nature, in neither poem, is permitted to accrue independent aesthetic value. Indeed, Wordsworth sees the possibility of nature unrelated to human morality as something he has outgrown. Both writers vindicate nature by humanizing it, and vindicate humanity by naturalizing it. Except for the first verse paragraph, Wordsworth pays little attention to the actual landscape, as he describes instead an outline, a foundation, and paradigm within which nature has human meaning and being human necessitates dependence on nature. Thelwall acknowledges a mortality that cannot be repressed, the naked scene without vegetation, and the deluge that spares nothing, just as 'Tintern Abbey' faces mortality in its last verse paragraph.

III

In conclusion, let me note briefly some of the inferences I draw from the two Thelwall essays. If one incorporates Thelwall into an expanded canon of Romantic literary history, one needs to develop models of literary development that do not depend on political disillusionment. Although Thelwall had discrete moments of disillusionment, his identity as a writer was affected far more by political repression and violence, actual or threatened. E. P. Thompson's ultimate disappointment in Thelwall as an ideal type of radical intellectual derived, I believe, from Thelwall's political rationalism. Thelwall's class bias, such as it was, is like that of Paine's or Godwin's or Condorcet's. It derives ultimately not from personal weakness but the philosophical conviction that reason is superior to superstition and custom, that authority should be constructed by means of the stronger argument, not rules of precedent or the will to power. Thompson rightly faults Thelwall for being insensitive to the customary but unwritten laws of the Welsh farmers and peasants he conflicted with or the English labourers he impatiently belaboured with questions. Actually, however, Thelwall was not a consistent rationalist in his politics. His politics criticized agricultural capitalism by defending rural customs and traditions of long standing. Thelwall never integrated or theorized adequately his rationalism and defence of customary tradition. Indeed, one aspect of his political thought, quite congruent with Romanticism but neglected by most of Thelwall's commentators, insists that democratic institutions are not innovations but restorations of older, previous cultural achievements (Saxon, Norman, Plantagenet, 'true' Whig). The real 'Jacobins', in the sense of violently destroying customs of long standing and ignoring ancient precedent, are Pitt, Grenville, Sidmouth, Burke, and Castlereagh, as well as the 'monopolizing' agricultural capitalists.[17] The tension between rationalism and popular traditions is precisely an object of theoretical inquiry that is very troublesome for contemporary reflections – including Thompson's – on the legacy of the radical Enlightenment in a postmodern world.[18]

The final matter I wish to address is formal, finally aesthetic. I have been treating Thelwall's essays throughout as worthy of *literary* attention, as though the loco-descriptive essay and travel journal were *literary* genres that not only communicate information but also provide aesthetic pleasure, that provide examples of both excellence and banality. 'Tintern Abbey' and the 'Dejection' ode are not just the texts for which Thelwall's essays are the context; those essays are also the texts for which Wordsworth's and Coleridge's great poems are contexts. Letting the more democratic Thelwall into the canon does not displace Wordsworth and Coleridge but expands and complicates the overall literary conversation.

Notes

1   Jon P. Klancher, *The Making of English Reading Audiences, 1790-1832* (Madison and London: University of Wisconsin Press, 1987), p. 41.

2   Recent work on Thelwall relevant to this essay includes the following: E. P. Thompson, 'Hunting the Jacobin Fox', *Past and Present*, 142 (1994), 94-140; and 'Disenchantment or Default? A Lay Sermon', in, Conor Cruise O'Brien & William Dean Vanech, ed. *Power and Consciousness* (London and New York: University of London Press, & New York University Press, 1969), pp. 149-81; Penelope J. Corfield and Chris Evans, 'John Thelwall in Wales: New Documentary Evidence', *Bulletin of the Institute of Historical Research*, 59 (1986), 231-39; Nicholas Roe, *Wordsworth and Coleridge: The Radical Years* (Oxford: Oxford University Press, 1988), pp. 234-62; 'Coleridge and John Thelwall: The Road to Nether Stowey', in Richard Gravil and Molly Lefebure, ed. *The Coleridge Connection*, ed., (Basingstoke: Macmillan, 1990), pp. 60-80; *The Politics of Nature. Wordsworth and Some Contemporaries* (Basingstoke: Macmillan, 1992), pp. 134-36; Vernon Owen Grumbling, 'John Thelwall: Romantick and Revolutionist', Unpublished doctoral dissertation (University of New Hampshire, 1977). Gregory Claeys' anthology, *The Politics of English Jacobinism. Writings of John Thelwall* (University Park: Pennsylvania State University Press, 1995) makes available to a wider public Thelwall's political essays.

3   E. P. Thompson, 'Hunting the Jacobin Fox', p. 105.

4   John Thelwall, 'The Phenomena of the Wye, During the Winter of 1797-98', *MM*, 5 (May 1798), pp. 343-46; 'A Pedestrian Excursion Through Several Parts of England and Wales During the Summer of 1797', *MM*, 8 (August 1799), pp. 532-33; 8 (September 1799), pp. 616-19; 8 (November 1799), pp. 783-85; 8 (January 1800), pp. 966-67; 9 (February 1800), pp. 16-18; 9 (April 1800), pp. 28-31; 11 (March 1801), pp. 123-25; 12 (September 1801), pp. 103-06; 12 (October 1801), pp. 198-200; 12 (November 1801), pp. 305-08. Further references to these essays will be cited in the text.

5   Nevertheless, the essays have undeniable a 'picturesque' dimension. The Wye essay explicitly cites the precedent of William Gilpin and the 'Pedestrian Excursion' refers to Thomas Gray's guidebook, *The Traveller's Companion, In a Tour Through England and Wales; Containing a Catalogue of the Antiquities, Houses, Parks, Plantations, Scenes, and Situations, in England and Wales, Arranged According to the Alphabetical Order of the Several Counties, a Catalogue, County by County, of Interesting Places to Visit. A New Edition* (London: G. Kearsley, 1800). As the edition I looked at was a 'new' edition, Thelwall's copy in 1797 would have been an earlier one. The edition I saw was pocket size.

6   John Thelwall, *The Champion* (6 June 1819), pp. 351-52.

7   For Thelwall's political and biographical context, see Michael Scrivener, 'The Rhetoric and Context of John Thelwall's "Memoir"' in G. A. Rosso & Daniel P. Watkins, ed., *Spirits of Fire. English Romantic Writers and Contemporary Historical Methods* (Rutherford: Fairleigh Dickinson University Press & Associated University Presses, 1990), pp. 112-130. The 'Prefatory Memoir' itself is in his *Poems, Chiefly Written in Retirement* (1801; reprinted. Oxford: Woodstock Books, 1989). Thelwall was editor of the *Courier* for only two weeks. The fullest, most recent treatment of the violent attacks on Thelwall in 1796-97 is by E. P. Thompson, 'Hunting the Jacobin Fox', pp. 94-140. Thelwall himself wrote about the experiences extensively, both at the time they happened and later. *An Appeal to Popular Opinion Against kidnapping and Murder, Including a Narrative of the Late Atrocious Proceedings at Yarmouth; 2nd edition*, (London: J. S. Jordan, 1796). In the *Champion* 24 (October, 1819), pp. 670-71, Thelwall describes a hitherto unrecorded episode of violence against himself at Stockport in 1797.

8   The July 14, 1797 letter is transcribed by Grumbling, 'John Thelwall: Romantick and
       Revolutionist', p. 215.

9   See the account in Roe's *Wordsworth and Coleridge*, pp. 248-62, and his 'Coleridge
       and John Thelwall: The Road to Nether Stowey'.

10   On the overall Thelwall-Coleridge relationship, see Roe, 'Coleridge and John
       Thelwall', and Vernon Owen Grumbling, who discusses in detail the Thelwall-
       Coleridge correspondence in Chapter Five of 'John Thelwall: Romantick and
       Revolutionist'. See also Warren Gibbs, 'An Unpublished Letter from John Thelwall
       to S. T. Coleridge', *Modern Language Review*, 25 (1930), 85-90, and Burton R.
       Pollin & Redmond Burke, 'John Thelwall's Marginalia in a Copy of Coleridge's
       Biographia Literaria', *Bulletin of the New York Public Library*, 74 (1970), pp. 73-
       94; Peter J. Kitson 'The Whore of Babylon and the Woman in White: Coleridge's
       Radical Unitarian Language' in Tim Fulford and Morton D. Paley, ed. *Coleridge's
       Visionary Languages* (London: D. S. Brewer, 1993), pp. 1-14.

11   Roe, *Politics of Nature*, p. 130.

12   William Gilpin, *Observations on the River Wye*, intro. Jonathan Wordsworth (1782;
       reprinted: Oxford and New York: Woodstock Books, 1991). Comparing *The
       Peripatetic* and the 'Pedestrian Excursion' yields many interesting similarities that I
       cannot pursue here for lack of space.

13   See Roe, *Politics of Nature*, pp. 127-29, Anne Wallace, *Walking, Literature, and
       English Culture. The Origins and Uses of Peripatetic in the Nineteenth Century*
       (Oxford: Clarendon Press, 1993), and Jeffrey C. Robinson, *The Walk. Notes on a
       Romantic Image* (Norman & London: University of Oklahoma Press, 1989), chapters
       five and six especially.

14   For the tradition of civic humanism, see Iain Hampsher-Monk 'Civic Humanism and
       Parliamentary Reform: The Case of the Society of the Friends of the People',
       Journal of British Studies, 18 (1979), pp. 70-89. For Thelwall's politics see Charles
       Cestre, *John Thelwall. A Pioneer of Democracy and Social Reform in England
       During the French Revolution* (London and New York: Swann Sonneschein &
       Charles Scribner's Sons, 1906); Grumbling's first two chapters; Geoffrey Gallop,
       Ideology and the English Jacobins: The Case of John Thelwall', *Enlightenment and
       Dissent*, 5 (1986), pp. 3-20, and Iain Hampsher-Monk, 'John Thelwall and the
       Eighteenth-Century Radical Response to Political Economy', *The Historical
       Journal*, 34 (1991), pp. 1-20. Claeys' introduction to his anthology of Thelwall's
       political writings is the most recent account of Thelwall's political theory, *The
       Politics of English Jacobinism*, pp. xiii-lx.

15   Prior to the Nore, there was another serious mutiny at Spithead; see E. P. Thompson,
       The Making of the English Working Class (London: Victor Gollancz, 1963
       [Harmondsworth, Penguin, 1968]), pp. 167-68. See also Arnold Schmidt, 'Alienation
       and Displacement: Wordsworth and the Naval Mutinies of 1797', *Nineteenth-
       Century Contexts*, 17 (1993), 204-13.

16   Roe, *Politics of Nature*, p. 136.

17   The political essays in *The Champion* (1818-21) draw upon consistently the Norman
       yoke mythology and exalt Saxon democracy. A typical essay is the lead article, 'Vox
       Populi, Vox Dei', *Champion* (30 [September, 1820], 625-26). Notions of the 'true'
       Whig principles, that included radical reform, are present in all of his political
       writing, early and late. He finds precedents for radical reform from the Norman and
       Plantagenet period in numerous essays, including *The Natural and Constitutional
       Right of Britons to Annual Parliaments, Universal Suffrage, and the Freedom of
       Popular Association* (London: John Thelwall, 1795), 27-28. See also Peter J. Kitson
       '"Sages and patriots that being dead do yet speak to us": Readings of the English

Revolution in the Late Eighteenth Century', in James Holstun, ed. *Pamphlet Wars: Prose in the English Revolution* (London: Frank Cass, 1992), pp. 205-30.

18   Thompson's *Customs in Common. Studies in Traditional Popular Culture* (New York: The New Press, 1993) especially but perhaps all of his historical writing discovers rationality in popular traditions. Without supporting Thompson's 'rigorously theoretical' opponents, the Althusserians, I believe that Thompson never adequately theorized his particular mixture of Marxism and populist traditionalism. In another direction, a central controversy for Jurgen Habermas and his critics is the normative status of reason, especially in relation to preexisting – customary – cultural and individual values.

7 Patriot Poetics and the Romantic National Epic: Placing and Displacing Southey's *Joan of Arc*

LYNDA PRATT

I

On 17 December 1796 Coleridge sent Thelwall a parcel of books, including:

> a Joan of Arc, with only the passage of my writing cut out for the Printers – as I am printing it in my second Edition, with very great alterations & an addition of four hundred lines, so as to make a complete & independent Poem – entitled The Progress of Liberty – or the Visions of the maid of Orleans (*CL*, I, p. 285).

Coleridge's dissection of Southey's first epic, the physical removal of his own contributions to the poem, was also an act of displacement. It represented a forthright, though by the end of 1796 not that astonishing, creative distancing of himself from private and public relationships with the man who was both his brother-in-law and, in the minds of the reviews and the reading public of the mid 1790s, his closest literary associate.[1] From a late twentieth-century perspective this mutilated copy offers a startlingly appropriate symbol of *Joan*'s current critical status. The poem exists uneasily as a hybridized fragment on the very margins of canonical Romanticism, a text which, though actually complete in itself, is read only for the few hundred lines contributed by Coleridge, the very same sections that were cut out of the copy sent to Thelwall.[2] Reading *Joan* in this way perpetuates, and re-enacts, Coleridge's mutilation and also misinterprets its place in early Romantic literary and political culture. When it is reconstructed, restored to its main author, and replaced in its proper context the real significance, and acute contemporaneity, of Southey's work emerges. In itself, and in the varied responses it provoked from sympathetic and hostile contemporaries, *Joan* was entangled in a complex series of placements, displacements, and replacements, acts whose very intricacies reveal the contested nature of the national epic in the 1790s.

The first step is to place *Joan* itself. Early readers virtually all pointed out the lack of respect shown to literary tradition and to notions of cultural decorum in the public declaration that this modern epic had been written in just over six weeks (*Joan 1796*, p. [v]).[3] In fact, and as Southey with his eye for literary controversy undoubtedly intended, this was a misreading of the poem's preface. *Joan* actually emerged over a period of two and a half years. It was begun in July 1793 and published by Joseph Cottle at the end of 1795 (*Joan 1796*, p. [v]).[4] As was to become highly characteristic of Southey's longer works, a complex process of drafting and redrafting, or placing and displacing, sometimes alone, at others with the help of friends, ensured that it changed dramatically during this time. Three pre-publication versions survive: the first is the original poem written in summer 1793; the second is a fair copy of this earlier draft made by Southey in November-December 1793 and incorporating one or two alterations; the third manuscript dates from 1795 and, as well as containing Coleridge's revisions, is substantially the text published at the end of that year.[5] A fourth draft of *Joan*, incorporating changes made by Southey and Robert Lovell in summer and autumn 1794, is now lost.[6]

Though they have been largely neglected, these manuscripts are crucial to any re-reading of *Joan* and to any reinstatement, or replacement, of its significance both for Southey's personal reputation and for the history of the national epic in the 1790s. What emerges from them is a much more interesting and consistent author than the uninspired figure of critical demonology, a poet who had strong views, and who was prepared to revise his poem in order to convey these. Even as he was finishing *Joan* (1793) Southey felt that its attacks on the forces of clerical 'Superstition' and royal absolutism were not thorough going enough and that he needed to 'enlarge on . . . [the] servility of the priests' (*Joan 1793*, XII, f.179). When he revised the poem later that year, the influence of Godwin's *An Enquiry Concerning Political Justice* focussed its concentration on the workings of 'Eternal Justice' and intensified its critique of monarchical and ecclesiastical 'Vice & Folly'.[7] Moreover, as well as assimilating ideas from Godwin, and demonstrating that revision was an integral part of Southey's poetics, the second surviving manuscript sheds new light on his relationship with Wordsworth.

It is commonly assumed that Southey's later social protest poetry was greatly influenced by his canonical contemporary.[8] Whilst this intertextuality cannot be denied, it is important to realize that, from the final months of 1793, before he was acquainted with either Wordsworth or his work, he had become interested in 'the private wretchedness occasioned by the war-systems of Europe' (*Joan 1798*, I, p. 18). The second version of *Joan* contains an embryonic version of what became a keynote of the published poem, Southey's ability to tell a 'plain tale' of the sufferings of ordinary men and women.[9] In one of the major revisions to this second version, the maid of Orleans herself reminds the dauphin of his social responsibilities:

> To thee elated thus above mankind
> Subjected thousands gaze; they wait thy will
> They wait thy will to quit their peaceful homes
> To quit the comforts of domestic life,
> For the camps dissonance, the clang of arms,
> The banquet of destruction . . .
> Glows not thy crimson cheek - sinks not thine heart
> At the dread thought of thousands in thy cause
> Mowed by the giant scythe of Victory?
> Of Widows weeping for their slaughtered husbands
> Of orphans groaning for their daily food?[10]

This may seem minor and undeveloped, but the emphasis on the horrors of warfare and the fate of nameless 'Widows' and 'orphans' represented a significant move from the oblique discourse on the nature of kingship found in *Joan* (1793) (*Joan 1793*, VI, line 27, f. 83). In a matter of months, Southey had moved towards the social protest poetry that was to characterize a great deal of his work in the mid- and late 1790s. The young writer had begun to find a voice of his own, not one appropriated from Wordsworth.

The manuscripts of Southey's first epic also help reformulate an even more complex relationship, that with Coleridge. The latter's involvement in the revisions to *Joan* (1795) and his contempt for the 'images imageless - these small capitals constituting personifications' which he had been 'forced to introduce . . . to preserve the connexion with the machinery of the poem previously adopted by Southey' are commonplaces of Romantic criticism.[11] However, they offer only a partial truth. Coleridge's participation in the 1795 revisions was, after all, relatively minor. He helped rework only the first four books and his own contributions to the epic run to some 359 lines in a ten book poem.[12] Moreover, Coleridge's critique of supernatural machinery obscures the fact that his fellow poet would undoubtedly have agreed with him. Southey had been cutting down on the number of supernatural incidents in *Joan* since late 1793, six months before meeting Coleridge, and by 1795 was increasingly frustrated with the 'clock work' nature of a device whose usefulness had been much debated in eighteenth century epic theory.[13] The public break between the erstwhile collaborators at the end of the year may have acted as the catalyst for the removal of all the epic's supernatural incidents, but it was just a catalyst, nothing more.[14]

The manuscripts and revisions of *Joan* allow a rethinking of Southey's poetics, and offer a more complex version of his creative, intertextual relationships with Coleridge and Wordsworth. They also reveal his effort to locate the poem, to define it as a new kind of national epic and himself as a new, radical type of national epic poet. In this case though, both text and author are placed through the conscious adoption of a rhetoric of displacement.

When Southey published a second, once again heavily revised, edition of *Joan* in 1798 he itemised those 'useless and wearying' features of previous epics that his own work had rejected:

> my readers will find no descriptions of armour, no muster-rolls, no geographical catalogues, lion, tyger, bull and bear similes; Phoebuses and Auroras (*Joan* [1798], I, p. 17).[15]

His comments, which ironically read like the type of catalogue he has repudiated, apply equally well to the earlier, published and manuscript, versions of *Joan* and demonstrate a self-conscious attempt at generic revisionism. Southey was determined both to displace traditional features of epic writing and, following William Hayley's clarion-call for a revival of national heroic literature in his *Essay on Epic Poetry*, to embark on a wholesale redefinition of the form for the 1790s.[16] Something of this ambition, and of the problems it entailed, can be found in the opening of *Joan*, originally drafted in *c.* July 1793 and published two and a half years later in substantially the same form:

> Wars varied horrors, & the troop of ills
> That mark (with blood) Ambitions [wasted] path of France
> [Destructive] –
> [I sing – of English laurels reaped amidst]
> [The fields of carnage –]
> By maiden hand delivered – whilst abashd
> Oppressive England bowd her humbled head
> I sing – nor thou [1 illegible word] Freedom scorn the Song -
> Breathe oer the harp energic – so thy fire
> Shall glow [amid the strain] <so unquenchd> to many a future age
> (*Joan 1793*, I, lines 1-7, f. 4).[17]

What is highly characteristic about these lines is their combination of placement with displacement. The formulaic 'I sing' opening, and the introduction of the nationalistic affiliations of the epic invoke familiar generic ancestors, a lineage which is simultaneously undercut and displaced when it is revealed that this writer, unlike Virgil and his heirs, is going to condemn bloodthirsty ambition and celebrate the ultimate defeat of his own nation.[18] The traditionally displaced, historicized politics of this poem will not affirm national greatness, but instead will prove that the 'Genius of Liberty' needs to 'defend the French from Ambition – Hatred – Slaughter Injustice and England' not only in the fifteenth century, the time of Joan of Arc, but also in the late eighteenth century, Southey's own day (*NLRS*, I, p. 28). However, the rhetoric of displacement is taken much further. This national English epic is geographically relocated to France, and a lower class French woman, not an aristocratic British man, becomes the embodiment of heroic virtue.[19] What *Joan* offers then is the beginning of a wholesale redefinition of the nature of the epic and the character of the heroism that the genre endorses, preferring the republicanism of Lucan's *Pharsalia* to the proto-imperialism of Virgil's *Aeneid*, and elevating the domestic virtues celebrated in Homer's 'good herdsman' Eumaeus above the martial codes endorsed by more traditional classical heroes such as Achilles or Aeneas (*Joan 1796*, p. vi).[20]

The displacements and redefinitions of the national epic offered by *Joan* and by its successor *Madoc*, which publicly rejected the genre's 'degraded title', suggest that in the 1790s, and from the point of view of a radical writer such as Southey, it was no longer possible to write an epic that was either set in Britain or which endorsed the virtues of British society by celebrating either its foundation or its glorious heroic past.[21] *Joan* transforms the foreign wars of Henry V, his lieutenants, and their late eighteenth-century descendants, into inglorious acts of barbarism and treachery. The hero of *Madoc* rejects a benighted Britain, and indeed Europe, in favour of establishing the new utopian society in Peru.[22] The implication is that physical and generic displacement are the only answers to the political and cultural demands of the age. However, as Southey himself was aware, this is a simplification.

Southey was extremely conscious of the links between literature and the nation. In his first published prose work *Letters Written During a Short Residence in Spain and Portugal* (1797) he stated explicitly that a country's political health was reflected in its culture – 'Books are the portrait of the public mind' (*SLSP*, p. 130). Nowhere was this more true than when it came to the condition of the highest of literary forms, the epic. Although Southey asserted that all Spanish and Portuguese poetry wanted 'taste and generally feeling', he reserved particular scorn for the 'Epic and Heroic' literature of both nations. *Letters*, following Hayley's lead in the *Essay on Epic Poetry*, supplies the reader with detailed summaries and copious quotations from two such debased efforts: Lope de Vega's *The Beauty of Angelica* and Tojal's *Charles Redeemed. England Illustrified* (*SLRS*, I, p. 26; *SLSP*, pp. 131-65, 331-55). Both accounts elaborate and expand his earlier critique of the traditional epic and anticipate the demolition of Chapelain's *La Pucelle ou La France Délivrée* in the second edition of *Joan* (*Joan 1798*, I, pp. 23-79). *Angelica* and *Charles Redeemed* are dismissed as examples of the very worst kind of heroic literature and, by inference, of exactly the type of bad writing Southey, as both consumer and producer of epics in the *Letters*, was personally determined to avoid. With their convoluted plots, improbable machinery and total subservience to monarchical and religious imperatives de Vega's and Tojal's poems are portrayed as the exact antithesis of what he had increasingly aimed at in *Joan*. This emerges most clearly in the introductory remarks on *Charles Redeemed*, addressed to both an imaginary correspondent and to the wider, epic reading, public audience of *Letters*:

> I will give you a complete account of a . . . Portugueze Poem. You will be surprised to hear that you must consider it as a national Epic Poem, - that Charles II. of England is the hero, that it is written neither upon his misfortunes, or his restoration, but upon his marriage with Catherine Princess of Portugal, and consequent conversion to the Roman Catholic faith (*SLRS*, p. 330).

Southey exposes the 'national vanity' behind a poem such a Tojal's, a 'vanity' 'which, though it may be very patriotic, is [also] very ridiculous' (*SLRS*, p. 373). It was, of course, a trap into which his own *Joan*, with its repudiation of nationalism as a 'trick to catch the vulgar', had not fallen (*NLRS*, I, p. 28). Or had it? After all, Tojal's relationship to England mirrors Southey's (as the English author of *Joan*) relationship to France. Both produce national epics which they displace onto other nations, and just as Tojal imposes his monarchical Catholicism onto England, so Southey could playfully suggest sending his *Joan* to France where it should be 'a national Poem' (*NLRS*, I, p. 122). The joke might have been lost on those French revolutionaries who, reading the historical figure of Joan of Arc in a very different way, as a royalist and clerical heroine, actually banned the celebration of her festival.[23]

   Displacing the national epic therefore had its own inherent problems. Indeed, though there is no doubt that Southey's *Joan* is primarily directed at an English audience in need of political and cultural reform, there is

94 *Placing and Displacing Romanticism*

evidence that he saw the short-comings of the anti-nationalistic national epic and came to realize that its oppositionist, displaced rhetoric could only be so effective. As he confessed in an undated commonplace book entry, ideally 'England should be the scene of an Englishman's poem' (*SCPB*, IV, p. 17).

Though his 1794 drama *Wat Tyler*, and his later inscription on the same subject, demonstrated that a radical appropriation of nationality was possible, Southey never managed to find a suitably English 'historic point on which to build' a national poem (*SCPB*, IV, p. 17).[24] His third and final epic *Roderick the Last of the Goths* (1814) displaces the conflicts of the peninsular war onto medieval Spain. Nevertheless, when asked, he knew exactly where to place his earliest attempt at the genre:

> my Joan of Arc has revived the epomania that Boileau cured the French of 120 years ago; but it is not every one who can shoot with the bow of Ulysses, and the gentlemen who think they can bend the bow because I made the string twang, will find themselves somewhat disappointed.[25]

As previous critics have observed, Southey ascribes responsibility for the tremendous revival of interest in the epic in the 1790s entirely to the impact of his own poem.[26] He defines himself not merely as the first writer of the modern epic but also, as the derisive remarks about his imitators suggest, as the foremost. If, as he claims, *Joan* was one of the most significant poems of the age how did its readers, in particular those who were also writers, respond to it? How, or where, did they actually place Southey's epic?

There is plenty of surviving evidence that Southey's contemporaries engaged in placing both *Joan* and its author. Coleridge, in another letter to Thelwall, this one from 19 November 1796, asserted, ' Of course, you have read the Joan of Arc. Homer is the Poet for the Warrior - Milton for the religionist - Tasso for Women - Robert Southey for the Patriot (*CL*, I, p. 258). Coleridge's appropriation of poet and poem for the cause of radical patriotism may well have been congenial to his brother-in-law. However, it was not the only point of view. In 1799 the *Anti-Jacobin's* review of the second edition of *Joan* offered a diametrically opposite assessment of patriotic poetics:

> The established rule for epic, that the subject be national, is, surely founded on true patriotism. To this rule ... [Southey] has acted in direct opposition and chosen ... the ignominious defeat of the English . . . Is there not a squint of malignity – a treacherous allusion in such a picture? And was it not rather a seditious rather than a poetic spirit that first contemplated the Maid of Orleans, as the heroine of an English epic? [27]

Characteristically, the *Anti-Jacobin* makes its point by quoting and rewriting Southey's controversial preface, literally turning his own language against him. This programmatic transformation of Coleridgean 'Patriot' into malignant subversive reveals the fundamental complexities of a period in which 'true patriotism' was claimed by both radicals and conservatives and was open to continuous, and contradictory, definition and redefinition.[28]

Their inability to agree on what constituted the patriot nation means that when they come to place *Joan*, Southey's contemporaries do so in ways which ensure that the national epic itself becomes a battleground for competing political (and literary) ideologies. In other words, the political divisions of the age mean that in the 1790s there was no consensus about what made the ideal, modern national poem. There was no single, absolutist definition of either the patriotic Briton or of patriotic poetics. The late eighteenth-century national epic therefore emerged out of a context of political and generic instability. Indeed, its very presence and prevalence is indicative of anxiety, of a period in which definitions of the nation, and of the kind of literature which embodied national consciousness, were subject to constant interrogation.[29]

II

The remainder of this essay will discuss two poems which, though written at the turn of the century, when optimism about the French Revolution had largely been replaced by anxiety over the rise of Napoleon and the threat of French invasion, both engage with, and attempt to place, *Joan*. Yet, though they are on identical subjects, the totally different ways in which they deal with it show the continued lack of political and cultural consensus. The first, Henry James Pye's *Alfred* (1801), attempts to offer a conservative alternative to Southey's radical poetics, relocating the national epic in the heart of a heroic British nation. The second, Joseph Cottle's work of the same name, published less than a year earlier in 1800, shows Southey what could be done with a radical appropriation of the matter of Britain, geographically re-placing the displaced nationalism of *Joan*, and rewriting Southey's epic in the terms of British national myth.[30]

Pye's conservative credentials were confirmed by his appointment in 1790 to the Poet Laureateship. Throughout the political upheavals of the following decade he served his patron, William Pitt, well. His *War Elegies of Tyrtaeus, Imitated: And Addressed to the People of Great Britain* (1795) appropriated the language of patriotism for a loyalist defence of the conflict with revolutionary France, and his *Naucratia, or Naval Dominion* (1798), though published in the year following the naval mutinies at Nore and Spithead, affirmed that in spite of the 'devious guile' of subversives who drew the nations 'truest patriots [sailors] from their country's cause': [31]

> Never shall Anarchy's mad daemon tread
> Insulting here, o'er Freedom's hallow'd head,
> While Freedom's sons in festive carol raise
> To George and Liberty their votive lays . . . [32]

This loyalist interpretation of patriot poetics, and belief in their importance in the nation's defence against the evils of Jacobinism, was at the heart of Pye's next major work – *Alfred*.

The conservative allegiances of Pye's *Alfred* are apparent from its opening pages. Dedicated to Pitt's successor, Henry Addington, the poem affirms the significance of its 'great national subject', and the literary credentials and political affiliations of its author:

> in celebrating the Founder of the Jurisprudence, the Improver of the Constitution, and the Patron of the Literature of my Country, I have endeavoured to appreciate, at their just value, the important blessings we derive from each . . . 'I am glad to have it observed, that there appears throughout my verses, a zeal for the honour of my country; and I had rather be thought a good Englishman, than the best poet, or the greatest scholar, that ever wrote' (*Alfred 1801*, 'Dedication').

Consciously opposed to the works of 'some poets of the present day', Pye reclaims both language and literary production for the loyalists, rewriting '"Senseless Equality's pernicious theme"' as '"the rights of man, -/ Man's real rights"', and exposing French and English Jacobin rhetoric as '"specious Sophistry"' (*Alfred 1801*, 'Dedication', p. 89). As befits a patriotic poem published in the year that saw the passing of the Act of Union, Pye's text physically enacts and embodies the '"THE FAVOUR'D EMPIRE OF THE BRITISH ISLES"', the new political entity of Great Britain and Ireland (*Alfred 1801*, p. 235).[33] The divinely sanctioned, united nation is characterized by loyalist myths of social harmony ('"Each rank supported, firm, by mutual aid"') and class co-operation in the upholding of '"the liberty of all"' (*Alfred 1801*, p. 90). At its heart is the monarch. Alfred the '"people's shield"' and 'patriot King' embodies national virtue. He is quite literally the 'ENGLISH HERO': lord and father of his people, just legislator, educator, great warrior, founder of British commerce, accomplished and patriotic poet (*Alfred 1801*, pp. [5]; 87-91; 101-4; 126; 132-3 and n.; 142).[34] Dedicated to his country, he will "'live her guardian, or her martyr bleed'" and all but one of his subjects offer him their unquestioning support (*Alfred 1801*, p. 131). The only exception, Ceolph, is a false patriot (he "'mask'd his black designs in patriot zeal'"), the ninth century equivalent of an English Jacobin (*Alfred 1801*, p. 26).

Pye's appropriation of British history, or his version of it, in order to promulgate loyalist myths of national unity and the national character reinforces the ruling dynasty's genealogical construction of their own Britishness. The Hanoverian kings claimed descent from Alfred and in the Laureate's epic George III ("'Briton-born'" unlike his grandfather and great grandfather) inherits not just the Anglo-Saxon monarch's throne, but, as his rightful heir, all of his national virtues:

> "And see, best glory of that patriot race,
> Her monarch [George III], Briton-born, Britannia grace;
> Loved, honour'd, and revered by all, save those
> Who, foes to freedom, to her friends are foes.
> But foes in vain – for Anarchy's wild roar
> Shall never shake this Heaven-defended shore,
> While Freedom's sons gird Freedom's sacred throne,
> With loyal Faith's impenetrable zone"(*Alfred 1801*, pp. 98-9).

The connections are obvious. The current struggle against the threat posed to national integrity by Napoleonic France is the equivalent of the ninth-century battle against Danish invaders. Pye's epic celebrates 'patriot King' and heroic defenders of Britain's 'sacred throne' at times of national emergency, both in the Anglo-Saxon past and in his own day (*Alfred 1801*, pp. [5]; 90). It puts 'into metre the popular political phrases of the time', punishing Saxon (and by implication English Jacobin) fifth columnists, praising landowners for their ancestral loyalty to the monarch, and justifying the Act of Union on the grounds that it recreated Alfred's vision of national identity.[35] The story of Alfred the Great therefore offers a convenient way of historicizing and commenting on the present, providing right-minded, loyalist patriots with the ultimate nationalistic justification for their defence of the monarchical, governmental, and social status quo. It confers historical legitimacy on the thoughts and actions of those loyal subjects, who, it insists, are merely upholding age old traditions, and also offers them the chance to participate, even if vicariously, in the modern day epic heroism of resistance to France. *Alfred*, the work of a self proclaimed "'daring muse'" "'fired by patriot zeal / For Freedom's favourite seat

[Britain]"', represents the apotheosis of loyalist politics and of the conservative reclamation of patriot poetics (*Alfred 1801*, p. 239). Moreover, Pye, proclaiming himself as a new, superior version of his epic predecessors Homer and Milton, takes on the mantle of national bard, the '"Truth"' sanctioned defender of '"Albion's weal" (*Alfred 1801*, pp. 238-9).[36]

Although the 'Dedication' suggests the possibility of other definitions of '"the honour of my country"', and the existence of subversive interpretations of patriotism and patriot poetics, Southey and his radical epic are not mentioned by name in the Laureate's poem. Yet, there is no doubt that the latter's loyalist contemporaries read it as a riposte to *Joan*. The *Anti-Jacobin* devoted twenty-four pages, spread over three separate issues, to *Alfred*, much more space than it allotted to any other epic poem of the period.[37] It compared the Laureate favourably to Homer, and prophesied that 'his success will place him in the foremost ranks of the poets of the day'.[38] But, most significantly of all, it juxtaposed his loyalist poetics and 'manly and judicious' defence of the 'good English man' with a very different type of modern epic, the radical version produced by Southey:

> The weak and worthless leader of the 'Isocratists,' who makes 'liberty' a cloak for his envy and 'truth' a cover for his malignity, will do well to consider it [*Alfred*] seriously before he insults his country a second time by an ostentatious display of the triumphs of her enemies.[39]

Alfred therefore offers a model which the unpatriotic poet would do well to learn from. It literally displaces Southey's unhealthy, envious, anti-national epic, offering up a healthy, masculine, national alternative in its stead. The cross-dressing Joan of Arc, whose gender indeterminacy recalls loyalist concerns about the French Revolution's erosion of traditional sexual boundaries, is replaced by the royal, heroic, unambiguous maleness embodied in Alfred the Great.[40]

Pye's reformulation of the national epic represents a relatively straightforward repudiation of *Joan*. Joseph Cottle's response is more complex. As is well known, Cottle was Southey's loyal supporter and was responsible for publishing his *Joan* (1796). His public membership of Southey's literary circle was consolidated by those reviewers of *Alfred* who explicitly linked it with the unconventional practices of certain 'modern writers'.[41] There are several similarities between the two epics: a plain, almost prosaic style identified by frequently hostile critics as characteristic of the 'new' school, whose public leader was Southey, and defended at great length by Cottle in the preface to the second edition of *Alfred* in 1804; controversial prefaces whose refutation of traditional generic practices led the *Monthly Review* to wish that Cottle had described his work as 'anything but an Epic Poem'; an interest in domestic life and a shared attempt to redefine the very nature of epic heroism; and a concentration on the terrible effects of war upon the lives of ordinary people.[42] However, *Alfred*'s intertextuality is not just based upon imitative admiration, on the publisher's uncritical, unassimilated borrowings from his controversial 'protégé'. In fact, as Stuart Curran has observed, it also reacts against the self-conscious anti-Englishness of Southey's epic, substituting the British Alfred for the French Joan.[43] Yet Cottle's choice of hero is more complex than this suggests, combining his determination to write on a national subject with his rejection of the militaristic code celebrated by so many of his predecessors (*Alfred 1800*, p. ii).[44] Alfred the Great is, this poet insists, chosen not simply because he is a British worthy but because he is the right kind of national hero. He is a man 'distinguished in private life for everything which was amiable', unlike the Aeneas condemned by Southey in *Joan*, and in his public life 'for all that was great' (*Alfred 1800*, p. [i]). Moreover Alfred is a supranational national figure, 'the admiration of other countries, and the peculiar glory of our own' (*Alfred 1800*, p. [i]). His defensive war against the invading Danes may coalesce with the demands of the times but, as Cottle's version confirms, the Anglo-Saxon monarch would never transfer his righteous 'sentiment of noble resistance to oppression' to 'causes less just . . . which partake . . . more of aggression than defence' (*Alfred 1804*, I, p. xxx). He is, as the poem shows, a man of peace rather than one of war, a redefined hero for a replaced and rethought national poem.

Cottle's *Alfred* therefore appropriates some of the characteristic features of the new, publicly-identified, radical Southeyan epic, and places generic experimentation back within a national context. However his vision of Britain is very different from the conservative nation celebrated and endorsed by Pye. The Laureate's Alfred is a noble embodiment of the physical fabric of his country, 'Amid distress and danger firm he stood,/ As Albion's cliffs defy the stormy flood', a 'patriot King' whose reign spreads 'peace and freedom wide o'er human kind' and anticipates the time when '"Britain's nations [are] join'd / A world themselves, yet friends of human-kind"'(*Alfred 1801*, pp. [5]; 139; 212). His subjects themselves are either loyal aristocrats, or stereotypical British yeoman who happily sacrifice their lives for an ideal social compact evoked in the epic's concluding lines:

> [Alfred] Feels the true duty of the royal mind,
> His first, his purest bliss, to bless mankind.

> Scorning the base degenerate power that craves
> A hard-wrung homage, from a horde of slaves . . .
> Happy to form, by Virtue's sovereign sway,
> A gallant race of freemen to obey,
> Respect by deeds of goodness to impart,
> And fix his empire o'er the willing heart;
> While patriot worth this godlike mandate taught,
> 'Free be the Briton's action as his thought'.
> Such the true pride of Alfred's royal line,
> Such of Britannia's kings the right divine (*Alfred 1801*, pp. 242-3).

With its sub-Burkean invocation of the glories of the British constitution, Pye's *Alfred* relies upon a series of patriotic platitudes and on a vision of national history which does not question the possibility that 'Britain's throne' could be 'Rear'd' on anything but a 'base of Liberty and Law' (*Alfred 1801*, p. 243). Its rhetorical nationalism is far removed from Cottle's vision.

Cottle's Alfred is not portrayed as the illustrious ancestor of George III, and he is much more interested in the physical well being of his poorer subjects than with dashing round his kingdoms in order to affirm the Act of Union. He endures personal hardship, learns much of the conditions endured by loyal Britons, who willingly sacrifice their own lives in defence of his throne, and eventually works out what it means to be a good king. The final contract he establishes with his people is a less high-sounding, but ultimately more pragmatic one:

> . . . "Each man whose sword was drawn
> In this his country's cause, and who requires
> A safe and quiet home, shall soon possess,
> Together with my smiles, a plot of land,
> A cottage that shall every good contain . . .
>   . . . I will rule
> In mercy, and my thought . . .
> Shall be to serve you, and to make you feel
> Protection and all joy" (*Alfred 1800*, p. 453).

Yet what we actually have in the king's closing words is another rewriting of Southeyan epic, an enactment of Joan of Arc's final advice to the newly crowned Charles:

> "King of France!
> Protect the lowly, feed the hungry ones,
> And be the Orphan's father! thus shalt thou

Become the Representative of Heaven,
And Gratitude and Love establish thus
Thy reign. Believe me, King! that hireling guards,
Tho' flesh'd in slaughter, would be weak to save
A tyrant on the blood-cemented Throne
That totters underneath him" (*Joan 1796*, p. 409).

The maid of Orleans offers a dire warning of the revolution that will eventually occur if the king fails to act on her advice, a revolution whose effects Southey and his contemporary audience were experiencing. Cottle's poem offers a much more positive, pro-active model. The Anglo-Saxon monarch, unlike the French, does not have to be told how to behave correctly to his subjects. He has learned from experience and now does right instinctively. This *Alfred* illustrates that the new heroics championed by Southey's radical displacements could actually be replaced in a revisionist interpretation of British history and of the national poem. It is the publisher of *Joan*, that placed, displaced, and replaced example of the late eighteenth-century epic, who ultimately shows his radical protégé exactly what could be done with the matter of Britain.

Romantic writers of very different political persuasions may have agreed on the necessity for a revival of the highest of literary forms and that, ideally, the 'subject for the epic should be national' (*Joan 1796*, p. vii). Yet, in theory and practice, as the calculatedly anti-nationalistic *Joan* and the responses it provoked illustrate, there was, amidst the political and literary conflicts of the 1790s, no consensus about what form that much needed national poem should take.

Notes

1   Evidence of public awareness of the Southey-Coleridge relationship can be found in John Aikin's review of *Joan 1796* in *Monthly Review*, ns. 19 (1796), pp. 194-5; and the *Critical Review*, ns 17 (1796) (p. 210) notice of S. T. Coleridge, *Poems on Various Subjects* (Bristol: J. Cottle, 1796). Although he joked to Thelwall that 'an admirable Poet might be made by *amalgamating* ... [Southey] & me', (*CL*, I, p. 294), by late 1796 Coleridge was becoming increasingly critical of Southey's work, especially *Joan 1796* and *Poems* (Bristol: J. Cottle: 1797); for example *CL*, I, pp. 290, 293-4. The dedication to his 'Ode to the Departing Year' can be read as a public statement of these misgivings. Certainly the *Monthly Visitor*, 1 (1797) (p. 273) suggested as much.

2   For example, R. Sternbach, 'Coleridge, Joan of Arc, and the Idea of Progress', *ELH*, 46 (1979), pp. 248-61. Thelwall's copy of *Joan 1796* does not seem to have survived.

3   For contemporary condemnations see Aikin's assessment, *Monthly Review*, 19, pp. 361-2, and Wordsworth to William Matthews, 21 March 1796 (*EY*, p. 169).

4   *NLRS*. I, p. 28.

5   The three manuscripts are: (i) Houghton Library, Harvard, MS. Eng. 265.3. The first draft written between mid-July and late September 1793. (*Joan 1793*) I thank the Houghton Library for kind permission to quote from this manuscript. (ii) Department of Rare Books, University of Rochester Library, Rochester, New York, MS AS727. The transcript, with some alterations, made from 7 November to 22 December 1793. (*Rochester MS*.) Quoted with kind permission of the Department of Rare Books, University of Rochester Library. (iii) British Library, London, Add. MS. 28,096. Completely revised by Southey between May and late October-early November 1795 and published at the end of the year. Coleridge helped with the first four books, and the manuscript contains some of the latter's alterations in his own hand (*Joan 1795*). Cited with kind permission of the British Library.

6   In July 1794 Southey arranged for Richard Cruttwell, the Bath-based publisher of William Lisle Bowles, to issue a subscription edition of *Joan*. The proposals for this were included on the endpapers of R. Southey and R. Lovell, *Poems* (Bath 1795). On 14 August 1794 Southey claimed to have fourteen subscribers and, with Lovell's help, to be taking 'infinite trouble' in revising it (*NLRS*, I, pp. 65-6). However, there is some doubt as to how extensive these alterations were and whether this version of *Joan*, unlike the other three, ever existed as an independent entity. The subscription edition never appeared and by autumn 1794 Southey had abandoned work on it in favour of *Madoc*.

7   *Joan 1793*, VI, f.83; *Rochester MS*, VI, lines 1-33 of new section intended to replace VI. lines 312-33. Southey read *Political Justice* in late 1793 (*NLRS*, I, pp. 40-1).

8   Mary Jacobus, in *Tradition and Experiment in Wordsworth's Lyrical Ballads (1798)* (Oxford: Oxford University Press, 1976), argues that a description of a war-widow in *Joan 1798* (I, pp. 110-2) 'may owe something to Wordsworth's "Ruined Cottage"' (pp. 143-4 n.4). Lucy Newlyn, in *Coleridge, Wordsworth, and the Language of Allusion* (Oxford: Oxford University Press, 1986), notes *The Ruined Cottage's* indebtedness to *Joan 1796* but insists that 'for Southey, borrowing amounts to little more than theft' (pp. 9-10; 17 n. 1). As the *Joan* manuscripts show, the situation is more complicated than this. Moreover, there is evidence from Southey's 1797-9 revisions to *Madoc* of an apparently contradictory retreat from descriptions of individual suffering.

9   It was a strength identified by Charles Lamb in 1797 (*Marrs*, I, p. 95).

10   *Rochester MS*, VI, lines 19-24, 25-29 of new thirty-three line section added in as replacement for VI, lines 312-33 initially transcribed from *Joan 1793*, f.83. This section was eventually used, though in a slightly different context, in *Joan 1796*, pp. 147-8.

11   Coleridge's annotations to *Joan 1796*, II. lines 398ff, quoted in Anon., 'Bibliomania', *North British Review*, 40 (1964), p. 82. In 1796 he had agreed with Thelwall that 'the 9th book [of *Joan 1796*, written by Southey and containing Joan's descent to the underworld and a surfeit of supernatural machinery] is execrable' (*CL*, I, p. 293). Southey removed this from *Joan 1798* and republished it separately as 'The Vision of the Maid of Orleans' in his *Poems*. 2 vols (Bristol: J. Cottle, 1799), II, pp. [7]-69.

12   For details of his contributions, G. Whalley, 'Coleridge, Southey and *Joan of Arc*', *Notes and Queries*, 199 (1954), pp. 67-9.

13 *Joan 1793*, III, IV and XI, as well as a number of separate incidents throughout this first draft, had been devoted to supernatural events. *Joan 1795* removed some of these, and none of the new material added to it was supernatural in character. See, *NLRS* I, pp. 136-8 for Southey's dissatisfaction with the 'clock-work' nature of the supernatural.

14 *Joan 1798*, I, p. 11, totally rejected the 'palpable agency of superior powers'.

15 For an earlier version of this list, see *NLRS*, I, pp. 137-8.

16 William Hayley, *An Essay on Epic Poetry* (London: J. Dodsley, 1782). Southey found the poem's extensive endnotes especially useful (*SLRS*, I, pp. 25-7). Hayley's influence on the Romantic epic is discussed in Stuart Curran, *Poetic Form and British Romanticism* (New York and Oxford: Oxford University Press, 1986), pp. 160-1; 239-40, n. 10.

17 *Joan 1793*, I, lines 1-7, f.4. Compare with *Joan 1796*, p. [5].

18 *Joan 1796*, p. vi described Aeneas as a 'villain' and also expressed Southey's preference for Statius over Virgil, p. vii, Coleridge later claimed that at the time he produced *Joan 1796* '"Southey had never read, or more than merely looked through"' the works of either '"except in school lessons"', 'Bibliomania', p. 79.

19 Southey was not the first to make a woman the hero of an epic, Chapelain and Blackmore had pre-empted him, H. T. Swedenberg, *The Theory of the Epic in England 1650-1800* (Berkeley and Los Angeles: University of California Press, 1944), pp. 23-4, 74. However, some of his contemporaries expressed reservations over the suitability of his choice. Aikin argued that Joan of Arc was unsuitable as Chapelain (unintentionally in his *La Pucelle ou la France délivrée* [1656]) and Voltaire (intentionally in his comic *La Pucelle d'Orléans* [1762]) had made her an object of public ridicule, *Monthly Review*, 19, pp. 361-8. Her potential lack of respectability even for writers with radical associations, is summed up in Charles Lamb's fear that, in revising his contributions to *Joan 1796* into 'The Visions of the Maid of Orleans', Coleridge would 'degrade ... [Joan] into a pot girl' (Marrs, I, p. 94).

20 The earliest version of *Madoc* explicitly replaces the Virgilian hero with one who 'the unfrequented path/ Of Justice, firmly treads', K. Curry, 'Southey's *Madoc*: The Manuscript of 1794', *Philological Quarterly*, 22 (1943), p. 362.

21 Robert Southey, *Madoc* (London, 1805), p. ix. See also Lynda Pratt, 'Revising the national epic: Coleridge, Southey and *Madoc*', *Romanticism*, 2 (1996), pp. 149-63.

22 Southey's original plan was to identify Madoc with the first Inca, Manco Capac, and to have him found an ideal society in Peru.

23 Marina Warner, *Joan of Arc. The Image of Female Heroism* (London: Weidenfield and Nicholson, 1981; reprinted, London: Vintage, 1991), p. 253. Her festival and cult were revived by Napoleon.

24 R. Southey, *Wat Tyler. A Dramatic Poem* (London: T. Broom, 1817). The 'Inscription. For a Column in Smithfield Where Wat Tyler Was Killed' appeared in the *Morning Post* for 12 February 1798, Kenneth Curry, ed. *The Contributions of Robert Southey to the Morning Post* (Alabama: University of Alabama Press, 1984), pp. 31-2.

25 *LCRS*, II, pp. 121-2. In 1799 Southey planned an 'Analysis of Obscure Epic Poems ... it will be valuable now, & daily becoming more so, as the books which it will rescue from utter oblivion daily become scarcer. Criticisms will be scattered thro it, the compressed narration of each poem will not be uninteresting, there will be many translations, & perhaps sometimes when I see a fine subject massacred I may throw off a passage of my own to show what could have been made of it', Southey to

Thomas Southey, 1 March 1799, British Library, London, Add. MS. 30,927 f.38. Quoted with kind permission of the British Library.

26 Bernard Wilkie, *Romantic Poets and Epic Tradition* (Madison and Milwaukee: University of Wisconsin Press, 1965), p. 41.

27 *The Anti-Jacobin Review and Magazine*, 3 (1799), p. 121.

28 The transformation of the nature of patriotism in the 1790s has been the subject of extensive recent debate, helpful introductions include Linda Colley, '"Whose Nation? Class and National Consciousness in Britain, 1750-1830' *Past and Present*, 113 (1986), pp. 97-117; and David Eastwood, 'Patriotism and the English State in the 1790s' in *The French Revolution and British Popular Politics*, ed. Mark Philp (Cambridge: Cambridge University Press, 1991), pp. 146-68. David Eastwood, 'Robert Southey and the Meanings of Patriotism' *Journal of British Studies*, 31 (1992), pp. 265-87 uses Southey's later works to portray his 'pivotal position' in 'this struggle for the language of patriotism'. Significantly, a previously unnoticed manuscript of *Wat Tyler*, describes it as a 'Patriotic Play by Coleridge', British Library, London, RP4533 part II.

29 The outpouring of national poems at the turn of the eighteenth century is discussed in Curran, *Poetic Form*, pp. 161-7.

30 Southey himself considered, but rejected, writing a poem on Alfred the Great. His reason for doing so was undoubtedly connected with his poor opinion of Cottle, and Pye's, epics. *SCPB*, IV. p. 17.

31 Henry James Pye, *The War Elegies of Tyrtaeus, Imitated; And Addressed to the People of Great Britain* (London: T. Cadell, 1795); Henry James Pye, *Naucratia; Or Naval Dominion. A Poem* (London 1798), p. 70.

32 Pye, *Naucratia*, p. 76.

33 Alfred receives support from the people of England, Scotland, Ireland, and Wales, and is portrayed as the great unifier of the four nations in a common struggle against the Danish invaders, 'Britain's sister isles in Alfred's cause conspire', *Alfred 1801*, p. 150. After the battle of Eddington he calls for national unity, 'Within its fence be Britain's nations join'd,/ A world themselves', p. 212.

34 This view of Alfred was the standard one of the late eighteenth and early nineteenth century, Lynda Pratt, 'Anglo-Saxon Attitudes: The Political and Literary Significance of Alfred the Great in the 1790s' in D. G. Scragg and C. Weinberg, eds. *Post-Conquest Views of the Anglo-Saxons* (Cambridge: Cambridge University Press, 1997), pp. 138-56.

35 See Southey's review, *Critical Review*, ns 34 (1802), p. 370. He also reviewed Cottle's *Alfred* (London: Longman and Rees, 1800), *Critical Review*, ns 31 (1801), 160-71. Pye traces the descent of the Wyndhams, Temples and Berties from supporters of Alfred (*Alfred 1801*, pp. 25 and n.; 125 and n). He also celebrates British landholders for their role in Magna Carta, 'the famous ... declaration of the rights of Englishmen' (p. 92n).

36 *Alfred 1801*, 239n. Pye cites Miltonic and Homeric authority for his work. *Monthly Review* 37 (1802), pp. 180-1 identifies some of his borrowings from his epic precursors.

37 *Anti-Jacobin Review and Magazine*, 9 (1801), pp. 232-4; 340-7; 10 (1801), pp. 12-21.

38 *Anti-Jacobin Review and Magazine*, 10 (1801), p. 20.

39 *Anti-Jacobin Review and Magazine*, 9 (1801), p. 232.

40 Concern at the erosion of traditional gender boundaries also provoked profound unease in revolutionary France, see Lynn Hunt, *The Family Romance of the French*

    Revolution (Berkeley and Los Angeles: University of California Press, 1992), pp. 113-23.

41   *Monthly Review*, 48 (1805), p. 437. The links between *Alfred* and the Southey circle had already been made in the *MM*, 11 (1801), pp. 603-4; *MM*, 11 (1801), pp. 395-6; and *Monthly Review*, 35 (1801), pp. [1]-9. Cottle's massive preface to *Alfred 1804* is an attempt to refute this criticism (I, pp. ix-l).

42   *Monthly Review*, 35 (1801), p. [1].

43   Curran, *Poetic Form*, pp. 168-9.

44   This was elaborated on in *Alfred 1804*, I, pp. xxxii-xl.

8 Re-placing Waterloo: Southey's Vision of Command

PHILIP SHAW

I

In November 1815, Robert Southey, journalist, historian and Poet Laureate, entered into an unwitting test of wills with a living legend: Arthur Wellesley, the Duke of Wellington.[1] Southey's version of the quarrel, which is set out in a letter to William Wynn (*NLRS*, II, pp. 124-8), – is concerned with the veracity of the Duke's account of the recent Allied victory over Napoleon. The revelation that the successful general and hero of the battle of Waterloo should turn out not to be the decorous figure of popular belief, takes its initial force from an editorial dispute. The story can be summarised as follows. In the weeks prior to his visit to the Netherlands – a trip which was to include a visit to the site of the famous battle – Southey had completed the second half of a laudatory article on the life of Wellington. The article was to have appeared in the *Quarterly Review* for July, but the publication of the July issue was delayed due to Southey's objections to the alterations that John Wilson Croker had made in his text. According to Southey, the Duke of Wellington, through Croker, had interpolated two large passages in which it was claimed that the Duke had not been surprised by the French Forces and that no merit was due to the Prussians in the victory. Faced with this wilful intervention in historical truth, Southey risked exposing himself to the full weight of the Duke's indignation and insisted that the papers be returned to him so that the 'falsehoods' could be 'struck out', and the truth 'reinserted'.

The author's version of the *Quarterly* essay was eventually published in November. Wellington was clearly dismayed and, although he did not respond directly to Southey or to Croker, he ensured that his feelings would be known. In a despatch to the Earl of Clancarty, for example, he calls upon the King 'to prevail on his Legislature to pass a good strong law of libel . . . does [he] not see that he is encouraging and fostering a nest of . . . libellers in his country, whose object is to overturn his government, and in the mean time to do him and his Allies all the mischief they can'. For Wellington,

106

The truth regarding the battle of Waterloo is this: there exists in England an insatiable curiosity upon every subject which has occasioned a mania for travelling and for writing. The battle of Waterloo having been fought within reach, every creature who could afford it, travelled to view the field; and almost every one who came who could write, wrote an account. It is inconceivable the number of lies that were published and circulated in this manner by English travellers . . . this has been done with such industry that it is now quite certain that I was not present and did not command in the battle of Quatre Bras, and it is very doubtful whether I was present in the battle of Waterloo. It is not so easy to dispose of the British army as it is of an individual: but although it is admitted they were present, the brave Belgians, or the brave Prussians, won the battle; and neither in histories, pamphlets, plays, nor pictures, are the British troops ever noticed. But I must say that our travellers began this warfare of *lying;* and we must make up minds as to the consequences.[2]

The passage is notable, not least for the way in which Wellington links the corruption of truth to that dangerously unstable form of Romantic subjectivity, the traveller. Within weeks of the battle the field of Waterloo had become a popular tourist attraction. And with the tourists came the profiteers: the souvenir collectors, showmen, painters and writers. The uncontainability of these bourgeois 'creatures' bears visible testimony to the fact that the field of victory can no longer be regarded as a private domain. As the ambassadors of commercial society swarm across the battle-field, set free by economic forces beyond the control of the Dukes and Earls, the lies begin to multiply: their number is 'inconceivable'; the 'warfare of *lying*' replaces the war for truth.[3]

Southey, then, is much more than an inaccurate historian. He is, first and foremost a representative of the mobile bourgeoisie; a middle-class traveller whose claim to distinction rests upon the relentless production of writing. Wellington, as is well known, was notorious both for the disdain with which he held his own despatches – writing was an embellishment; a corruption of the truth – and for his Byronic dislike of professional writers. Unlike Byron, however, he knew which side of the commercial divide to inhabit. His hatred of authors is based on a simplistic distrust of the levelling effects of the public sphere. He had, as he explained later in his life, been 'too much exposed to authors'[4]. One of them, seeking the Duke's guidance for a projected account of the campaign, was sternly advised to leave well alone: 'you may depend upon it that you will never make it a satisfactory work'. To another he cursorily remarked: 'I can refer you only to my own despatches published in the "London Gazette"'.[5] Wellington's hatred of writers is bound up, it seems to me, with a desire to control both the meaning of the battle and his own status as a privatized, autocratic subject. The illimitable spread of writing threatens to undo the discursive hierarchy on which the Duke's idea of individual and national authority depends. To write the battle in defiance of this authority is to stake a claim on an autonomy no longer based on distinction and command but on the tacit acknowledgement that a 'public sphere' exists and that differences and exclusion can be converted, at the level of discourse, to a formal system of equality.[6]

Writing and travel are linked, therefore, to a complex system of deference and consensus. Within this system the accessibility of the field of Waterloo enables the bourgeois traveller to identify with its noble author; to stand on the spot where Wellington once stood and thus to convert an emblem of landed property into the experience of common property. Whether the tourists wrote their names on the walls of La Belle Alliance or more purposefully converted the field into an abstract space of self-assertion – from Wordsworth's *Thanksgiving Ode* to Byron's *Pilgrimage* – the site could no longer be regarded as Wellington's own.

Southey's dispute with the Duke touches, then, on a series of questions to do with property, authority and identity. Nowhere is this more apparent than in the controversy over the name of the victory. Throughout his correspondence and in the *Journal of A Tour in the Netherlands,* Southey had expressed his desire that the battle be known by the name of Belle Alliance. In the *Journal* he invokes the voice of the peasant who guided him on the field: 'He was very angry that Waterloo should give name to the battle; call it Hougoumont, he said, call it La Belle Alliance, or La Haye Sainte, or Pepelot, or Mont St. Jean – anything but Waterloo!'.[7] Similarly, in the letter he claims that, 'One of the passages which I struck out was a sentence saying that the good sense of Europe had rejected the name of Belle Alliance for the battle as being in some degree false. I have since discovered that in the Duke's dispatches he underlined the word *Waterloo,* this for the same mean motive' (*NLRS,* II, p. 216).

Southey's preference for the Prussian name emerges out of a vexed contemporary debate. As soon as the news of the allied victory reached England, journals as various as the *Anti-Jacobin Review* and the *Political Register* scrambled for authoritative copy. The editors of these journals, in a bid to satiate public interest, printed Wellington's authenticated despatch – first published in the *London Gazette* – alongside its nearest competitor: the more substantial and mellifluous report of the Prussian General Gneisenau.[8] Readers such as Sir John Sinclair were quick to express their disappointment with the Duke's account: 'By its side stands the Prussian Report, like oriental poetry, compared to the firm and vigorous language of the North; it breathes life and fire, all is as it were painted; the feelings are roused, and in the conclusion, there is a species of romantic chivalry ... '. Such a distinction was anathema to the Duke. Not only had Sinclair violated the law of property in approaching a 'foreign' source – von Müffling but also, in the appendices, the eyewitness account of de Coster, Napoleon's peasant guide – he had also committed the unpardonable sin of poetization. For Sinclair's evaluation of the Prussian and English prose turns on the stock romantic distinction between the exotic south and the austere North. Rather like Southey, whose work was also invested in this distinction, Sinclair wishes to recast the victory as a form of chivalric romance. And also like Southey, his approach to the battle incurred the wrath of its self-proclaimed author.[9]

Shortly after its publication, Wellington informed Sinclair of his objection to the people of England 'being misinformed and misled by those novels called "Relations", "Impartial Accounts", &c. &c., of that transaction, containing stories which curious travellers have picked up from peasants, private soldiers, individual officers, &c. &c., and have published to the world as the truth'.[10] It is possible that Wellington has a number of such 'novels' in mind – from Simpson's *Visit to Flanders* (1815) to Charlotte Eaton's *Narrative of a Few Week's Residence in Belgium* (1815).[11] But given the recent dealings with Croker it is tempting to think that Southey is the real target. The dispute over the name of the battle is a particular sticking point. Wellington had already snubbed Müffling for speaking of the 'Battle of *La Belle-Alliance*'[12] – this too presented a challenge to his authority. Were the victory to be re-named Belle Alliance it would cease to be the sole property of Wellington and the British establishment; an internationalist history would be the result. Moreover, it would legitimate the existence of a non-paternal bourgeois public sphere. In short, the significance of the war against revolutionary France would not have been decided not by an autocracy – the political equivalent of Coleridge's 'infinite I AM' – but by an increasingly dominant professional class.

Despite his title, therefore, a writer such as Sinclair places himself in the service of the very forces that were eroding the older, chivalric codes of aristocratic privilege. His appeal to the Burkean rhetoric of chivalry – enacted in his preference for La Belle Alliance over the English-sounding Waterloo – is an attempt to recoup his material losses. Like Sinclair, Southey is also interested in symbolic recuperation. But his passage from tractable bourgeoisie to poetic page of state has its own, unique contours. Beginning with an early letter to John Rickman, Southey divides his feelings between a private rhetoric of romance and a more social tone of bellicose patriotism: 'The name which Blücher had given it will do excellently in verse – the field of Fair Alliance! but I do not like it in prose, for we gave them such an English thrashing, that the name ought to be one which comes easily out of an English mouth' (*LCRS*, IV, p. 119). As with Sinclair, prose is equated with Englishness and with Wellington; poetry with the spirit of romance and Blücher.

The Rickman letter was written in July – some weeks before Southey made the journey that is recorded in the *Journal* and that also provides the inspiration for his verse Romance, *The Poet's Pilgrimage to Waterloo*. Looking back on this trip in his December letter to William Wynn, only this time writing with the unofficial knowledge of one of Wellington's libellous travellers, Southey places much more emphasis on Blucher's appellation rather than on the Englishness of Wellington's. But with Southey's literary outpourings in mind, perhaps what is most interesting about this revaluation is the way in which history lends support to the poetry. Once again, the authority of the peasant guide is invoked: 'tell the people in England it ought not to be called Waterloo' (*NLRS*, II, p. 126). Thus, in a letter dated 19th December 1815, a few days after the letter to Wynn, 'The Poet's Pilgrimage to La Belle Alliance' is the favoured title of his commemorative poem (*NLRS*, II, p. 128). But here, picking up on the distinction he had made to Rickman, he values the title, not only for the way in which it does justice to the historical fact that the victory is a shared one, but also, quite simply, because it is more aesthetically pleasing.

In consolidating the historical significance of the battle, therefore, Southey is keen to ensure that it takes on a pleasing form. His choice of Edward Nash as the official illustrator of the poem was thus a carefully considered one. As befits a composition written under the aegis that 'A battle can only be made tolerable in narration when it has something picturesque in its accidents, scene, &c. &c', Nash has produced engravings that 'are all sufficiently picturesque' (*LCRS*, IV, p. 118). I will have more to say about the use of the visual in connection with the field of battle later on. For now I wish merely to observe that for Southey there is something distinctly unpicturesque about Wellington's chosen name for the battle. Compared with the sonorously iambic La Belle Alliance, Waterloo somehow fails to capture what is most poetic and thus most significant about the event.

In the passage that follows, Southey goes on to outline his plans for a national epic on the age of George III: 'The subject . . . is nothing less than a view of the world during the most eventful half century of its annals, – not the *history*, but a philosophical summary, with reference to the causes and consequences of all these mighty revolutions. There never was a more splendid subject, and I have full confidence in my own capacity for treating it' (*NLRS*, II, p. 129). The move from history to philosophy is a telling and not unfamiliar strategy of the Romantic temper. Southey's purpose is to make the significance of the war with France come alive for a national mind preoccupied not so much with history as with its more pressing economic effects. In the *Pilgrimage*, by emphasizing the picturesque through the framework of a philosophical summary, with history invoked as a final arbiter of truth, Southey is exercising nothing less than his right, as Poet Laureate, to poeticize the political; to tell the story of British national history as it *ought* to be and therefore as it *is*. Left to the merely prosaic imaginations of Croker, Wellington and Rickman, the battle risks losing what Byron refers to as 'that undefinable but impressive halo which the lapse of ages throws around a celebrated spot' (*Childe Harold's Pilgrimage* III, 29n: *BCPW*, II, p. 303). Unlike Byron, however, Southey is less equivocal about the attempt to transform the prosody of the present into the poetry of history. If the battle is to survive as a triumphant event in British history, he seems to be saying, it must first of all sublate the chaos and confusion of its linking phrases – the dissonant voices, from Cobbett's stridently materialist *Political Register* to the *Examiner's* Whiggish 'history hath only one page' argument – into a politically transcendent proper name. In 1815, La Belle Alliance becomes much more than an empty designator of reality;[13] for Southey it is an index of an abstract truth: the belief that the antinomies of nation states, classes and ultimately of individuals can be subsumed in a name that is itself a legitimate synthesis of the historical and the poetic.

Behind these public concerns, however, there lies a more personal truth. To validate his own right to distinction at a level beyond that of the abstract principle of discursive equality, Southey must square the Romantic ideal of an heroic, privatised subjectivity with the reality of his social status as a member of the very class that is learning to convert this ideal into a marketable commodity. To address *this* aspect of Southey's work we must consider the context that William Hazlitt created for the reception of the Laureate's work in the pages of the *Examiner*.

II

In his review of *The Lay of the Laureate*, Hazlitt makes no bones about what he sees as the poet's inveterate egotism: '"Once a Jacobin and always a Jacobin" . . . every sentiment or feeling that he has is nothing but the effervescence of incorrigible over-weening self-opinion' (*Howe* VII, p. 86). All of this is worked into a coruscating analysis of the Lay's rhetorical ambition, the Proem of which opens thus:

> There was a time when all my youthful thought
> Was of the Muse; and of the Poet's fame,

> How fair it flourisheth and fadeth not, ...
> Alone enduring, when the Monarch's name
> Is but an empty sound, the Conqueror's bust
> Moulders and is forgotten in the dust.[14]

What follows is as psychologically perceptive as it is politically inflammatory. In Hazlitt's view, the impropriety of expressing such thoughts in a poem addressed to the King is only matched by the degree of egotism that it reveals:

> He endeavours to prove that the Prince Regent and the Duke of Wellington (put together) are greater than Bonaparte, but then he is by his own rule greater than all three of them. We have here perhaps the true secret of Mr. Southey's excessive anger at the late Usurper. If all his youthful thought was of his own inborn superiority to conquerors or kings, we can conceive that Bonaparte's fame must have appeared a very great injustice done to his pretensions (*Howe*, VII, p. 88).

Southey, in other words, is of the devil's party without knowing it. His avowed hatred of the scourge of Europe is prompted by a structure of self-assertion that owes its being to the very imperialism that it denounces. For, Hazlitt asks, on what does Southey's claim to greatness depend? If it is on the official symbol of the laureate wreath then it is of no great matter. The crown is not, as Southey contends, an object of great envy. Thus, having first of all set up the poet as a type of inverted Napoleon, Hazlitt makes the further move of identifying his quest for fame with an un-Napoleonic sense of characterless inconsistency: 'Whether he is a Republican or a Royalist, – whether he hurls up the red cap of liberty, or wears the lily, stained with the blood of all his old acquaintance, at his breast, – whether he glories in Robespierre or the Duke of Wellington', in Hazlitt's prose Southey is nothing less than a rhetorical shifter, a paper 'I' caught between violent antitheses, only himself when he is expressing an antipathy to the 'principles' and 'prejudices' of others: 'Such is the constitutional slenderness of his understanding, its "glassy essence"' (*Howe*, VII, p. 86).

From a certain sociological point of view, Hazlitt has every right to dissolve his subject in anaphoric vitriol. What this virtuoso display denies, however, is the psychological complexity of Southey's response to the abdication of Napoleon. To John May and Walter Scott, Southey writes of the event as the final curtain on a 'tragedy of five-and-twenty years': 'Much as I had desired [the abdication], and fully as I had expected it, still, when it came, it brought with it an awful sense of the instability of all earthly things'. What the tragedy lacked, however, was a satisfying 'after-piece': 'I thought he would set his life upon the last throw; or that he would kill himself, or that some of his own men would kill him; and though it had long been my conviction that he was a mean-minded villain, still it surprised me that he should live after such a degradation, – after the loss, not merely of empire, but even of his military character'. As it is, the 'sudden termination' of the Napoleonic narrative leaves Southey with a peculiar feeling of insecurity: 'it seemed like a change in life itself' (*LCRS*, IV, pp. 68-9) – akin to the discovery that the story of one's life had never, after all, really been one's own:

> for I could not but remember how materially the course of my own life had been influenced by that tremendous earthquake, which seemed to break up the very deeps of society, like a moral and political deluge. I have derived nothing but good from it in every thing, except the mere consideration of immediate worldly fortune, which to me is dust in the balance. Sure I am that under any other course of discipline I should not have possessed half the intellectual powers which I now enjoy, and perhaps not the moral strength (*LCRS*, IV, p. 66).

The material course of Southey's life has been fashioned under the influence of Napoleonic 'discipline'. Now, in the absence of this power – a younger Southey had pronounced the general 'the greatest man that events have called into action since Alexander of Macedon' (*NLRS*, I, p. 222) – he begins to exhibit uncomfortable signs of mourning. In a special sense, therefore, as much as Byron, Hazlitt or Scott, Southey recognizes his enemy as internal to his own ego, a part of his relationship to himself.[15] But it is the lack of a satisfactory end to the *drama* of this relationship that troubles Southey the most. In Lacanian terms, whether the emperor functions as the subject of tragedy or of romance, the lack of a satisfactory 'after-piece' exposes a gap in the real that can only be filled with the totality of the signifier. In the absence of such a signifier the Napoleonic text remains incomplete.[16] Where, then, is the figure who will take the emperor's place?

By December 1814, the gap is all too apparent: 'We make war better than we make peace . . . Europe was in such a state when Paris was taken, that a commanding intellect, had there been such among the allies, might have cast it into whatever form he pleased' (*LCRS*, IV, p. 96). The echo of Coleridge's 'commanding genius' is a reminder that Southey was constitutionally determined to frame the course of his own life and that of European history in terms drawn from the discourse of high Romanticism. To do justice to the enemy, and thus to oneself, all that the drama needed was the intervention of a British genius and a decisive conclusion. At first Wellington and Waterloo would appear to fulfil this aim. But Southey, due to the extent of his investment in the Napoleonic romance, was destined to perpetuate his feelings of dissatisfaction: 'it surprised me that he should live'.

In 1815 history has opened a fissure that only literature can negotiate. Both the pusillanimous end of the emperor and the prosaic dealings of the Duke point towards the inability of history to live up to Southey's romantic script. But if the narrative cannot be completed it can at least be regulated. Southey's response to the gap in the real is to fill it with his own system of fictional power: the consolidation of his cultural position as a one-man textual industry. Hence the ceaseless production of more romances, histories, political essays, definitive editions, and, crucially, of laureate pieces. What the leaders of men sully in the field of statesmanship, the laureate will recoup in the field of culture.

> Literary fame is the only fame of which a wise man ought to be ambitious, because it is the only lasting and living fame. Bonaparte will be forgotten before his time in Purgatory is half over . . . Pour out your mind in a great poem, and you will exercise authority over the feelings and opinions of mankind as long as the language lasts in which you write' (*LCRS*, III, p. 144).

Thus, from the *Lay* through to the *Pilgrimage* Southey's interest in the significance of contemporary events is prompted by a deeper desire to fashion himself as a power in English literature. Such ambition did not go unnoticed. As Francis Jeffrey remarked, echoing Hazlitt: '[the poet-laureate] has very distinctly manifested his resolution not to rest satisfied with the salary, sherry, and safe obscurity of his predecessors, but to claim a real power and prerogative in the world of letters, in virtue of his title and appointment'. The claim to 'real power' encompasses both his relation to literary power – the great poets of the past from Spenser to Milton – but also to political power:[17] 'it is easy to see the worthy Laureate thinks himself entitled to share in the prerogatives of that royalty which he is bound to extol'.[18] From the letters to the *Quarterly Review* articles, and from the *Journal of a Tour* to the *Poet's Pilgrimage to Waterloo,* what we encounter is the transformation of geo-political reality into the abstracted space of literature. In what amounts to a virtual re-mapping of Waterloo, Southey strives to convert a public heterotopia into a private bibliotopia. The one hinges on the other: both the officially sanctioned mouth-piece of a triumphant and newly invigorated nation state *and* the unofficially elected voice of a national poetic tradition.

III

That Southey aimed for something more than the short term view is born out in a letter to his fellow Waterloo bard, Walter Scott. 'My poem will reach you in a few weeks; it is so different in its kind, that, however kindly malice may be disposed, it will not be possible to institute a comparison with yours. I take a different point of time and a wider range, leaving the battle untouched, and describing the field only such as it was when I surveyed it' (*LCRS*, IV, pp. 152-3). The point of comparison is an apt one. Where Scott indulges his talent for conducting an action – the anaphoric structure of headwords in conjunction with definite articles, imperatives and active verbs – Southey is concerned with the allegorical aspects of battle. Thus, where Scott's poem is passionately factual, Southey's poem is plangently mythical. The former is written within an epic framework, the latter is conceived as a romance. Despite its immediate historical focus, therefore, there is a sense in which the *Pilgrimage* can be seen as a continuation of Southey's earlier quest romances. With its emphasis on the recuperative effects of the journey, the transformation of the traveller into a steadfast hero and the key intervention of a mythical female guide, the poem is yet another reworking of Book I of *The Faerie Queene* – filtered, of course, through the Puritan matrix of Bunyan. Here, once again, we must mark Southey's departure from Scott. For where Scott confines himself to an historically specific account of the 'matter of Waterloo', Southey, true to the aims of his projected national epic, ranges quite freely through the imaginative realms of time and space.[19] This should not be taken to mean that the *Pilgrimage* elides or suppresses matter. Nor does it entail its transcendence. In Southey's texts, the realm of the psyche is constituted not as an evasion of history but through a direct engagement with it. By re-writing Wellington's account of Waterloo through the context of a Spenserian privileging of poetry over history – privatized romance over state-sanctioned fact – and then using this reconstituted history, in turn, as a sanction for his aesthetic ends, the poet aims for nothing less than the totalizing vision on which high Romantic identity depends.

In the letter to Scott, the reference to the poem's 'wider range' in connection with the rhetoric of surveying ('describing the field only such as when I surveyed it') recalls the context in which images of Waterloo were produced and consumed in this period. Advertisements in *The Times* for the period 1815 to 1818 signalled the availability of battle narratives, guide books, poems and, most significantly, maps. Of these, the most authoritative was undoubtedly the 'detailed plan' of the field of battle executed by W. M. Craan, the official map maker of the King of the Netherlands. Craan's map was notable both 'for the accuracy of its detail, and for the exact positions and respective movements it describes of every regiment during the day'.[20] Readers were thus able to orientate themselves in relation to a truth that could be described as objective and neutral. But the map did more than simply name, recount and locate. It also operated as a form of territorial discourse, reproducing political imperatives in the guise of scientific disinterestedness. The 'silent lines' of Craan's plan encouraged readers to locate themselves above the chaos and confusion of battle and thus to consume the field as an object of knowledge/power.[21] Southey's act of 'surveying' points towards a similar impulse. With its echo of Cowper – 'I am monarch of all I survey, / My right there is none to dispute' (*PWC*, I, p. 403) – the rhetoric of command and comprehension has an obvious analogy with the discourse of romantic self-fashioning. But is also suggests the wider equation between literary authority, subjectivity and visual power. In Southey's view the fragmented perspectives of Waterloo have to be monitored by a 'dominant overseeing eye',[22] for the danger of losing the 'wider range' is that of becoming absorbed in the pathos of minute particulars: the 'marks of wreck . . . for those who closelier peer'.[23]

Southey's visual strategy turns, therefore, on a delicate negotiation of topographical power. To elevate the eye above the landscape the poem must recreate the panoramic vision of the map-maker. To do so, however, is to risk an unfortunate encounter with the structure of false or Napoleonic seeing. As Southey the historian was aware, for the first half of the battle the emperor had been stationed at the top of a tall wooden tower. Southey the journalist refers to this in his *Quarterly* essay: 'In the early part of the day he had reconnoitred the ground, and directed the movements from a sort of scaffolding, observatory, or telegraph, which had been erected from some ichnographical purposes'.[24] In fact the platform had been commissioned by the King of the Netherlands to enable Craan to draw up a detailed map of the surrounding territory. The image of Napoleon on the observatory became a popular feature of guide books and histories. In Thomas Kelly's *History of the French Revolution* (1819), for example, the emperor is depicted at the top of the tower surveying the battlefield with the aid of a telescope (Figure 8.1).[25] To dissipate the force of the emperor's eye, the surrounding text goes on to distinguish between the gaze of Napoleon (artificially elevated and curiously preoccupied with the 'beauty' of enemy forms) and that of Wellington ('his penetrating eye detected the first error').[26]

The distinction between false or Napoleonic seeing and the 'penetrating eye' of Wellington was to become a stock feature of Waterloo-related literature. From William Thomas Fitzgerald's 'The Battle of Waterloo':

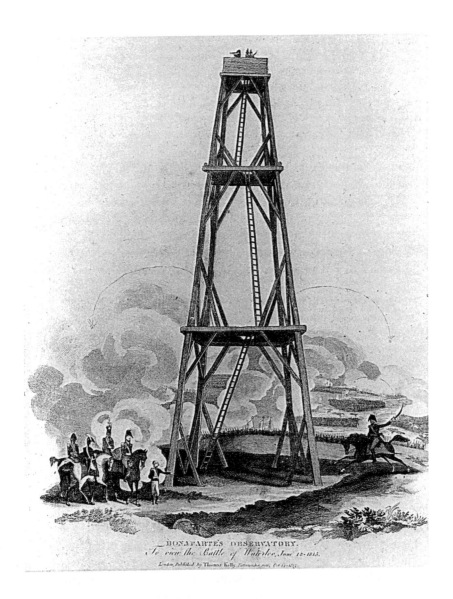

8.1   **'Bonaparte's Observatory' from Thomas Kelly,**
History of the French Revolution (1819)

His eagle eye discerns from far
The moment which decides the war . . . [27]

To Southey's *Pilgrimage*:

Deem not that I the martial skill should boast
Where horse and foot were station'd here to tell,
What points were occupied by either host,
And how the battle raged, and what befell,
And how our great Commander's eagle eye,
Which comprehended all, secured the victory (I, iii, lines 32-37).

In Southey's case, however, the comparison between the task of the historian and the task of the poet also serves as a means of distinguishing one form of surveillance, associated with military command and aristocratic privilege, with another, superior form of seeing: the elevated vision of the bard. Taking an Aristotelian distinction at its most literal, Southey deploys the rhetoric of deference only to assert the 'natural' superiority of poetry over history. Thus, where poets such as Fitzgerald defer to 'Laurelled Wellington':

But where's the BARD, however grac'd his name,
Can venture to describe GREAT WELLESLEY'S fame?
Such Bard, in strength and loftiness of lays,
May soar beyond hyperbole of praise,
And yet not give the tribute that is due
To BRITONS, WELLINGTON, led on by you!!
For to the plains of WATERLOO belong
The magic numbers of immortal song (II, iii, lines 20-27).

Southey seeks to ensure that poetic laurels take precedence over victory laurels. To do so, however, he must separate his own form of elevation from that of the commanders.

Structurally the poem takes the form of a contest between the cold eye of French materialist philosophy, represented by the duplicitous figure of earthly Wisdom, and the 'scope unconfined' of divine providence, represented by the 'heavenly muse' (II, iii, line 48). Here, divinity triumphs over techne. But the assertion of god-like vision is, itself, not without its technical problems. The initial encounter with the field of battle is, in topographical terms, an unpromising one. Waterloo is described as 'a little lowly place', raised by the glory of its recent fame (I, iii, line 3). It is only when the poet reaches Part II, 'The Vision', that the rhetoric of quest romance is allowed to compensate for the geographical deficiencies of the actual field. Musing in 'solitude' (II, i, line 1) the poet travels across an endless plain, a waste land of dolorous tombs and mouldering ruins, his destination, an allegorical representation of Waterloo. It is at this point, in what amounts to a parodic allusion to the melancholic landscapes of *Childe Harold's Pilgrimage*, that the vision of the poet is arrested by the sight of an 'aspiring Tower' (II, i, line 8), an 'eminence sublime' (II, i, line 12) upon which resides the figure of earthly Wisdom.

The doctrine that Wisdom teaches combines the worst of materialist philosophies, from Voltaireian cynicism to Byronic fatalism. Handing the poet a telescope to aid his 'faulty vision', the poet surveys a field of 'darkness'. The creed he is expected to derive from this exercise is straightforwardly egotistic: since there is nothing more to see, and nothing else to do, it is best to cultivate 'pleasure' and 'the Self', 'the spring of all' (II, i, lines 20-22). This, of course, is not only a Byron's creed, it is also Napoleon's. Having reached the limit point of Romantic narcissism, Southey's poet counters with an invocation of a well-worn Southeyian theme, the rallying of the martyrs for apocalyptic glory, 'Victorious over agony and death' (II, i, line 43). Wisdom replies with a speech that is directly comparable with Byron's 'history hath one page argument':[28]

> Assuming then a frown as thus he said,
> He strech'd his hand from that commanding height,
> Behold, quoth he, where thrice ten thousand dead
> Are laid, the victims of a single fight!
> And thrice ten thousand more at Ligny lie,
> Slain for the prelude to this tragedy!
>
> Thus to the point where it began its course
> The melancholy cycle comes at last ...
>
> The present and the past one lesson teach;
> Look where thou wilt, the history of man
> Is but a thorny maze, without a plan! (II, ii, lines 719-00).

The names of history – Voltaire/Byron/Napoleon – question the values of heroic martyrdom, but it is a questioning that also proclaims the death of tragedy. The field is a 'stage' and war a 'dreadful drama' (II, ii, line 10). Here there is no catharsis, no relief from the 'vague and purportless' folly of mankind (II, ii, line 20). Like the Southey of 1814, Napoleon's mourners gaze on a world of death and defeat; a world that elides the life-giving principles of growth and change. Supremely sterile, the best that Wisdom can offer is a masturbatory round of physical and political entropy.

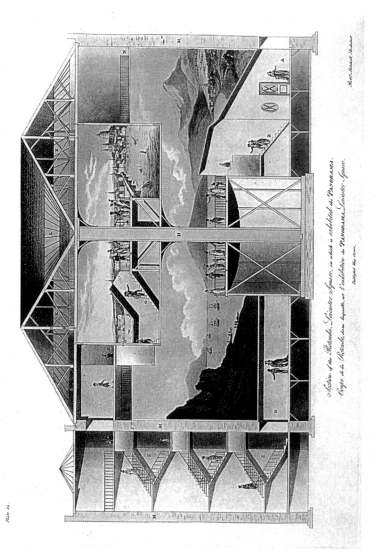

8.2   Robert Mitchell, 'Plans and Views in Perspective on Buildings Erected
       in England and Scotland', plate 14.
       Selection of the Rotunda, Leicester Square, in which is exhibited the Panorama (1801)

The denial of heroic death is linked, in part, to Southey's vexed sense of the failure of the Napoleonic drama. But what I want to focus on here is the poem's more problematic visual dynamic, and the politicization of its claims to distinction. The notion of the 'melancholy cycle', of a serial perspective of history, revolving around the focal point of the spectator's eye is a key metaphor of the period. It is literally manifested in the enormous popularity of the panorama: a 360 degree painting housed in a purpose built rotunda (Figure 8.2). It was Henry Aston Barker, the son of the inventor of the panorama, who travelled in the same year as Southey to cash in on the latest patriotic spectacle.[29] Poetry, not even Southey's, could compete with the popular appeal of this phenomenon. It is hardly surprising, therefore, that the *Pilgrimage* should contain so many references to visual elevation and to 'magic' or 'moving' pictures (II, iv, line 40), both as terms of disparagement – in the Earthly Wisdom passages – and as terms of appraisal – in the vision of the Sacred Mountain. Indeed, the concluding section is centred on the description of a circular pageant, a panoramic view of futurity in which the 'Hopes of Man' turn around a centred self. Here, in a benign repetition of 'The Tower', the poet gazes 'with scope unconfined of vision free' (II, iii, line 48). The world lies beneath him, as it had for Wisdom, 'like a scroll' or map, as if the distinction between the realms of the visible and readable had been erased: 'so ample was the range from that commanding height' (II, iii, line 50).

To relate the panorama to Southey's view of the melancholy pleasures of Bonapartism is doubtless to do violence to artistic and historical propinquity. In doing so I wish simply to register the sense in which Southey, like Napoleon and Wellington, becomes subject to panoramic fantasies of self-aggrandisement and paradoxical self-abnegation – fantasies that question the very systems on which they depend. It is common to speak of Romanticism's antipathy towards bodily or gross seeing, but in Southey's case we witness a poet whose familiarity with the visual – in his letters he refers to the panoramic print of Waterloo; he augments his work with picturesque engravings – is suggestive of a positive interest in the 'superficial' pleasures of visual consumption.[30] It is an interest that places the idealized notions of command and distinction in jeopardy. For as much as Southey seeks to elevate his own mountain top perspectives from the artificially stimulated vistas of the panorama his text is subject to the same contradictions.

With this idea in mind it is worth turning to the panorama itself. The key that accompanied Barker's Waterloo painting presents us with an initial

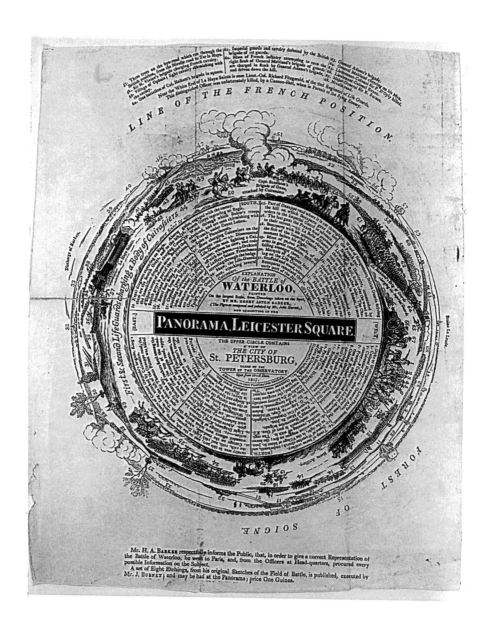

8.3   John Burnet after Henry Aston Barker,
Explanation of the Battle of Waterloo

puzzle (Figure 8.3). The strange thing is that for all the talk of presenting the viewer with a total vision; of placing the I in a stable and controlling subject-vision (significantly, the closest figure to the viewer is Wellington),the fact remains that the panorama is consumed with detail. The viewer does not survey a whole picture; rather the eye is arrested, as in Kelly's depiction of Napoleon, by picturesque fragments. Like Southey's view of liberal history, the spectacle is a thorny maze in need of a plan. The key, as William H. Galperin notes, would appear to fulfil this need. By allowing patrons to read and thereby control what they could otherwise only see, the disorientating aspects of the visible are contained. A feeling of displacement is tempered by one of re-placement. But self-control should not be confused with self-empowerment. At another level the key serves only to remind the middle-class professional of his difference from the subjects portrayed in the painting. The key singles out the notables: the Marquisses, the Dukes and the Earls – the figures who are really in command. There are no references to foot soldiers. In the end, therefore, the patrons of the Waterloo panorama would have rejected the sensationalism of the visual display for a more 'stubborn structure' of deferential behaviour.[31]

Like Barker's panorama, Southey's *Pilgrimage is* also preoccupied with detail. Part One, 'The Journey', reads like a poeticized version of the *Journal.* The accumulation of curios, irregularities, minutia and 'rough objects' – from the 'marks of wreck' to the sprouts of corn – are all indicators of the piquant pleasures of picturesque travel. But if this part disappoints, it does so because it places its reader/viewer as one of Gilpin's 'disempowered travellers'.[32] Whilst the gradual disclosure of the ruins of Hougoumont has its charms, the love of novelty can only be sustained for a short while. After a time, the disparity between Nash's broken pastoral and the visual totality which it elides becomes all too apparent (Figure 8.4). To satisfy the drive for proprietorial mastery – to signify the shift, in other words, from the voyeuristic gaze of the tourist to the comprehensive eye of the laureate – the poem must move on to other, more lasting scenes.[33]

Part Two, 'The Vision', attempts to transcend the transitory pleasures of the picturesque through a practice of visual consummation. It does so by re-introducing a relationship with the feminine. The poet's legitimate union with the Muse or goddess contrasts with the morally ambiguous companionship of Earthly Wisdom. But it is in the context of the previous section's investment in the picturesque that this union takes on its deeper significance. Unlike the fleeting spatio-temporal particulars of Part One, the panoramic visions of the Sacred Mountain are complete and sustained. It is as if the satanic connotations of Napoleon's 'commanding height' have been redeemed.[34] In addition to this, with the socio-economic constraints of

8.4   C. Bell, 'Entrance to Hougemont' (1816)

Barker's rotunda consigned to the abject matter of history, Southey is free to imagine the higher reality of literary or poetic seeing: A 'living picture moved beneath our feet. / A spacious City first was there displayed' (II, iv, line 33). The city turns out to be London – a popular feature of panoramic displays throughout the period. In Southey's vision, London forms the apex of a vast perspectival plain. From here the poet's gaze reaches beyond Britain to the fields of Europe and still further to the imperial domains of the East. As the transitory gaze of the tourist gives way to the eternal eye of God, the poet would appear to have attained his goal: the triumph of an encompassing vision and the glory of an integrated and distinctive subjectivity:

> And thou to whom in spirit at this hour
> The vision of thy Country's bliss is given
> Who feelest that she holds her trusted power
> To do the will and spread the word of Heaven,
>
> Hold fast the faith which animates thy mind,
> And in thy songs proclaim the hopes of mankind (II, iv, lines 61-66).

Somewhere along the way the 'eagle eye' of the commander has been subsumed. At this point it seems only natural that the poem should end with the crowning of a cultural victor: Robert Southey, Poet Laureate.

But there is more to this vision than meets the eye. In addition to the uncomfortable reminders of the commercial picturesque, and of the false or Napoleonic seeing, the poem also contains a panoramic 'key' in the form of detailed footnotes. These are mostly concerned with matters of literary elucidation and historical actuality. Here, once again, the peasant guide's complaint is cited – 'call it anything but Waterloo!' – only this time it has been emptied of its geo-political force. By the time of the poem's publication the name of the battle had become a rigid designator. In the end, therefore, a poem entitled *The Poet's Pilgrimage to La Belle Alliance* has been framed by the politics of deference – to state history, to the market-place and, ultimately, to the authority of Wellington. Romantic vision, at least in this version, would remain confined, re-placed by an autocracy that it cannot quite command.

Notes

1   The analysis of the relationship between Wellington and Romanticism has been somewhat overshadowed by discussions of the 'commanding genius' Napoleon. That Napoleon should continue to appear as a centralized object of power in Romanticism

is symptomatic of a dominant tendency within Romantic criticism to reify the politics of the past. For a notable exception to this rule see the following essays by Eric C. Walker: 'Wordsworth, Wellington and Myth' in *History and Myth: Essays on Romantic Literature* ed. Stephen C. Behrendt (Detroit: Wayne State University Press, 1990), pp. 100-15 and 'Wordsworth, Warriors, and Naming' in *Studies in Romanticism*, 29 (1990), pp. 223-40.

2   *Supplementary Despatches, Correspondence and Memoranda of Field Marshal Arthur Duke of Wellington, K.G.*, ed. by his son the Duke of Wellington, 15 vols (London: John Murray, 1858-72), XII, p. 155. Henceforth *Supplementary Despatches* followed by volume and page number.

3   The Duke guarded the site of his greatest victory with jealous pride. When, on revisiting the field in 1821, the Duke saw the Lion Mound erected by the Dutch he is reported to have exclaimed: 'They have spoiled my Battlefield'. Sir William Fraser, *Words on Wellington* (London, 1889), p. 247. Cited in Elizabeth Longford, *Wellington: The Years of the Sword* (London: Weidenfield and Nicholson, 1969), p. 79.

4   Wellington, quoted in Elizabeth Longford, *Wellington: The Years of the Sword*, p. xv.

5   *Supplementary Despatches*, X, p. 509.

6   For a useful introductory discussion of Habermas's concept of the 'public sphere' see Terry Eagleton, *The Function of Criticism: From 'The Spectator' to post-structuralism* (London: Verso, 1984), p. 9. A more detailed analysis of the relation between deference and consent in the 'growth of early bourgeois society' can be found in *The Ideology of the Aesthetic* (Oxford: Basil Blackwell, 1990), p. 23.

7   Robert Southey, *Journal of a Tour in the Netherlands in the Autumn of 1815* (London: Heinemann, 1902), p. 91.

8   The brief reference in the British despatch to the 'timely assistance' of the Prussians was regarded as discreditable even at the time, prompting more than one observer to criticize the Duke for his lack of beneficence. (See Longford, *Wellington: The Years of the Sword*, pp. 485-6). Wellington, however, remained unrepentant. As late as 1842 he felt able to refer to his own despatch as the definitive account of the battle: 'The report of the battle made at the time by the Duke of Wellington to the British and the Allied governments of Europe has long been before the public. In that report he does full justice to the exertions made by his colleague the Prussian commander-in-Chief and by the General officers and troops to aid and support him, and to the effectual aid which they gave him'. Following a long extract from the text of 1815 he adds: 'Historians and commentators were not necessary' *Supplementary Despatches*, X, pp. 529-30.

9   F.C.F. von Müffling, *History of the Campaign of 1815. Introductory observations and appendices by Sir John Sinclair*, ed. Major-General B. P. Hughes from the original edition of 1816 (Wakefield: S.R. Publishers, 1970), p. vii.

10 *Supplementary Despatches*, X, p. 507.

11 I would like to thank Jeanne Moskal of the University of North Carolina for drawing my attention to Eaton's *Narrative*.

12 Quoted in Longford, *Wellington: The Years of the Sword*, p. 484.

13 For the theoretical background to this discussion see Jean-Francois Lyotard, *The Differend: Phrases in Dispute*, trans. by Georges Van Den Abbeele (Manchester: Manchester University Press, 1988).

14 Robert Southey, *Poetical Works of Robert Southey, Collected by Himself*, 10 vols (London: Longman, 1838-40), X, p.139.

15   Jacqueline Rose offers an exacting analysis of the psychology of war in her essay 'Why War?', reprinted in *Why War? – Psychoanalysis, Politics, and the Return to Melanie Klein* (Oxford: Blackwell, 1993), pp. 15-40.

16   For the discussion of Lacan and Napoleon I am indebted to Jerome Christensen, *Lord Byron's Strength: Romantic Writing and Commercial Society* (Baltimore & London: John Hopkins University Press, 1993), pp. 127-32.

17   I have explored the question of Southey's relation to both the official and unofficial power of the Laureate tradition in my essay 'Commemorating Waterloo: Wordsworth, Southey and the "Muses Page of State"', *Romanticism*, 1 (1995), pp. 50-67.

18   Francis Jeffrey, unsigned review of the *Lay of the Laureate, Edinburgh Review*, June 1816, XXVI, 441-9. Reprinted in *Robert Southey, The Critical Heritage*, ed. Lionel Madden (London: Routledge & Kegan Paul, 1972), pp. 215-18 (p. 216).

19   The phrase is Simon Bainbridge's. See his perceptive essay 'To "Sing It Rather Better": Byron, The Bards, and Waterloo' in *Romanticism*, 1 (1995), pp. 68-81, (p. 72).

20   Advertised in *The Times*, 6 January 1817, no. 10,037, p. 1.

21   J.B. Hartley offers a penetrating analysis of the relations between maps and power in his essay 'Maps, knowledge, and power' included in *The Iconography of Landscape: Essays on the Symbolic Representation, Design and Use of Past Environments*, ed. Denis Cosgrove and Stephen Daniels (Cambridge: Cambridge University Press, 1988), pp. 277-312.

22   See Michael Charlesworth, 'The Ruined Abbey: Picturesque and Gothic Values' in *The Politics of the Picturesque: Literature, Landscape and Aesthetics Since 1770*, ed. Stephen Copley and Peter Garside (Cambridge: Cambridge University Press, 1994), pp. 62-80.

23   Robert Southey, *The Poet's Pilgrimage to Waterloo* (London, Longman & Co., 1816), I, iii, 39, p. 68. All further references to this work will be to this edition.

24   Robert Southey, 'The Life of Wellington', *The Quarterly Review*, 13 (April & July, 1815; 2nd edn, 1816), pp. 448-526 (p, 517).

25   Thomas Kelly, *History of the French Revolution*, 2 vols (London, 1819), II pp. 70-3.

26   As with Burke's categorization of the sublime and the beautiful in the *Philosophical Enquiry*, it is interesting to note in passing that in this description the boundary between the sublime and the beautiful is contestable. Here, Napoleon emerges as an androgynous figure: strong in so far as he manifests his power through eternal images of the 'masculine' sublime; weak with respect to his emotional investment in the transitory forms of feminine 'beauty'. In many respects the ambiguity of Napoleon's vision corresponds to the textual erotics of the picturesque: a psycho-sexual discourse that speaks equally of possession and dispossession; of both the control of feminized forms and of a submission to feminine 'tyranny'. For an illuminating discussion of the gender politics of picturesque discourse see Vivien Jones's essay 'Politics and the Picturesque in Women's Fiction' in Copley and Garside, ed. *Politics of the Picturesque*, pp. 120-44.

27   The poem was published in three different journals, *The New Monthly Magazine, The Gentleman's Magazine* and the *European Magazine*. Reprinted in *British War Poetry in the Age of Romanticism: 1793-1815* (New York & London: Garland, 1976), pp. 592-4. Simon Bainbridge points out this comparison in 'To "Sing It Rather Better"', p. 74. I would also like to record a more personal note of gratitude for helpful comments following the delivery of an earlier version of this essay at the Fourth International B.A.R.S. conference at the University of Wales, Bangor in July 1995.

28   This point is made by Malcolm Kelsall, *Byron's Politics* (Brighton: The Harvester Press, 1987), pp. 78-9.

29   Barker's panorama, *The Battle of Waterloo,* was first exhibited at the Leicester Square rotunda in 1816. For more information about the Barkers and panorama painting see Scott B. Wilcox's essay 'Unlimiting the Bounds of Painting' in *Panoramania!*, ed. Ralph Hyde (London: Trefoil, 1988), pp. 13-44.

30   For an informed discussion of Romantic ways of seeing together with a probing analysis of the panorama phenomenon see William H. Galperin, *The Return of the Visible in British Romanticism* (London & Baltimore: Johns Hopkins University Press, 1993).

31   Galperin, *Return of the Visible*, p. 44.

32   The distinction between Gilpin's picturesque of dispossession and the proprietorial 'drive to mastery' of Uvedale Price and Richard Payne Knight is explored by Kim Ian Michasiw in 'Nine Revisionist Theses on the Picturesque', *Representations*, 38 (1992), 76-100. See also Copley and Garside, ed. *Politics of the Picturesque, ad passim.*

33   It should also be noted that in Part Two the rhetoric of the poem shifts from pastoral to romance – from a world of temporal pathos to one of transhistorical steadfastness.

34   Wordsworth explores the connection between Milton's satanic vision and Barker's panorama in a section from Book VII of the Prelude. See my 'Mimic sights': A Note on Panorama and Other Indoor Displays in Book 7 of the Prelude' in *Notes and Queries*, 40 (1993), pp. 462-4. See also Galperin, *Return of the Visible*, p. 55.

9 Subverting the Command of Place: Panorama and the Romantics

MICHAEL CHARLESWORTH

C. R. Maturin published his gothic novel, *Melmoth the Wanderer,* in 1820. At the centre of the book, the Wanderer, who has acquired supernatural powers, transports himself to an island in the Indian Ocean, where he encounters a young, beautiful female noble savage, named Immalee. Immalee is extremely naive, having lived alone, and the Wanderer undertakes to show her the world and to explain everything. To this end, he suggests that they climb a high hill on her island, intending to begin the educational process by showing her part of the world from its top. This idea excites and dissatisfies her: 'But I would like to see the whole, and all at once!' she says. At the top, however, the promised panorama fails to materialize; at least, it is not described to the reader nor even mentioned. Instead, the Wanderer takes out his telescope. Once she has mastered the telescope, Immalee focuses in turn on four buildings on the nearby coast of India, which, as the Wanderer explains, are religious buildings and thus, 'are indicative of the various modes of thinking of those who frequent them'. Immalee sees, in turn: first, 'the black pagoda of Juggernaut', surrounded by 'the bones of a thousand skeletons', with worshippers being crushed under the wheels of Juggernaut's wagon; secondly, 'the temple of Maha-deva', where women hang their newborn children in baskets from trees to perish with hunger, and throw their aged parents in the river to be eaten by crocodiles; thirdly, a mosque, where Turks mistreat some poor Hindu beggars; and finally a small Christian chapel, the sight of which instantly converts Immalee to Christianity, which is the last thing that the Wanderer wishes, so he abruptly departs.[1] The Wanderer returns in the following chapter, however, to narrate two starkly contrasting visions of European imperialism. He describes first 'the gallant and well-manned vessels of Europe, that came on like the gods of ocean, bringing fertility and knowledge, the discoveries of art, and the blessings of civilisation, wherever their sails were unfurled and their anchors drops, – he could tell

129

9.1   **Thomas Sandby,** *Fort Augustus*

all'.[2] We turn the page, however, to find him 'fraught with far different visions':

> There came on the European vessels full of the passions and crimes of another world, – of its sateless cupidity, remorseless cruelty, its intelligence, all awake and ministrant in the cause of its evil passions, and its very refinement operating as a stimulant to more inventive indulgence, and more systematized vice. He saw them approach to traffic for 'gold, and silver, and the souls of men;' – to grasp, with breathless rapacity, the gems and precious produce of those luxuriant climates, and deny the inhabitants the rice that supported their inoffensive existence; – to discharge the load of their crimes, their lust and their avarice, and after ravaging the land, and plundering the natives, depart, leaving behind them famine, despair and execration; and bearing with them back to Europe, blasted constitutions, inflamed passions, ulcerated hearts, and consciences that could not endure the extinction of a light in their sleeping apartment.[3]

There is no narrative resolution of this stark contrast.

What exactly is going on here? What does it mean that the promised panorama fails, that the Wanderer, its proprietor, loses control of the telescope – the technology that he has provided to make sense of the prospect? What does it signify that these events are the prelude to an elaborate and entirely subversive view of European imperialism? What does the episode tell us about vision and representation in the nineteenth century, and their connections with power?

This essay is dedicated to suggesting that the loss of control over panoramic vision is a *precondition* for the subversive view of colonization; and that of the two views, it is of course the subversive view that is the romantic one. To begin to address the questions that have just been posed, however, we need first to take a view of the history of panoramic representation before 1820. In brief, the main points to emphasize are as follows.[4]

Panoramic representation for military purposes was practised by the artist Thomas Sandby during the Hanoverian campaign against the Jacobite rebellion of 1745-46, and immediately afterwards in 'Butcher' Cumberland's European campaign, 1746-48. Sandby drew broad views of battlefields, landscapes and military camps seen from elevated positions. In doing this he was providing a visual form of military intelligence (Figure 9.1). This type of drawing was taught to officer cadets by his brother Paul Sandby, who was Chief Drawing Master at Woolwich Military Academy from 1768 until 1797, when he was succeeded by his son Thomas Paul (who taught there until 1828). Panoramic drawings involve, in general, exaggerated breadth in relation to their height (often a ratio of 1:4 or more), high vantage-points, and clarity of detail combined with an absence of atmospheric or meteorological effects. Mist and cloud recorded in such images could only serve to obscure the representation of details on which men's lives could be staked in military operations.

Such views were promoted and cultivated by the military and strategic institutions of the Hanoverian state, the most important of which were: the Board of Ordnance, which began the Ordnance Survey in this era;[5] the Royal Military Academy at Woolwich, which trained artillery and ordnance officers; the East India Company Army's training college at Addiscombe, for which Robert Dawson took parties of cadets on trips sketching what he called 'panorama views' in the mountains of North Wales;[6] and the Royal Navy, which developed panoramic views of coastlines exemplified by William Westall's views in Australia for the Flinders expedition. The Navy views seem to have evolved out of the strategic necessity of drawing coastal profiles as an aid to navigation.[7] Within each of these institutions junior officers were taught how to draw such strategically useful views, or landscape artists such as Westall were hired to provide them.

The panoramic visual field as a form of intelligence-gathering was given monumental commemoration by the first Marquess of Rockingham when he built a symbolic and real watchtower, the Hoober Stand, in the garden of his house, Wentworth Woodhouse, near Rotherham, in 1748. Hoober Stand is a viewing platform which gives immense views in all directions. The inscription on it celebrates the suppression of the Jacobite rebellion, the 'Forty-Five', and by tacit implication Rockingham's important part in that: as Hanoverian Lord-Lieutenant of the County of the West Riding of Yorkshire during the Jacobite rebellion, he turned his huge house into an intelligence-gathering station where he personally transcribed reports from the field and speeded them on their way to the Hanoverian army by providing fresh horses to messengers. He even went so far as to spy on the activities of a neighbouring landowner, the Roman Catholic Duke of Norfolk. When Thomas Sandby visited Wentworth Woodhouse with a group of artists in 1774, they ascended the Hoober Stand and the Marchioness of Rockingham thoughtfully provided them with a large reflecting telescope to enhance their optical overlordship of the surrounding terrain.

By its form, the Hoober Stand relates, as a precursor, to the Panorama entertainment, the purpose-built structure patented in 1787 by Robert Barker. In the novel interiors of the Panorama entertainment, visitors ascended a central viewing tower to emerge on a viewing platform where the immense impact of painted views extending around them for three hundred and sixty degrees would strike them all at once. The difference from the Hoober Stand was that the Panorama's views were painted on canvas, while those at Hoober were real countryside. Panoramas were made in Edinburgh, London, and Dublin, rapidly spreading abroad, first to Paris by 1800.[8] Once purpose-built structures had been built to house them, certain ratios of height to width became standard. Thomas Girtin's 'Eidometropolis' or panorama of London, for example, measured eighteen feet by one hundred and eight feet, or a ratio of 1:6. The paradigm set up at Hoober Stand, where immense view alternated with telescopic details, passed into the Panorama entertainment in two ways. First, it enters in terms of the highly detailed finish of the paintings, where everything was painted, in John Constable's words, 'minutely and cunningly'.[9] This crisply seen finish meant that, despite their more constricted dimensions, easel paintings could also borrow something of the panoramic visual field. As the art historian Alan Wallach has pointed out with regard to panoramic U.S. landscape paintings by Thomas Cole, the exceptionally clear details in such paintings amount to the equivalent of a telescopic dimension in a visual field otherwise distinguished by its breadth.[10] Second, the telescope features in Panorama entertainments in a more literal way: at the Colosseum in London, in 1829, built to house a huge Panorama of London, visitors were provided with small telescopes for a closer inspection of details of the prospect.[11] This alternation between broad view and telescopic detail has become the basic paradigm of panoramic representation.

Panoramic drawings for military purposes were a form of encoded and stored information. This function, too, was taken over by Panorama entertainments and came to be thought of as their *raison d'être*. As early as 1789, the magazine 'Woodfall's Register' recommended the 'benefits of the Royal Family gaining knowledge of foreign lands through the panorama'.[12] By then the imperial possessions of the Hanoverian dynasty were extending themselves all over the world and were here given their symbolic apparatus of consumption. Military officers returning from abroad became a chief source of new ideas and visual information for the Panorama entrepreneurs. This relationship was part of the symbiosis between Panorama entertainments and colonialism: S. C. Brees' Panorama of New Zealand was advertised in London in 1849 as 'not the work of a mere artist, but of a surveyor, whose business it was to explore and set down with topographical accuracy the natural features of the colony'.[13]

The Sandbys therefore amount to two examples among many of the institutionalisation of panoramic representation, its servicing of Hanoverian imperialist aspirations, as well as its transition into a form of landscape art. Their careers cover the years in which panoramic views were enshrined by

Hanoverian military and strategic institutions as the most valuable ways of depicting landscape. Such institutions helped equate the maintenance of political power with the panoramic point of view. This equation was first worked out against rebellious domestic populations (the Highland Scots) before being exported to prove instrumental in extending Hanoverian dynastic power across the globe in the second half of the eighteenth century. Although I used the word 'information' in connection with panoramic drawing and the Panorama entertainments, three related points need to be emphasized. The first is that panoramic representation gives only certain types of information about a place. That is to say, it gives information that the army deems to be of value, such as the rise and fall of the land, location of woodlands, divisions of terrain, broad economic functioning such as agriculture, logging, quarrying, fishing, and the location of villages and towns. There is therefore an ideological problem that arises as soon as panorama becomes de-contextualised and comes to be classed as entertainment (when we rely, as it were, on the military for our fun). Allied to this problem is that of the change of audience that occurs at the moment when the panoramic visual field enters the Panorama entertainments. The audience for a military drawing was a small group of military commanders planning the next stage of a campaign, not preoccupied, particularly, with visual pleasure, and interesting in perceiving only certain types of information. While panoramic vistas sometimes occur in the more general representation of landscape in the era before Panorama entertainments, they did so without the spectacular impact and the concentrated rhetorical force of the entertainments themselves, which have become part of our amused sense of early nineteenth-century showmanship. In Stephan Oetterman's term, the entertainments were a 'mass medium' servicing a large middle-class audience of people who attended them in order to be entertained, and to find out information, with no highly specialised sense of the edited character of that information or of the strategic purpose or ideological position served by the particular Panorama under scrutiny. The third related point is therefore that, rather like the visitors to the Hoober Stand, when we look at these panoramas, because of their complicity with overlordship, we are forced to look at them from a position of identification with the point of view of the rulers, the political masters (I am of course using 'point of view' in both a literal and a figurative sense). They encourage a sense of identity of outlook between viewer and those in power, and one that excludes, by distancing and superiority of station, the possibility of identification with the subjugated.[14] The ideology inheres in the way the visual field is constructed.

9.2   **J.M.W. Turner,** *View of London from Greenwich*

That is the background and I now wish to place certain Romantic figures in the foreground to gauge Romanticism's dealings with the panoramic field. The grand era of Panorama entertainments was from the early 1790s until the late 1840s, and it would be possible to argue that, so thoroughly did this new means of representation permeate culture, any artist or writer working in Britain or the U.S. during that era would have been aware of it. However, all the cases discussed below are those in which an overt awareness of panorama is signalled by the artists themselves.

I wish to turn firstly to a painting from 1825 by J.M.W. Turner, only recently rediscovered in 1994 in New York (Figure 9.2). It shows a view of London from Greenwich, and at first sight it seems to be a panoramic image, revealing a broad vista from an elevated position. Reinforcing this idea are two black-coated figures who, between them, enact the two stages of response that we have already seen Immalee, in *Melmoth*, experiencing. The left hand figure is evidently enraptured by the whole view revealed to his sight at once, while the right hand figure – possibly the same figure at a later stage of the viewing process – grasps his telescope to isolate details from the big picture – in this case a close-up of the steamships making their way down-river past Greenwich. We can discern in the left hand bottom corner some cursorily handled intimations of the 'boosterish chamber-of-commerce concern' that has been alleged to dog panorama.[15] In this case they seem to refer both to the historical growth of London and to grandiose plans for its redevelopment. The inscriptions on the maps and papers read:

> London 1526 Reign of Elizabeth Regn.
> London 1825 Reign . . George IV.
> Plan for . . London.
> St Paul's Cathedral Sir C. Wren.
> Designs of . . London

And the two labels on the adjacent objects read 'N. Pole' and 'New World'. The painting's foreground is made up of dimly discerned maps and papers on two of which 'Grand Junction Paddington Recent Canal' and 'Thames - SEA' (with the blue line of a river between) can be read.

While a celebration of London's greatness, and of steam power as a means of improving the financial and industrial 'circulation of the state', can be interpreted as typical themes of Turner,[16] I would argue that, like Melmoth's text, 'View of London from Greenwich' is an image that challenges or questions, rather than reinforces, panoramic representation. The painting was made during the decade when Thomas Hornor was undertaking his entrepreneurial scheme for the biggest Panorama of all –

the view of London from St. Paul's – mounted in the purpose-built London Colosseum. Articles relaying Hornor's progress to an expectant public were constantly in press. Turner's image seems to be executed in a comic or satirical mode (I'm referring to the style of the figures, some spindly and gouty, and their antics). And the labels on the bundled objects, 'N. Pole' and 'New World' seem to lead the syntagmatic verbal chain that evokes London into fantastic regions. More important, however, is the fact that we are presented with a view of London in which we can see very little clearly. London may look beautiful, but it also looks mysterious, and the beauty to some extent relies on the mystery. The atmosphere of smoke and haze that lies over the city prevents detailed clear seeing. This forces attention back onto the very effects of atmosphere that baffle the clear seeing; it is they that now become the point of the painting. What baffles these painted characters' ability to see every detail is mist and smoke; but what prevents us from doing so is Turner's ability and desire to paint effects of smoke and mist, and it is in that desire that we get Turner's comment on the relative merits and value of panoramic views and Turnerian views.

Turner doubtless chose Greenwich as his vantage point because of the view it afforded of the city, but there is an additional association that is important to note. Next door to Greenwich is Woolwich, where the Royal Military Academy is situated. As I have emphasized, the Academy was one of the training schools of panoramic drawing throughout Turner's lifetime, and its cadets could be found in Woolwich and on the neighbouring hills of Greenwich, practising their art, as in the case, for example, of drawings by George Heriot, who was trained at Woolwich by Paul Sandby in the early 1780s.[17]

Another major figure in Romanticism who used similar terms to call into question panoramic seeing was William Wordsworth, in his two Black Combe poems of 1813 (published in 1815): 'Written with a Slate Pencil on a Stone, on the side of the mountain of Black Comb', and 'View from the Top of Black Comb'. The latter seems at first to be an orthodox celebration of the panoramic views that the mountain, in the southern extremity of the Lake District some five miles north-west of Millom, afforded, over Wales, over the headwaters of the Trent, southern Scotland, the Pennines, Anglesey and the coast of Ireland. The satisfactions provided by such views are summarised in the last three lines:

> A revelation infinite it seems;
> Display august of man's inheritance,
> Of Britain's calm felicity and power!

The telling nationalism of the last line of course serves to diminish the promise of 'infinite revelation', while it locates the panoramic view in its characteristic ideological source. There is a clear reducing progression from 'revelation infinite' via 'man's inheritance' to 'Britain's felicity and power', as the promise of the first phrase is progressively constricted and the sublime spectacle subsumed within geopolitical desires. Wordsworth's doubts about the cultural values of panoramic seeing go further than this, however, in the events reported in the other Black Comb poem, 'Written with a Slate Pencil'. Here he exults in the bafflement of panoramic vision that happened to a 'geographic Labourer' who had pitched his tent on the top of Black Combe for an extensive period of surveying for the Ordnance Survey of England (a military endeavour, we should remember, which necessitated from the surveyor a 'lonely task, / Week after week pursued' as Wordsworth phrases it). The poet recounts an incident when the mighty powers of nature, during daytime hours, obliterated all daylight:

> all around
> Had darkness fallen – unthreatened, unproclaimed –
> As if the golden day itself had been
> Extinguished in a moment; total gloom,
> In which he sat alone, with unclosed eyes,
> Upon the blinded mountain's silent top!

Wordsworth's relish for this incident, when natural forces can baffle the human will to dominate, is apparent, indeed is the point of the whole poem. Who was this 'geographic Labourer'? He was a pivotal figure in the growth of strategic and military modes of vision and representation in the first decades of the nineteenth century: General William Mudge, Director of the Ordnance Survey, Lieutenant-Governor of the Royal Military Academy at Woolwich, and Superintendent of Addiscombe College, whose cadets for the East India Company's army roamed Wales, in the same decade, with Robert Dawson, practising their panorama sketching. Mudge had himself been trained by Paul Sandby at Woolwich from 1777 to 1779.

Many more challenges to panoramic representation could be discussed, from throughout the nineteenth century.[18] One that seems to bear in a more directly inimical way than do Wordsworth's poems on panorama's associated ideological freight is Edouard Manet's panoramic view of the French dictator, Napoleon III's, 'Exposition Universelle' of 1867 (Figure 9.3). This oil painting is subversive not only of the official engraved panorama of the exhibition,[19] but, on a deeper level, it is subversive because the universal exhibition takes the panorama as its controlling metaphor, as it brings its subject (national technologies) within

9.3 **Edouard Manet,** *L' Exposition universelle, Paris 1867*

one comprehensive overall view (within the exhibition grounds) while offering close-up examinations of details through individual booths and sites. There is often a central viewing tower – the Eiffel Tower, in 1889, the one in Montreal in 1967, the six hundred feet high Tower of the Americas in San Antonio, Texas – to go with the 'telescopic' booths or pavilions. Such a viewing tower is visible near the centre of Manet's painting. The *Exposition* of 1867 was so important to Napoleon III that he installed a family member in the important chief administrative post, to make sure that the event reflected exactly what he wanted. It also took place at the time of Napoleon's Haussmanization of Paris, by which the physical fabric of the city was being superficially reconstructed, with, for example, the forming of the famous glittering facades on the city's new boulevards. T.J. Clark has argued that Manet's painting takes issue with the spectacular aspect of this transformation. Clark suggests that the specific transformation of the area shown in the painting (both foreground and, of course, middle distance), in order to stage the *Exposition,* amounts to a synecdoche of Napoleon's capitalist remodelling, and that the remodelling serves partly to conceal the structural shifts and splits in Parisian life, inhibiting us from seeing a profounder level of economic, cultural and political functioning clearly.[20] Manet has addressed this situation by painting a very nice panorama of the Exhibition, which explicitly thematizes panoramic viewing not only in its own point of view, but by depicting the viewing tower and the photographer Nadar's balloon, which intimates a more perfect panoramic vantage-point, to be achieved through flight. However, in Manet's painting it is impossible to see anything clearly, and that, of course, is precisely the point and the substance of Manet's attack on the ideologically-driven changes to French life that Napoleon III had engineered. Haussmanization was undertaken in great part to destroy the revolutionary potential of the Parisian working class.[21] In return, Paris received a spectacular superficial façade. It is the resulting obfuscation of the city and its political tensions that is mirrored in Manet's image.

Manet goes beyond the stage of relying on weather conditions to subvert panoramic representation, and, in his overt espousal of a frankly unfinished, sketchy brushwork in a completed image, intimates that the opening up to the viewer of the technical processes of representation amounts to an ideological, as well as an artistic, counter-strategy and way forward. (We should remember that this was also the era in which Napoleon III's regime tended to favour highly finished paintings with an immaculate seamless surface).

An alternative to the invocation of the limitations of meteorology was achieved in literature, too, though with a different result, and to help elucidate this I want to turn to the stories of Edgar Allan Poe; in particular, to 'The Balloon Hoax' (1844) and 'A Descent into the Maelstrom' (1841). The description of the view from the balloon as it passes over the Welsh mountains, in 'The Balloon Hoax', suggests that Poe was familiar with the visual phenomenon of the unrolling aerial Panoramas which featured in pantomimes and similar theatrical presentations of the time to dramatize journeys.[22] But it is in 'A Descent into the Maelstrom' that Poe fully opens up an alternative to the panoramic dimension, and in doing so offers a key to descents in various other stories.

The story begins with a conversation between a guide and the narrator on a panoramic vantage-point, 'the top of the loftiest pinnacle . . . a sheer unobstructed precipice of black shining rock, some fifteen or sixteen hundred feet from the world of crags beneath us'.[23] The guide tries to get the narrator to admire the immense view, which he locates with geographic precision mixed with intimations of awe:

> we are now close upon the Norwegian coast – in the sixty-eighth degree of latitude – in the great province of Nordland – and in the dreary district of Lofoden. The mountain upon whose top we sit is Helseggen, the Cloudy. Now raise yourself up a little higher – hold on to the grass if you feel giddy – so – and look out, beyond the belt of vapour beneath us, into the sea.

But the narrator is oppressed by a sense of terror which prevents him from enjoying the vista:

> A panorama more deplorably desolate no human imagination can conceive. To the right and left, as far as the eye could reach, there lay outstretched, like ramparts of the world, lines of horridly black and beetling cliff, whose character of gloom was but the more forcibly illustrated by the surf which reared high up against it its white and ghastly crest, howling and shrieking for ever.

The panoramic impulse has here brought us, quite literally, to the end (or the edge) of the world, at the north cape of Norway, and there seems, perhaps, nowhere else to go except to a number of barren-looking offshore islands. The dimension that immediately opens up at our feet, however, provides an unexpected avenue of exploration – and one very different from the panoramic, not least because of its literal direction, being vertical – towards the centre of the earth – rather than horizontal. It is the dimension of the maelstrom itself.

What can this mean, the sudden opening up of the vertical dimension at the moment of the apparent absolute triumph of the 'deplorably desolate' panoramic horizon? That Poe had the intention of playing with the balance between the literal and the metaphorical is clear from the epigraph he set at the head of the story, in which Joseph Glanville writes of 'the vastness, profundity, and unsearchableness of [God's] works, *which have a depth in them greater than the well of Democritus*' (Poe's italics). If the panoramic impulse, closely complicit with the colonizing process, aspires to search, to know, to model the literal and material world, then another dimension suddenly emerges from Poe's use of this epigraph.

To help construe this dimension, I want to turn to the work of the living French landscape architect, Bernard Lassus. In his design projects Lassus has used a conceptual structure that he has further elaborated in purely theoretical work.[24] He draws a structural distinction between the horizontal and the vertical dimension, and thinks of the latter not, primarily, as vertical but as immeasurable (*demesurable*). The horizontal thus implicitly becomes the measurable, and in Lassus's view of history that implied measurement has been quite literal. In his hypothesis, the immeasurable dimension has been increasingly exploited as western colonization has successively removed the blank, white, unexplored areas from the maps of the globe. As the horizontal surfaces of the earth have been progressively explored (a process that became much accelerated during and after the eighteenth century), gardens and parks, from Studley Royal or Stourhead in early eighteenth-century England to Buttes-Chaumont in Paris, have developed and elaborated the garden grotto, the chasm or sudden cleft, as an alternative space. Indeed, the Parisian park of Buttes-Chaumont, a product of the late 1860s fashioned in an abandoned gypsum quarry, contains both a panoramic platform of vision (the temple on the highest pinnacle which gives a wide view of adjacent Paris) and a large grotto, which are juxtaposed in this report from 1869 by William Robinson:

> [the vestige of the quarry] forms a wide and imposing cliff, 164 feet high, or thereabouts, in its highest parts, and from these you may gradually descend to its base by a rough stair, exceedingly well constructed, and winding in and out of the huge rocky face. At the base of the cliff . . . there is a lake . . . and in one bay has been constructed a large stalactite cave, about sixty feet high from its floor to the ceiling, and wide and imposing in proportion. At its back part the light is let in through a wide opening, showing a gorge reminding one of some of those in the very tops of the Cumberland mountains, and down this trickles the water into the cave, ivy and suitable shrubs being planted along its course above the roof of the cave. The effect is remarkably striking.[25]

As Lassus points out, the twentieth century has added an upward to this downward movement towards untramelled imaginative play, as science fiction has burgeoned. The hypothesis allows Lassus to develop garden and landscape designs of considerable power and playfulness. Yet it is surely the vertical as a measureless (in Poe's interesting word, 'unsearchable') dimension given over to the unrestricted exercise, not of God's power, perhaps, but of the human imagination, that is signalled in 'A Descent into the Maelstrom' and exploited by Poe in such stories as 'The Black Cat', 'The Cask of Amontillado', 'The Pit and the Pendulum', and 'The Fall of the House of Usher', in which the place of revelation is the cellar, basement, vault or dungeon. Poe is hardly alone, in the era during which he wrote, as an explorer of such places as a domain of Romanticism. In *Melmoth*, to return to my starting point, physical safety, and what is far more important to him, understanding of the Wanderer, come to the Spaniard, Monçada, only after he has penetrated to the subterranean apartment of Adonijah the Jew, down a passage almost 'as long and intricate as any that ever an antiquarian pursued to discover the tomb of Cheops in the Pyramids'.[26] (Moreover, in an implied comment not only on word and image relations but on the limitations of vision, knowledge comes to him from *reading* rather than *looking* or viewing).

What is at stake in the opening up of this vertical, measureless dimension, is therefore a different type of knowledge, and so of understanding, than that purveyed through the panorama. As Kevin Egan has summed up, in 'A Descent into the Maelstrom' the mariner eventually gains from his traumatic experience 'a perception of the order underlying an apparently anarchic natural world . . . a higher plane of knowledge'.[27] The knowledge offered by a descent into the vertical dimension may therefore embrace, yet is hardly limited to, knowledge of the natural world. In Poe's stories, it is in the cellars that we encounter axe-murder, burial alive, immurement and demonic cats. Perhaps we can therefore suggest that it is also knowledge of human motivations, fears, mistakes, momentary impulses, and attempts to conceal the dire consequences of their actions, that is laid out in Poe's cellars and vaults. In other words, these places are the settings for psychological knowledge – indeed on a psychotic level. They are places chosen for crimes and punishments by Poe's characters in part because of the concealment they afford (they are literally 'unsearchable' by panoramic surveillance). Bringing such crimes to the light of knowledge demands penetration and exploration of the vertical dimension – the dimension of the imagination and the psyche. For Monçada, the apartment of Adonijah the Jew, who has himself spent sixty years there evading the threat of physical oppression by concealment, offers what he needs: work, food, and sanctuary. By his textual discoveries there, the apartment also provides him with what he needs on another level perhaps even more urgently (or perhaps it is what the book itself needs): final knowledge of his tormented tormentor, the Wanderer.

My conclusion is that, during the era of Western exploitation of the rest of the world, Romanticism developed the vertical dimension as an enabling dimension of the imagination, and did so partly to avoid the imperial investment in the panoramic view as the visual field of useful knowledge. Making this turn enabled Romantic artists to explore a field still relatively untouched by science and to pioneer yielding encounters with the psyche.

Notes

1   Quotations are from the lengthy passage on pp. 386-96 of Maturin's *Melmoth the Wanderer: A Tale*, ed. Alethea Hayter (Harmondsworth: Penguin Books, 1977). Subsequent references are to this edition.

2   Maturin, *Melmoth*, p. 398.

3   Maturin, *Melmoth*, p. 400.

4   The summarised account that follows is condensed from my 'Thomas Sandby climbs the Hoober Stand: the politics of panoramic drawing in eighteenth century Britain', *Art History* 19.2 (June, 1996), pp. 247-66. Another source that deals with some of the issues is my 'Elevation and Succession: the representation of Jacobite and Hanoverian politics in the landscape gardens of Wentworth Castle and Wentworth Woodhouse', *New Arcadian Journal*, 31/32 (1991), pp. 7-65.

5   See N. Alfrey and S. Daniels, eds., *Mapping the Landscape: Essays on Art and Cartography* (Nottingham: University Art Gallery, Castle Museum, 1990) esp. pp. 13-27.

6   Quoted in Sir Charles Close, *The Early Years of the Ordnance Survey* (Chatham: Institution of Royal Engineers, 1926), p. 80.

7   See Bernard Smith, *European Vision and the South Pacific* (1966; 2nd edn: Newhaven: Yale University Press, 1985), pp. 3-9, 18.

8   The most authoritative work on the Panoramas is Stephan Oetterman, *Das Panorama: die Geschichte eines Massenmediums* (Frankfurt, 1980). See also the important article by Eric de Kuyper and Emile Poppe, 'Voir et regarder' *Communications*, 34 (1981), pp. 85-96.

9   Quoted by Scott B. Wilcox, 'Unlimiting the Bounds of Painting' in *Panoramania!*, catalogue of the exhibition at the Barbican Art Gallery, London (1988-89), p. 33.

10   In a paper given at the Art Historians' Association annual conference in London, 1989.

11   For the Colosseum, see Ralph Hyde's exemplary study, *The Regent's Park Colosseum* (London: Ackermann, 1982).

12   cited by Wilcox, 'Unlimiting the Bounds of Painting', p. 38.

13   cited by Wilcox, 'Unlimiting the Bounds of Painting', p. 37.

14   The argument in my 'The ruined abbey: Picturesque and Gothic values', in *The Politics of the Picturesque: Literature, Landscape and Aesthetics since 1770*, ed.

Stephen Copley and Peter Garside (Cambridge: Cambridge University Press, 1994) is of obvious relevance here.

15   Richard Quaintance, 'Vistas of Persistent Promise: an England evermore about to be', in *Glorious Nature: British Landscape Painting 1750-1850*, ed. K. Baetjer, M. Rosenthal et al. (New York: Hudson Hills Press and Denver Art Museum, 1993), p. 57.

16   See, for example, Stephen Daniels, *Fields of Vision: Landscape Imagery and National Identity in England and the United States* (Princeton: Princeton University Press, 1993), pp.112-45.

17   See Gerald E. Finley, *George Heriot 1759-1839* (Ottawa: National Gallery of Canada, 1979).

18   Philip Shaw's essay in this volume, pp. 112-31. Another example in which Robert Southey and Lord Wellington are the protagonists.

19   'General View of Paris and of the Universal Exposition of 1867, taken from the heights of the Trocadéro' by Charles Pinot and Sagaire, illustrated in F. Frascina, N. Blake, B. Fer, T. Garb and C. Harrison, *Modernity and Modernism: French painting in the nineteenth century* (New Haven: Yale University Press, 1993), p. 106.

20   T. J. Clark, *The Painting of Modern Life: Paris in the Art of Manet and his Followers* (Princeton: Princeton University Press, 1984), esp. pp. 60-66. I am simply emphasizing the *Exposition's* connection with panorama more than Clark did.

21   In addition to Clark on this, see D.H. Pinkney, *Napoleon III and the Rebuilding of Paris* (Princeton: Princeton University Press, 1958). While Pinkney consistently downplays the class politics, the very evidence he presents shows its importance.

22   See Richard D. Altick, *The Shows of London* (Cambridge, MA: Harvard University Press, 1978).

23   'A Descent into the Maelstrom' in *Tales and Sketches 1831-1842*, Vol. II of *Collected Works of Edgar Allan Poe*, ed. Thomas Mabbott (Cambridge, MA: Harvard University Press, 1978), p. 585. All quotations are from this edition.

24   The best introductions to Lassus's work are provided by Stephen Bann, in 'The landscape approach of Bernard Lassus', *Journal of Garden History*, 3.ii (1983), pp. 79-107, and 'The landscape approach of Bernard Lassus, Part II', *Journal of Garden History*, 15.ii (1995), pp. 67-106. Also important is Bann's 'From Captain Cook to Neil Armstrong: Colonial exploration and the structure of landscape', in *Projecting the Landscape*, ed. J. C. Eade (Australia National University Humanities Research Centre Monograph No. 4), pp. 78-91.

25   William Robinson, *The Parks, Promenades, and Gardens of Paris* (London, 1869), pp. 59-60.

26   Maturin, *Melmoth*, p. 352.

27   Kenneth Egan, 'Descent to an Ascent: Poe's use of perspective in "A Descent into the Maelstrom"', *Studies in Short Fiction*, 19.ii (1982), pp. 157-62, quote p. 157. This article emphasizes sight, especially what the mariner is able to see from the maelstrom.

10 Displacing Romanticism: Anna Seward, Joseph Weston, and the Unschooled Sons of Genius

JOHN WILLIAMS

I

In his article of 1954, 'The Contemporaneity of the *Lyrical Ballads*', Robert Mayo set Wordsworth's *Lyrical Ballads* of 1798 in the context of what he called 'the common taste' of the period.[1] In the process he stimulated debate around the nature of the originality of the *Ballads*, while he also revealed the extent to which the magazines of the period provided an important but relatively untapped field of research. To displace the idea that because the *Lyrical Ballads* had attracted controversy, they must therefore have been to a significant degree original in concept, was to displace a commonly-held assumption about the identity of British Romanticism. If Wordsworth's poems of 1798 could not be said to have heralded 'a new orientation of literary, social, ethical and religious values', then British Romanticism itself was left looking for a new home.[2]

What has happened in the wake of Mayo's research is perhaps best considered in terms of the fine tuning of the kind undertaken by Paul D. Sheats, among others, in 1974.[3] In 1981, Marilyn Butler, in *Romantics, Rebels and Reactionaries*, moved on from the poems of 1798 to Wordsworth's 'Preface' of 1800 to question even more radically the identification of Wordsworthian theory and practise with the 'popular notion' of the term 'Romanticism'. She described the 'Preface' as the work of 'a true son of the Enlightenment', where 'Wordsworth articulated the classical taste in a version less up-to-date than some. He represented strands of thinking and of taste typical of the last half century . . .'.[4]

Relocating Wordsworth within an Enlightenment context of theoretical literary debate rendered a traditional perception of British Romanticism untenable in just about every respect. Despite this, the notion of a 'Preface' that is understood to have broken the mould of orthodox aesthetics with its revolutionary literary theory – a blueprint for Romanticism no less – has proved to be deeply ingrained in critical thought. Students continue to be fed this assumption by textbooks describing the 'Preface' as containing ideas that 'are of crucial importance in the identification of Romantic Poetry', as opposed to the poetry of an earlier Augustan generation.[5] As recently as 1993, William Keach justifiably characterized the 'Preface' as a document that 'has long been regarded as the founding critical document of English Romanticism'.[6] This essay will argue that, important as the 'Preface' undoubtedly is, it came late in the day for Romanticism.

The *Ballads* attracted controversy virtually from the moment of their publication, but Marilyn Butler argues that the controversy they stimulated in the 1790s, a controversy that intensified after 1800 and the appearance of the 'Preface', was a consequence of the political context in which they appeared, and had little to do with the poetry *per se*, or for that matter with the theory of poetry that came with the poems.

In 1802 Francis Jeffrey attacked the 'Preface' in a way that very clearly did politicize the poetry in the light of the French Revolution and the threat of Jacobin infiltration. He described the Preface as a 'manifesto' presented on behalf of 'a sect of poets' who liked to think they had 'broken loose from the bondage of ancient authority, and reasserted the independence of genius'. Jeffrey purported to quote from Wordsworth's 'Preface', though in fact he was paraphrasing in a way designed to reveal to his readers the hidden – or displaced – political agenda lurking behind the aesthetics. 'It was their capital object' he wrote of the Lake Poets, '"to adapt to the uses of poetry, the ordinary language of conversation among the middling and lower orders of the people"', end 'quote'. 'What advantages are to be gained by the success of this project', he archly concluded, 'we confess ourselves unable to conjecture'.[7]

Regardless of how the controversy has come to be analysed, therefore, the impact of the French Revolution – specifically after 1792 – is generally recognized as seminal both for that collection of poems, and for the forging of a British Romantic Movement. In Butler's view, it was the Revolution that caused a still essentially neo-classical Wordsworth to be perceived by Jeffrey and others as the leader of a new sect of poets bent on a rejection of 'ancient authority'. For reasons that must therefore be described as many and various, and by no means satisfactory, the aura of controversy associated with the 1798 *Ballads* and the 1800 'Preface' remain key points of reference not only for the location of Wordsworth within the Romantic Movement, but equally for the way Romanticism has tended to be placed in literary historical terms. Inevitably, it seems, we are bound to conclude that the still frequently expressed view that Wordsworth is in some way the founding father of British Romanticism is seriously flawed.

If we take controversy as a necessary prerequisite in the evolution of Romanticism, we can investigate the problem further by considering literary controversies that were engaging public attention prior to 1789, controversies with political agendas that were every bit as urgently pursued as those which followed them.

II

Literary controversies no less volatile than that which materialized between Jeffrey and Wordsworth had flourished throughout the eighteenth century. A few have continued to attract scholarly attention; discussion of the disputes occasioned by the literary careers of James Macpherson, Thomas Chatterton and Robert Burns persist primarily because the careers of these men satisfy long held assumptions about what it is to be both precursors and practitioners of Romanticism. They all appeared to challenge the dictates of Augustan taste and decorum with respect both to what they wrote and how they lived. Less well remembered and rarely if ever mentioned is the dispute that took place between Joseph Weston and Anna Seward over the relative merits of Dryden and Pope as classicists. This ran for the best part of a year in the pages of the *Gentleman's Magazine* in 1789.

To read once again those interminable articles from Seward and Weston (interspersed with contributions from a mysterious third party who joined the fray on behalf of Pope, signing himself 'M.F.'), is to appreciate the extent to which much of what Jeffrey had to say about Wordsworth some five years later, belongs to a controversy around literary modernity that crucially predates the years of crisis created by the fear of French Jacobinism in the 1790s.

At some point prior to 1788, J. Morfitt, a barrister much respected for his refined literary taste among the literati of Birmingham, privately circulated a latin poem, 'Philotoxi Ardenae' (otherwise the 'Woodmen' or 'Bowmen of Arden'). His friend, Joseph Weston, equally acclaimed for his literary activities among the worthies of Birmingham, persuaded him to publish it. He added two translations of the poem, one in the manner of Pope, the other after Dryden, and he also wrote a lengthy Preface discussing the merits of his own (rather than Morfitt's) labours.

The poem is an insubstantial piece in praise of the patriotic landowners in the forest of Arden through the ages. It celebrates the yeomen archers who have always been ready to defend their homeland against invaders. Morfitt registers what for the period is a familiar enough warning on the subject of England's current slide towards decadence. The bowmen of Arden conjure up for us 'The glory of a sinking nation'.[8]

What sparked the controversy was not the poem, but Joseph Weston's 'Preface'. Weston emerges through his various published writings as a man whose strong views on the degeneracy of contemporary taste in literature had hardened into a neurotic conviction that his own efforts in verse had been marked down for ridicule by the rest of the critical fraternity. Friends and acquaintances – Anna Seward among them – could be moved to sympathy for his condition as frequently as they became profoundly exasperated by what for them (certainly for Seward) seemed a perverse dismissal of modern poetry. Weston's opposition to modernity had undoubtedly been influenced by the critical reception of his own mediocre work.

Long before the 'Woodmen' debate got underway, he was a familiar correspondent with the *Gentleman's Magazine*, usually complaining that his poetry had been scurrilously misquoted. On the eve of Anna Seward's attack on his 'Woodmen' Preface he is to be found complaining that 'The editors of the news-papers are my constant persecutors . . . This, Mr. Urban, is the third time that I have been dragged, most unwillingly, into public notice, through the medium of your Magazine; and every time to my disadvantage' (*GM*, 58 [December 1788], 1059). When in the 'Preface' he describes Pope as having blasted Dryden's reputation in the interests of furthering his own career, it is hardly surprising that his defence of Dryden takes on a very personal note indeed. Weston was more than ready to cast himself in the role of a latter day beleaguered Dryden, surrounded by unprincipled modern poets and critics. He singled out in particular the tendency of poets to become 'elaborately correct', 'delicately polished' and 'systematically dignified'; modern poetry has become 'stiffened polished and refined' until all is 'equal smooth and mellifluous', the moderns have thus become 'cold, mechanical versifiers', they have no spontaneity, no brilliance, they produce only 'Tinsel phrases'.[9]

What Weston finds in Dryden, and craves in modern poetry, is what he describes as harmony, a variety of 'Pause, Accent, Cadence and Diction'; poetry, he complains, has lost its creative relationship with prose, with the result that the exhilarating 'discords' to be found in Dryden have disappeared, along with a sense of dignity, unaffectedness and variety.

There is no longer any true sublimity in poetry, nor is there any 'simplicity'.[10]

Weston's diatribe against modernity cannot but invite comparison with Wordsworth's attack on the popular poetry of the day to be found in the 1800 'Preface' to *Lyrical Ballads*. Wordsworth and Weston do appear to have a good deal in common, and Butler's claim that Wordsworth's taste in Classicism was 'less up-to-date than some' comes to mind. In 1788-9 the political orientation of aesthetic views of this kind was clear. Railing against the new poetry, Weston asks 'Why must Poetry adopt a preposterous Plan of *Equalisation* unknown to Nature and to Art?'.[11] With Morfitt, Weston's politics were profoundly reactionary. Morfitt, however, was capable of second thoughts. After actively campaigning against Joseph Priestley under the pseudonym of 'John Nott, Button Burnisher', he changed his tune significantly around 1797 when he feared an internally divided nation would be unable to mount an effective campaign against Napoleon. In his 'Observations on the Present Alarming Crisis' (1797) he wrote, 'Would there not be much wisdom and magnanimity in annihilating religious animosities, and shaking hands with dissenters of all denominations?' The problem in hand for a nation under siege was more properly 'the unfeeling avarice of the rich, the supineness of the great, and the folly of both'.[12]

Seward's onslaught on the 'Woodman' Preface came in the *Gentleman's Magazine* for April 1789. It must have come as quite a shock to Weston if for no other reason than that he was in the regular habit of dispensing simpering, flowery encomiums on Seward's verse in his public literary correspondence. In the first instance, addressing primarily, one suspects, the problematic personality of Weston himself, Seward seeks to clear Pope's name of the charge of having behaved badly towards Dryden. Weston had once again praised Seward in his Preface, and she was therefore anxious to distance herself from any assumption that she shared the views of a man 'whose prejudices are as strong as his talents'. She then goes on to develop a defence of modern poetry, 'the poetic glory of the last half century' (*GM*, 59 [April 1798], p. 292).

Seward's first letter does little more then announce her intention, in the process providing a long list of 'MODERNS' by way of refuting Weston's generalization about the universally poor quality of 'the modern style of versification'. Her purpose here is plainly to exhibit the great variety of production since the 'Augustan age', beginning with Gray, Hayley and Mason, including seven 'celebrated female poets', and concluding with five 'unschooled sons of genius', Burns, Newton, Yearsley, Reid, 'and the greatest of these wonders, the ill-starred

CHATTERTON' (*GM,* 59 [April 1789], p. 292). In her second letter she launched a defence of Pope that left Weston's critique in shreds. Seward's position was underpinned by her belief in the inevitability of cultural progress. From Dryden to Pope to the present day there has been a progressive refinement of poetry that only the most perverse of critics can fail to have noticed. Her article employs a series of quotes designed to display Dryden's loutishness against Pope's delicacy (and Weston's sleight of hand when it comes to selecting quotes from Dryden). Helen in Dryden's *Aeneid* is a 'Cheapside Miss', Pope's Eloisa is a 'charming nun'. Dryden is described in her following letter as 'slovenly', Pope as ' elegant' (*GM,* 59 [May 1789], p. 931; [June 1789], p. 511). In her third instalment Seward further draws attention to Dryden's mercenary politics, 'Even Mr. W. allows that he formed his critical opinions according to the hour, callous to all the self-contradictions into which such meanness betrayed him'. Worked into Seward's argument is thus a claim that modernity reflects and encourages political responsibility and stability, not to mention domestic virtue: Pope 'watching, with filial tenderness, beside the couch of his aged mother'(*GM,* 59 [June 1789], pp. 510-11).

Weston allowed Seward to make her case, and came to his own defence in August. His first problem, he explains, is that he has been attacked by a woman, 'And what a pitiful figure does one of Homer's Heroes make while wounding a Goddess!'. In the meantime, however, a mysterious new male assailant had arrived, signing himself 'M. F.' On a man to man basis, Weston declared himself more than ready to 'try his strength' to the full. But how to respond to the woman he had so regularly, and with such condescending unction, praised for her literary talent? Here he could only ever bring himself to 'parrying some of this *literary* Amazon's most dangerous thrusts . . . while with one hand she shakes her glittering spear, with the other lifts her beaver, and discovers a countenance that melts down all opposition, and eyes that dim the radiance of the gems that spangle-o'er her burnished helmet' (*GM,* 59 [August 1789], pp. 680-3).

Both Seward and M.F. replied at once to Weston's prolix introduction. M.F. responded primarily to Weston's 'comfortable sense of his own importance'; Seward was quick to reaffirm her thesis on the diversity and refinement of poetry since Dryden over against Weston's preference for the old: 'the poetic writers of this day have done honour to their art, by avoiding the botching vulgarities of Dryden's style' (*GM,* 59 [September 1789], pp. 818, 820). In response, Weston concentrated on a defence of his character against M.F., and his letter swiftly degenerates into a characteristic expression of persecution mania. This is followed by a near hysterical diatribe against Pope:

...this Cromwell, who has injured the poetical constitution he pretended to ammend . . . shall this usurper, I say, who, having thus wickedly gained the throne, vilified the abilities, and assassinated the reputations of those whose claim to it might interfere with his own, and gibbeted all their adherents and abettors, rest undisturbed in the dust?'(*GM,* 59 [October 1789], p. 876).

His following letter continued in the same self-pitying vein, several times informing the reader that he had not been feeling at-all well of late. It was not until the fourth and final letter in the series that he offered anything like a coherent argument. This constituted regurgitating virtually all of the 'Woodman' Preface, pointing out that he was too ill to add substantially to what he had already clearly stated. He insists that, Seward's list of modern poets notwithstanding, poetry has declined specifically in terms of style, 'Poetic diction, and that alone, is the object of my reprobation' he writes, and what he seeks from poetic diction is clarity; modern poetry has become p. 1105).

Perhaps it would be ungenerous to suggest that Wordsworth, even at his most petulant in the 'Essay, Supplementary to the Preface' of 1815 or the 'Letter to a Friend of Robert Burns' of 1816, might remind us of Weston at his most querulously neurotic, fending off repeated attacks by modern literary Philistinism, even as Wordsworth sought to trample Jeffrey under foot. Yet certainly there is much in Weston's critical position – opposed to any idea of the inevitability of social or cultural progress, committed to clarity, to simplicity, even to the prosaic as against modern metrical sophistication – to suggest that Wordsworth's views were informed by the same climate of critical opinion that fostered critics of Weston's persuasion, rather than 'moderns' like Seward.

Weston and Wordsworth coincide in their attempt to find a way back to first principles for poetry, dismissing what for them is the superficial sophistication that surrounds a belief in progress encouraged by the Enlightenment. It is an essentially reactionary position, against which Anna Seward and Francis Jeffrey stand defined as modern progressives, with Seward happy to entertain an eclectic range of modern poetic achievement, including the work of women, and even those 'unschooled sons of genius' (one of whom is a woman). Given that both sets of critics are concerned to make room for this latter source of poetry, clarifying the different ways in which they do so becomes a significant task in the complex business of locating Romanticism.

III

British Romanticism was born out of a series of interlinked controversies around the issue of modernity. These arguments were rooted in long running eighteenth-century debates relating to the concept of progress; in consequence there were those who seriously questioned the merits of social and political evolution since the late seventeenth century. Only late in the day did this debate collide with the spectre of Jacobin populism. Those who distrusted modernity distrusted also the received wisdom that Enlightenment science had rendered social and political evolution since the Whig Revolution of 1688 an inevitable progress toward perfection. The intervention of what Seward had called the 'unschooled sons of genius', notably Thomas Chatterton, signified a challenge to a literature that had yoked itself to Enlightenment culture, and in consequence to a belief in the inevitability of progress. In going beyond the orthodox cultural terms of reference for his models and methods, Chatterton offered an alternative view of what poetry was, and whom it was for. The edifice of cultural stability was shaken, as were existing notions of what was healthily modern and progressive.

As a modern, we have seen that Seward displayed a liberal, progressive attitude that found room for such poets. Yet with the power that such an act of inclusion gave her, she was also effectively excluding them with the title 'unschooled' so condescendingly bestowed upon them. Such poets, pinned onto the end of her list, were consequently rendered tame freaks securely caged for observation.

By comparison, the Wordsworthian response to Chatterton and Burns (signalled, for example, in 'Resolution and Independence' and 'At the Tomb of Robert Burns') is far more serious, far more deeply felt; here was evidence of a creative power capable of changing, indeed of revolutionizing the poetic sensibility. Weston too, making the link from Dryden to the unsophisticated verse of such poets, displayed a commitment very different from that of Seward. In his 'Memoir' of another 'unschooled son', Robert Bloomfield, published in 1824, he praised the poet's 'sweetness, simplicity, and feeling', he was '*always* just and *true* . . . set up to defend our poetry against that tide of extravagance and nonsense which keeps pouring in from every point of the compass'.[13]

Faced with a new political agenda shaped by events in France after 1792, and abundant evidence of copycat subversion at home, Francis Jeffrey claimed to be able to trace the origins of Wordsworth's insidious poetic principles to several more or less contemporary sources of discontent: the political theories of Rousseau, the modish sentimentalism of

Kotzebue and Schiller, Cowper and Ambrose Phillips, and the eccentricities of the metaphysical poets.[14] But we should not lose sight of the fact that Jeffrey only ever describes this as what the poets themselves perceived to be new; he is sketching a caricature of what he claims the Lake Poets had mistakenly come to believe in as 'modernity'. From the vantage point of the Weston-Seward controversy it is possible to see Jeffrey's position as that of a true late eighteenth-century modernist, rather than a reactionary. His response to the Lake School of Jacobin poetry in fact originated in the beliefs he openly expressed when he later attacked Byron. Byron was called to account for his regressive, anti-modern tendency in reintroducing primitive poetry. Peter J. Manning has argued that Jeffrey saw Byron's appeal as 'at once a throwback and an innovative reaction to that diffusion of cultural standards of which his own journal [the *Edinburgh Review*] was the principal agent'. Byron was the reactionary, dealing in 'the old vulgar ballads', behaving, in effect, like an 'unschooled son of genius'. Jeffrey was the modernist, committed in the *Edinburgh Review* to what Manning summarises as the modernist credo of 'the impersonal laws of commerce, state religion, and respectability'.[15] The scene is of course set for a Waverley novel.

As the 'Preface' to *Lyrical Ballads* makes clear, Wordsworth was arguing against the modern poetry of his day, poetry with its roots in an increasingly modern materialist society' poetry that was immensely popular. Though Jeffrey – under political pressure – may seem to locate the Lake Poets, and thus Romanticism, with what was new in cultural and political terms, Romanticism in Britain was in fact evolving from an increasingly shared experience of cultural alienation from the contemporary literary life of the nation; as Byron was later to suggest, modern poetry was set upon 'a wrong revolutionary poetical system, or systems, not worth a damn in itself'. Compared to Pope, 'the little Queen Anne's Man', the new generation of poets (excepting perhaps Crabbe and Rogers) are 'of the Lower Empire'.[16] Seward's pantheon of modern poets dates the end of Augustanism and the beginning of modernism around 1750. Using this model, British Romantics might be placed as the poets who discover themselves to be displaced or exiled with the onset of modernity; the Romantic poet becomes the poet who remains unmodernized, a poet who belongs within the space otherwise reserved for Seward's 'unschooled sons of genius'.

To the progressive modern mind faced with the threat of chaos from republicanism and the commoner run riot after 1789, the existence of any such group will be deeply suspect, and for good reason. The emergent Romantics, displaced by post Augustan modernism, follow a path beaten to the edge of 1789 by (among others) Weston and Morfitt, a path which leads on into revolutionary politics at the point where Weston steps hastily to one side, while Morfitt is drawn half a step further down the way, and where Wordsworth's generation, having followed thus far, continue to explore further.

It is not to be wondered at, therefore, that as an aspiring poet at Cambridge, Wordsworth is attracted to the literary criticism of the Quaker poet John Scott. It was a short step to take from the critical milieu of Weston to Scott's advocacy of clarity and simplicity, and his dislike of embellishments in modern poetry. Ideologically, however, this signified a considerable shift from a defence of simplicity grounded in the reactionary political position of Weston and Morfitt to the dissenting politics of Scott, who had publicly defended Wilkes in 1770: 'The doctrines of divine hereditary right, and passive obedience to the will of kings', he scornfully explained, 'were doctrines readily adapted by those who believed the comet and the eclipse, prognostications of public calamity'.[17] It was from this politically sensitised agenda of determined demystification that Scott's aesthetic of simplicity derived.

The new politics proceeded to help shape a developing Romantic identity, and in due course they resulted in ideological fragmentation; but as Jeffrey eventually came to understand, it was not radical politics that had initially created a Romantic identity; that had taken place within the context of a much earlier debate around the credibility of a belief in modernity and progress rooted in the claims of Enlightenment culture.

Notes

1   Robert Mayo, 'The Contemporaneity of the *Lyrical Ballads*', *PMLA*, 69 (1954), pp. 486-522. Reprinted in *William Wordsworth: Penguin Critical Anthologies*, ed. Graham MacMaster (Harmondsworth: Penguin, 1972), p. 402.

2   Mayo, 'Contemporaneity', p. 421.

3   Paul D. Sheats 'The Lyrical Ballads', in *English Romantic Poets*, ed. M. H. Abrams (Oxford: Oxford University Press, 1975), pp. 133-48.

4   Marilyn Butler, *Romantics, Rebels and Reactionaries* (Oxford: Oxford University Press, 1981), pp. 60-1.

5   J. R. Watson, *English Poetry of the Romantic Period* (Harlow: Longman, 1985).

6   William Keach, 'Romanticism and Language', in *The Companion to British Romanticism*, ed. Stuart Curran (Cambridge: Cambridge University Press, 1993), p. 107.

7   Francis Jeffrey, *The Edinburgh Review*, 1 (October 25, 1802), pp. 63-6.

8   Joseph Weston *Philotoxi Ardenae: The Woodmen of Arden* a Latin Poem by J. Morfitt, with an Introduction and Translations by J. Weston (Birmingham 1788), p. 15.

9   Weston, *Philotoxi Ardenae*, p. ix.
10   Weston, *Philotoxi Ardenae*, p. x.
11   Weston, *Philotoxi Ardenae*, p. xi.
12   J. Morfitt 'Observations on the Present Alarming Crisis' (London, 1797), p. 7.
13   Robert Bloomfield, *The Remains of Robert Bloomfield, with a Memoir by Joseph Weston* (London, 1824), pp. vii-xvi.
14   Francis Jeffrey, *Edinburgh Review*, I (October 25 1802), p. 64.
15   Peter J Manning, '*Don Juan* and the revisionary self', in *Romantic Revisions*, ed. Robert Brinkley and Keith Hanley (Cambridge: Cambridge University Press, 1992), p. 214.
16   Byron, 'Letter to John Murray', 15 September 1817, *Lord Byron: Selected Letters and Journals*, ed. Leslie A. Marchand (London: John Murray, 1982), pp. 166-8.
17   John Scott, 'The Constitution Defended' (London, 1770), pp. 1-2.

11 Keats and the 'Poetical Character'

MICHAEL O'NEILL

Stuart M. Sperry wonders whether 'the poet of "Negative Capability" can prove congenial to most postmodernist criticism with its driving political commitments and theoretical priorities'.[1] Sperry underplays the capacity of much theory-propelled criticism to discover its own likeness wherever it looks. But he raises an issue – how 'congenial' is Keats to current criticism? – relevant to a volume concerned with 'Placing and Displacing Romanticism' and with Keats's recent bicentenary in 1995. Whether the bicentenary should encourage us to celebrate the grand march of critical intellect, to hail, Oceanus-like, a fresh perfection achieved by Jerome McGann, Marjorie Levinson and others after the Saturnian reign of Sperry, Walter Jackson Bate, and Christopher Ricks, is a question which might give us pause.

The application of historical and theoretical perspectives to Keats's poetry has resulted in loss and gain: gain in that we are more aware of the poetry's often ambivalent dealings with history and of the difficult issues involved in thinking about poetry in general; loss in that we risk denying, or repressing our awareness of, what Helen Vendler calls 'the existence of aesthetic power and aesthetic response'.[2] The Bakhtinian idea that 'Every concrete utterance is a social Act' offers a potentially exciting lens through which to view Keats's poems.[3] But the result has not always been a refreshed sense of Keats's poetic achievement. This is partly because the notion of 'poetic achievement' is itself under hermeneutic suspicion in certain quarters; there are those who, over-scrupulously, see the aesthetic as a repressive solution to extra-aesthetic tensions. For my part, I would be happier if current criticism of Keats's work borrowed some of the poet's own intermingled capacity for admiration and self-teasing irony in his dealings with the 'aesthetic', as when, in the same letter, he moves between writing 'I am sometimes so very sceptical as to think Poetry itself a mere Jack a lanthern to amuse whoever may chance to be struck with its brilliance' and proclaiming 'passages of Shakspeare' to be among the category of 'Things real' (to Benjamin Bailey, 13 March 1818: *Gittings*, p. 73).

In what follows I shall highlight a topic which is subtilized out of existence, overlooked or downplayed in current accounts of the poet, though it is both discussed and contested in the writings of Helen Vendler and Barbara Everett, possibly the most alert and sensitive readers of Keats's poetry in recent years: this topic is the creative and critical intelligence shown by Keats in exploring the significance and limits of poetry. My point of departure is Keats's account of the 'poetical Character' in a letter to Richard Woodhouse of 27 October 1818:

> As to the poetical Character itself, (I mean that sort of which, if I am any thing, I am a Member; that sort distinguished from the wordsworthian or egotistical sublime; which is a thing per se and stands alone) it is not itself – it has no self – it is every thing and nothing – It has no character – it enjoys light and shade; it lives in gusto, be it foul or fair, high or low, rich or poor, mean or elevated – It has as much delight in conceiving an Iago as an Imogen. What shocks the virtuous philosop[h]er, delights the camelion Poet. It does no harm from its relish of the dark side of things any more than from its taste for the bright one; because they both end in speculation. A Poet is the most unpoetical of any thing in existence; because he has no Identity – he is continually in for – and filling some other Body – The Sun, the Moon, the Sea and Men and Women who are creatures of impulse are poetical and have about them an unchangeable attribute – the poet has none; no identity – he is certainly the most unpoetical of all God's Creatures (*Gittings*, p. 157).

Keats is a poet whose language is 'continually in for – and filling some other Body'. We respond unreservedly to his poetry because it gives us what Barthes (only half-mockingly) calls 'the hallucinatory relish of "reality"',[4] the illusion, if you like, of presence. Through his use of language Keats is able to 'reproduce', in Shelley's words, 'the common universe of which we are portions and percipients' ('A Defence of Poetry': *SPP*, p. 505). 'The hare limped trembling through the frozen grass' (line 3)[5] at the start of *The Eve of St Agnes*, where the rhythm limps in sympathy with the trembling creature, is one example. A second, more far-reaching, instance occurs in the lines about Ruth in the Nightingale Ode: 'Perhaps the self-same song that found a path / Through the sad heart of Ruth, when, sick for home, / She stood in tears amid the alien corn' (lines 65-7): more far-reaching because not only do the words 'found a path / Through' make of Ruth's sad heart an aching, penetrable space but also because the initial 'Perhaps' signals to us the poet who is 'filling some other Body', or indeed for whom another body is filling in. The 'sole self' ('Ode to a Nightingale', line 72) is just round the corner of these seemingly so self-forgetful lines – as it is in the sentence after the passage in Keats's letter just quoted, which amusingly returns to the apparently selfless self: 'If then he has no self, and if I am a Poet, where is the Wonder that I should say I would write no more?'. And here the 'compositions and decompositions', in Keats's phrase, begin (to B. R. Haydon, 8 April 1818: *Gittings*, p. 83). For Keats the poet of 'no Identity' is also Keats the poet of the 'sole self'. Keats the unshockable 'camelion' poet is also concerned that the act of writing should, in ways his poetry moves us by only feeling its way towards, engage with issues of 'right'.

Again, the poet who would be 'continually in for – and filling some other Body' seems at times to flinch from the demands imposed by such absorption in otherness. Keats defines his 'poetical Character' with eloquent bravura, refusing to count the cost which obedience to the implicit progamme he outlines may exact. Yet the poetry's enactment of this cost keeps at bay the danger of aestheticising self-regard and lies close to the heart of Keats's achievement as a poet. So at the start of 'Ode to a Nightingale' Keats begins in an evidently depressed state. Or does he?

> My heart aches, and a drowsy numbness pains
>   My sense, as though of hemlock I had drunk,
> Or emptied some dull opiate to the drains
>   One minute past, and Lethe-wards had sunk: (lines 1-4).

The first three words assert the presence of the suffering, affective self; yet this impression is modified by what follows, where what 'pains' is a 'drowsy numbness': numbness and pain refuse either to support one another fully or to be wholly distinct. The condition of 'drowsy numbness' lapses from, and prepares for, a heightening of consciousness. The subsequent similes elaborate, yet draw away from, the original sensation which refuses fully to define itself; in so doing (or not doing so) the opening four lines are in keeping with Keats's sense of the 'poetical Character' as living in 'light and shade'. But at the start of the Ode this living in light and shade is less an Olympian, delighted relishing than an uncertain if potentially creative inhabiting. Keats goes on to write: ''Tis not through envy of thy happy lot, / But being too happy in thine happiness' (lines 5-6), where 'too happy' casts a paradoxically self-conscious glance at the poet's asserted absorption in the bird's 'happiness'. Empathy as imaginative burden rather than release is a theme minimized in the account of the 'poetical Character', but it threatens to come to the fore in the Ode, and should be seen as central to the poem's achievement, more so, perhaps, than the theme of longing for escape. Certainly, the longing for escape instantly raises the problem (that is also the saving grace) of empathy; Keats is able vividly to throw himself into imaginings of escape, but these imaginings take on a force that counterpoints the escapist impulse. In the second stanza of 'Ode to a Nightingale' the poetry dwells inside a pastoral haven in the act of longing for 'a draught of vintage' (line 11). This haven is at once a place made possible by poetry and the repetition in a finer tone of the world which Keats asserts his desire to leave. Desiring to go, he lingers with alliterative longing over the 'beaded bubbles' (line 17) in the drink which he trusts will allow him to 'leave the world unseen' (line 19).

Throughout 'Ode to a Nightingale' the poetry is detained by such acts of imaginative empathy from its dark goal of escape, cessation of consciousness; it is detained desirably and yet unwillingly. In stanza 5 the 'guessing' of 'sweets' (line 43) turns into a premonitory scenting of process and mortality as the poet imagines 'Fast fading violets covered up in leaves; / And mid-May's eldest child, / The coming musk-rose' (lines 47-9). The violets may be 'Fast fading', but the line, opening with two heavy stresses, pauses over the departure of the flowers. The subsequent 'And' breathes even-toned acceptance of transience; process is transformed, as so often in Keats's great poetry, into procession. And yet 'covered up in leaves' suggests, by analogy, how imaginative involvement can feel like being buried alive. Keats's comment on Milton's Satan entering the serpent (*Paradise Lost*, IX.179-91) is illuminating here: 'Whose head is not dizzy at the prosaible speculations of satan in the serpent prison – no passage of poetry ever can give a greater pain of suffocation'.[6] As Nicola Trott remarks, 'Satan-in-the serpent suggests an egotistical poet in chameleon's clothing'.[7] Indeed, Keats is a poet who relishes and suffers his own gift of identification with pain and pleasure, joy and suffering. That gift presents him with a poisoned chalice in *The Fall of Hyperion*. Forced to sustain a perilously unaided vision, Keats portrays himself as driven to the limits of endurance: 'Oftentimes I prayed / Intense, that death would take me from the vale / And all its burthens' (I.396-8). In these lines 'gusto' turns sour, and yet the tasting of that sourness is what gives the poem 'gusto'.

'It lives in gusto': Keats's sense of the 'poetical Character' is shaped by the criticism of William Hazlitt. In 'On Poetry in General', an essay which left its traces on *Lamia* and 'Ode on a Grecian Urn', we find perhaps the nearest thing in Romantic literature to Keats's simultaneous trust in imagination and his fear that 'the progress of knowledge and refinement has a tendency to circumscribe the limits of the imagination, and to clip the wings of poetry'.[8] Keats steals the last phrase for *Lamia* where he laments that 'Philosophy will clip an Angel's wings' (II.234); and nowhere in Keats is gusto more powerfully or more tragically displayed than at the end of *Lamia*. Here Keats drives a sword through the heart of his conviction that

'What the imagination seizes as Beauty must be truth – whether it existed before or not' (to Benjamin Bailey, 22 November 1817: *Gittings*, p. 37). Gusto is present in the way the couplets are a steady-paced match for the poem's final metamorphosis of the 'tender-personed Lamia . . . into a shade' (II.238). As 'tender-personed' indicates, the poem's sympathies are for Lamia; but it hands her over to Apollonius's rationalist gaze. The final paragraph traces the step-by-step vanishing of Lamia; like Lycius the reader protests, 'Shut, shut those juggling eyes, thou ruthless man!' (II.277). But the poem leaves us like Lycius' arms 'empty of delight' (II.307) – save for the pleasure we take in the art with which Keats implies how vulnerable beauty is once it is regarded as mere illusion. *Lamia* is, in Amy Clampitt's words, a 'weird trophy / hung among the totems of his own ambivalence'.[9] Yet 'ambivalence' notwithstanding, the poem is indeed a 'trophy': aesthetic spoil wrested from, and sad, reminding relic of, a bruising imaginative conflict.

Hazlitt was admired by Keats for 'the force and innate power' of a rhetorical style which 'yeasts and works up itself' (journal letter to the George Keatses, 14 February-3 May 1819: *Gittings*, p. 226). But Keats's fineness lies less in stylistic bravado than in his movement between moods and idioms, in his ability to inhabit contradictions, in the sense his poems give of creative articulation emerging out of manifold impulses. Barbara Everett notes perceptively of 'To Autumn' that its 'inter-stanzaic pauses are like crevasses, vital landmarks in the poem's spiritual geography'. Whether the result in this poem and other Odes is a 'harmony of differences'[10] is questionable. Undertows of disturbance are often present, as in the movement in 'Ode on a Grecian Urn' from stanza 3 to stanza 4. Stanza 3 concludes with the lines, 'All breathing human passion far above, / That leaves a heart high-sorrowful and cloyed, / A burning forehead, and a parching tongue'; stanza 4 starts with the question, 'Who are these coming to the sacrifice?' (lines 28-31). It is one of the most elusive transitions in Romantic poetry, quite different from the transitions in, say, Wordsworth's 'Ode [Intimations of Immortality]': '– But there's a Tree, of many one' (line 51), for instance, or 'O joy! that in our embers / Is something that doth live' (lines 132-3) (*WW*, pp. 298, 300). In the way they move against a preceding mood, these lines take the reader to the centre of the lyric self. In 'Ode on a Grecian Urn' the start of stanza 4 obliges the reader to work, as it were, grammatically. When did the poem last use a question? The answer is, in stanza 1 ('What men or gods are these? . . . What wild ecstasy?' [lines 8-10]). What happened to those fantasizing questions about the 'wild ecstasy' imagined on the Urn? They led into a two-stanza exploration of the tentatively held notion that 'Heard melodies are sweet, but those unheard /

Are sweeter' (lines 11-12). That notion began to undo itself in stanza 3 where the reiterated use of 'happy' ('More happy love! more happy, happy love!' [line 25]) suggests Keats's increasing desperation, and where the final lines (quoted above) have an impact at odds with their overt significance. What attracts is 'breathing human passion', not what lies 'far above'; 'aboveness', loftiness, is quickly seized back by and for the 'high-sorrowful' heart.

There is, then, a tacit admission at the start of stanza 4 that a course of enquiry has run its course; and now Keats moves more circumspectly, almost reverently. Gone is the imaginative grasping, the latching on to erotic fantasy, which quickly met its opposite in the icy stillness of the urn as artefact. 'Who are these coming to the sacrifice?' is a line that ramifies. By the end of the poem we may feel that all of us – in so far as we give up our lives to art, or do not do so – are, in some sense, 'sacrificed'. And it is an aspect of Keats's power that further possibilities inhering in a phrase or line or passage communicate, even as they allow more evident meanings to occupy centre-stage. At this stage love is left behind for the rituals of religion, the hope of private ecstasy for the depiction of collective ceremony; but what hangs in the air is the phrase 'breathing human passion'. The stanza is driven to discover that the breath of those who dwelled in the 'little town' (line 38) has been stilled; the writing drops its questioning guard, addressing the little town in lines of great pathos (lines 38-40), discovering that there is no possible reply to the question which began the stanza or to further questions, 'not a soul to tell / Why thou art desolate, can e'er return' (lines 39-40).

Always in Keats there is consciousness in and about the act of making; yet it is not the consciousness of Coleridge's Shakespeare who in *Venus and Adonis* is 'a superior spirit more intuitive, more intimately conscious, even than the characters themselves, not only of every outward look and act, but of the flux and reflux of the mind in all its subtlest thoughts and feelings . . . himself meanwhile unparticipating in the passions' (*BL*, II, p. 21). Rather with Keats's Odes there is often a brief withdrawal, in the 'inter-stanzaic' space, followed by renewed immersion in the poem's experience, an immersion which always exacts a cost, a cost which is often audible in the words. The cry 'Cold Pastoral!' (line 45) in the final stanza of 'Ode on a Grecian Urn' is a famous example, and the whole of that stanza is at once a retreat, a coming to terms and a regrouping. The inscrutable last two lines are, it is vital to remember, part of a long sentence. And this sentence begins with an internal rhyme that links the only end of 'old age' (line 46) with the 'Cold' nature of art, and continues with an emphatic stress that says 'old age *shall* this generation waste' (line 46); it knows, too, that 'other woe / Than ours' (lines 47-8) will persist. Yet it asserts that 'Thou shalt remain' (line 47), where 'shalt' is stressed as emphatically as the preceding 'shall'. 'Thou shalt remain' reasserts the hope that art is 'a friend to man' (line 48), a friendship shown by the way it takes the edge off 'waste' by what it 'say'st (line 48) and the edge off 'woe' by what it can be said to 'know' (line 50). The final two lines are, I take it, entirely Urn-speak; they mouth a demonstrable falsehood (demonstrable in terms of what this poem knows; it knows about many other things, including 'waste' and 'woe') and a privileged insight; they reassert the value of the special, vulnerable experience that art offers.

'To Autumn' chooses acceptance, immersion in the transient, and yet this immersion is sealed aesthetically. Almost toneless, the final lines refuse to let any note of lament prevail. The last line, 'And gathering swallows twitter in the skies' (line 33), reads in drafts as, 'And gather'd Swallows twitter in the Skies'.[11] The alteration to 'gathering' – allowing for activity, the possibility of purpose – does much to release the poem from anything too doom-laden. But Everett is suggestive when she sees in this poem a perfection of technique, tone and diction bought at a great cost: she writes, 'At moments it seems "good" in the way that a child will be called "good", when what is really meant is that its spirit is broken'.[12] Though this overstates the case, and is unnecessarily reductive, Everett sensitizes one to the immense grace under pressure exhibited by the writing. What has gone from 'To Autumn' are the gestures of protest that are assertions of self in the other Odes. The end of 'Ode to a Nightingale' is a case in point. In one sense the stanza is muddled, its categories of 'vision' and 'waking dream' (line 79) cobbled together after the event, after mental events that will not be pigeon-holed. Moreover, its scepticism about 'fancy' (line 73) has about it a false jauntiness, as of someone denying the seriousness of his feelings. What is affecting here, though, is that the lines reassert a freedom from the burden of imaginative experience, even as the long 'Adieu's' (lines 73, 75) are expressive of loss. After all, the poem has known inwardly for some lines that the fancy does not 'cheat' (line 73) at all; the lines about Ruth swing the voyaging fancy back decisively from the notion of the immortality of the bird's song to the perennial presence of suffering. But the poem will not remain steadily with one attitude or perception; the 'magic casements' (line 69) conform with an easier notion of imagination as leading to escapism, and permit the poem the sorrowful but necessary voyage back to the 'sole self'. In 'To Autumn' the abandonment of a split between different kinds of experience gives rise to a persistence in one kind, to a state that is courageous but muted, unflinching yet almost trapped. *The Fall of Hyperion*, written in the months leading up to 'To

Autumn', contains lines that flush out into the open the unseen seer of the Ode: 'Without stay or prop, / But my own weak mortality, I bore / The load of this eternal quietude' (I.388-90). If a significant absence for 'To Autumn' is desired, it lies, I would suggest, in these lines rather than in the working conditions of gleaners or the aftermath of Peterloo. *The Fall of Hyperion* harrows by including these lines; 'To Autumn' seems such a brave poem by refusing to gloss its creator's mood.

I shall conclude with four points about Keats's poetry which emerge from reflecting on his 'poetical Character'. First, it commits itself with exemplary courage to distinctive acts of verbal and, by implication, epistemological invention: 'That which is creative must create itself', he writes to J. A. Hessey (8 October 1818: *Gittings*, p. 156), and the most valuable criticism of his poetry focuses on the way it 'creates itself'. Second, it is an arena for the staging of internal debate; the poetry itself compellingly dramatizes Keats's ambivalences about poetry. When Leigh Hunt writes, in connection with a couplet from 'The Eve of St Agnes', that 'poetry, in its intense sympathy with creation, may be said to create anew, rendering its words more impressive than the objects they speak of, and individually more lasting',[13] he praises Keats precisely, and yet his praise, unintentionally, names a dilemma as well as an achievement: the dilemma being that 'intense sympathy with creation' may jostle uneasily with the pleasure taken in creating a surrogate 'creation' that outdoes the original. However, it is Keats's poems themselves that dramatize this uneasy discovery. Third, Keats's poems embody the belief, or doubting trust, or desperate hope that poetry has its own kind of 'intelligible relation to life', in Vendler's phrase,[14] a relation which outflanks the discoveries of 'consequitive reasoning' (to Benjamin Bailey, 22 November 1817: *Gittings*, p. 37) without collapsing into irrationalism, escapism, or imaginative arrest. Fourth, Keats creates a poetry with high aesthetic finish that is alert to its own processes and to the need for poetry to negotiate with process. In his 'Bright star!' sonnet he allegorizes two modes of poetry: the contemplative and the involved. The description of the star's 'lone splendour' (line 2) carries a very positive charge as the poet imagines himself into the bright star's condition of being like a 'patient, sleepless Eremite' (line 4). He rejects the bright star's state for the erotic entanglements of the sestet; and yet one notes here the desire to be 'still steadfast, still unchangeable' (line 9), to exist in a perpetual 'for ever' (lines 11, 12) that is not a deathly imaginative fixity, but is rather a state in touch with 'breathing human passion', when he is able 'Still, still to hear her tender-taken breath' (line 13). In *Adonais*, Shelley imagines for Keats a canonical permanence which Keats has surely won partly through his very ambivalence about the sealed, the unchangeable, the fixed:

> The splendours of the firmament of time
> May be eclipsed, but are extinguished not;
> Like stars to their appointed height they climb. . .
>
> (lines 388-90: *SPP*, p. 403).

Notes

1   Stuart M. Sperry, *Keats the Poet* (1973; Princeton: Princeton University Press, 1994), p. 346.
2   Helen Vendler, *The Music of What Happens: Poems. Poets Critics* (Cambridge, Mass.: Harvard University Press, 1988), p. 1.
3   Quoted by Jerome J. McGann in *The Beauty of Inflections: Literary Investigations in Historical Method and Theory* (Oxford: Clarendon Press, 1988), p. 19.
4   Roland Barthes, *The Pleasure of the Text*, in *Barthes: Selected Writings*, ed., and intro., Susan Sontag (London: Fontana/Collins, 1982), p. 408.
5   All poems by Keats are quoted from *John Keats: The Complete Poems*, ed. John Barnard, 3rd edn. (Harmondsworth: Penguin, 1988); hereafter *Poems*.
6   Quoted from *Poems*, p. 526.
7   Nicola Trott, 'Keats and the Prison House of History', in *Keats and History*, ed. Nicholas Roe (Cambridge: Cambridge University Press, 1995), p. 263.
8   In William Hazlitt, *Lectures on the English Poets: The Spirit of the Age: or Contemporary Portraits*, intro. Catherine MacDonald Maclean ([1907]; London: Dent, 1967), p. 9.
9   'The Isle of Wight', a section of 'Voyages: A Homage to John Keats', in Amy Clampitt, *What the Light Was Like* (London and Boston: Faber and Faber, 1985), p. 64.
10   Barbara Everett, 'Keats: Somebody Reading', *Poets in Their Time: Essays on English Poetry from Donne to Larkin* (1986; Oxford: Clarendon Press, 1991), p. 157; hereafter Everett. To be fair to Everett, she writes of the Odes' 'recreation of the movement of the living mind, remaking itself at every pace forward, so that every new stanza is also a self-losing', p. 157.
11   See *Gittings*, p. 295; see also *John Keats: Poetry Manuscripts at Harvard: A Facsimile Edition*, ed. Jack Stillinger, With an Essay on the Manuscripts by Helen Vendler (Cambridge, Mass.: Harvard University Press, 1990), p. 224-5.
12   Everett, pp. 146-7.
13   James Henry Leigh Hunt, *Imagination and Fancy* (London: Smith, Elder, & Co., 1891), p. 307.
14   Vendler, 'Keats and the Use of Poetry', p. 125.

12 Masking in Keats

THOMAS MCFARLAND

In *Childe Harold*, Byron memorably specifies what it is that a poet or other artist is hoping to do by his endeavours:

'Tis to create, and in creating live
A being more intense, that we endow
With form our fancy, gaining as we give
The life we image, even as I do now.
What am I? Nothing; but not so art thou
Soul of my thought! (Canto III, lines 46-51: *BCPW,* II, p. 78).

Yet Byron does not point to what will here be seen as an inevitable accompaniment to the endowing with form of our fancy. Perhaps he implies it, however, by the words 'gaining as we give / The life we image'. The poet before the poem is identified as 'Nothing'; but the soul of the poet's thought, which is a new life supervening on the poet's nothingness, has a being more intense. It is a life not only better than that of the poet before the poem, but it is clearly a life that stands in opposition to that nothingness.

Likewise Milton, in declaring that 'a good book is the precious life blood of a master spirit, embalmed and treasured up on purpose to a life beyond life',[1] almost seems to imply that the master spirit does not become a master spirit until the good book is written; for the 'precious life blood' is nowhere evident except in the book. Though he does not say, as Byron does, that before the artistic production the poet is Nothing, there is perhaps at least that implication, an implication directed by the metonymic placement of a preceding statement: 'Many a man lives a burden to the earth'. Life as a burden to the earth, like life as Byron's Nothing, is contrasted to the richer life that supervenes after the good book or the poem is produced. That richer and supervening life is characterized as a 'being more intense', as 'soul', as 'precious life blood'.

Milton and Byron agree, therefore, in conceiving a decisive contrast in the existence of the writer before the artefact and the existence of the writer after the artefact. The writer after and through the artefact masks, as it were, his old being by a new and radiant being. Though such a masking pertains to all artistic production whatever, it is in John Keats that it assumes its most dramatically defined and essential form. For Keats's

166

greatness as a poet is attained in large and decisive part by the successful assumption of two different masks, what may here be called the Mask of Hellas and the Mask of Camelot.

It is of course true that Romantic Hellenism and Romantic medievalism are important threads in the general fabric of Romanticism; but in Keats they eventuate in such a richness of texture and brightness of colour as to transume themselves into nothing less than the defining instance of a more intense being and a precious life blood. Heine, asking the question, 'What was the Romantic School in Germany?', provided medievalism as his answer: 'It was', he said, 'nothing other than the reawakening of the poetry of the middle ages as it manifested itself in the poems, paintings, and sculptures, in the art and life of those times'.[2] Yet nowhere in German literature does the attempt to assume the medieval mask produce an art so high as in the poetry of Keats. *Mutatis mutandis*, the same holds true for his commitment to the Mask of Hellas. With the sole exception of Hölderlin, no Romantic writer achieved so greatly with the materials of Greece as did Keats.

Indeed, it was because of the unique focus and vividness of Keats's use of the medieval and Hellenic masks that the special phrases Mask of Camelot and Mask of Hellas have been assigned to him alone. Almost all writers of the nineteenth century participated to some extent in Hellenic and medieval imagining; such participation, however, frequently rose scarcely above the banal. In a recent study of Wordsworth, the present author notes that a late and inferior poem 'utilizes a laboured framework of banalities about classical mythology', and the discussion goes on to say that:

> It is revealing that when his poetic faculty was no longer kept green from the reservoir of 'Home at Grasmere', Wordsworth tended to turn to such pre-packaged modes as Romantic Hellenism or Romantic medievalism. Both modes, so congenial to the vision of Keats, were alien to the source and structure of Wordsworthian intensity.
>
> Wordsworth did manage to achieve a modest success with the former mode in the passages in *The Excursion* that so intrigued Keats. And he was proud of 'Laodamia', noting significantly that it 'cost me more trouble than almost anything of equal length I have ever written'. He also noted, again significantly, that it was 'written at the same time as *Dion* and *Artegal and Elidure*', for the former is an adventure in Romantic Hellenism based on Plutarch ('Avaunt, inexplicable Guest! – avaunt' is, sadly, one of its lines), while the other is a foray of 242 lines into Romantic medievalism; but even at that not so egregious as 'The Egyptian Maid; or, The Romance of the Water Lily', an Arthurian piece that drones on for 386 lines. 'Laodamia' is better than all this, yet it is not only laboured, but really, one is constrained to think, not very good.[3]

In such considerations, to juxtapose Wordsworth's medievalism and Hellenism against those of Keats is to become aware of fundamental truths about masking. When one places a mask over his face he presents himself as another self. He hides and thereby repudiates the first face, replacing it with a second face that automatically becomes the presented self. Although I am not an admirer of the work of the late Erving Goffman, Goffman deserves praise for pointing to how various and inevitable are the presentations of a social self, in contradistinction to a purely subjective self. One sees this in the smiles and bonhomie of politicians, *a fortiori* in the roles of a powerful actor, Daniel Day Lewis, say, whose insipid suitor in *A Room With a View* is not in any way the same person as the confident homosexual lover in *My Beautiful Laundrette* or the tormented cripple in *My Left Foot*.

But Wordsworth's masked self is never able to obliterate his subjective self, and that is why his medievalism and Hellenism are so unsuccessful in producing great poetry. Behind every manifestation of his poetic genius there stands ineluctably what Keats himself described as 'the wordsworthian or egotistical sublime' (*KL*, I, p. 387), which is precisely Wordsworth's immensely powerful sense of a primary self. Only when the truth-telling certainty of that primary self flows with unblocked intensity does the great Wordsworthian poetry emerge. Keats, on the contrary, had nothing of the egotistical sublime – thought, indeed, that the poet has 'no identity', 'has no self' (*KL*, I, p. 387). He achieves his own greatness not through the truth-telling of a primary self, but through the masks of a presented self speaking from the worlds of Camelot and Hellas. Of his four greatest poems, one, 'The Eve of St. Agnes' is a total realization of the Mask of Camelot, another, the 'Ode on a Grecian Urn', is an equally total realization of the Mask of Hellas, and the two remaining, 'To Autumn' and the 'Ode to a Nightingale' are both if not explicit at least indirect utterances from the Mask of Hellas. Again, *Hyperion*, which Shelley thought Keats's greatest work, is entirely an utterance that issues from the Mask of Hellas.

But the tremendous qualities of the poems just mentioned are achieved only through Keats's total success in assuming the mask, and by the same token that success is achieved only by the repudiation and obliteration of the primary self. For the irreducible character of the mask is to be an opposite to the self. In Yeats's Great Wheel of twenty-eight phases, one of the four interpenetrating realities, mask, is defined entirely by opposition. 'The being becomes conscious of itself as a separate being', Yeats says, 'because of certain facts of Opposition and Discord', and the first of these is 'the emotional Opposition of *Will* and *Mask*'.[4] Again, under the rubric 'Relations' he lists 'Those between Will and Mask, between Mind and Body of Fate' as being 'oppositions, or contrasts'.[5] Such a statement is especially pertinent to Keats, whose will to be a poet exhibited a natural desire for the Mask of Camelot and the Mask of Hellas. And this essay's statement above that 'the writer after and through the artefact masks, as it were, his old being by a new and radiant being', is illuminated by Keats's insistence that 'by being is understood that which divides into *Four Faculties*'. He continues by noting that 'individuality' is 'the *Will* analysed in relation to itself', but 'Personality' is 'the *Will* analysed in relation to the free *Mask*'.[6]

We need not restrict ourselves to the world of vortex and gyre, nor spin round the ever-changing alignments of the Great Wheel, to realize that Yeats's preoccupation with the central reality of mask was a pervasive concern, one not restricted to the cryptic formulations of *A Vision*. As he said in his *Autobiographies*, 'What I have called 'the Mask' is an emotional antithesis to all that comes out of their 'internal nature' – and by 'their' he refers to the selves of subjective men.[7] Indeed, long before *A Vision* he wrote a poem called 'The Mask', which, composed between August 1910 and May 1911, became a lyric in *The Player Queen* of 1922. In that poem, an interlocutor says 'It was the mask engaged your mind, / And after set your heart to beat, / Not what's behind'.[8] The statement accords exactly with *The Vision*'s assertion that the 'personality' is 'the *Will* analysed in relation to the free *Mask*'.

In terms of the foregoing formulation, whereby personality does not emerge until the mask is conceived, it is permissible to say that John Keats did not become John Keats until he assumed his masks. He certainly did not become John Keats the great poet before then; but he also, and more radically, did not become John Keats the personality. 'The Author himself – that somewhat decrepit deity of the old criticism –', insists Roland Barthes, 'can or could some day become a text like any other: he has only to see himself as a being on paper and his life as a *biography* (in the etymological sense of the word), a writing without referent, substance of a *connection* and not of a *filiation*: the critical undertaking (if we can still speak of criticism), will then consist in *returning* the documentary figure of the author into a novelistic, irretrievable, irresponsible figure, caught up into the plural of its own text'.[9] No observation could apply more exactly to that episode in cultural history signified by the filing code John Keats. As a documentary figure become novelistic, caught up into the plural of its own text, John Keats has been, almost more than any other figure, treated as a hybrid of poetry and personality.

Shakespeare, in contrast, resists such treatment, as is vividly apparent in the words of Arnold, in that sonnet so much scorned by Leavis: 'Others abide our question. Thou art free. / We ask and ask – Thou smilest and art still, / Outtopping knowledge'.[10] It is quite the contrary with Keats. Amy Lowell has sometimes been patronizingly dismissed (read H. W. Garrod's comments) as having palpably fallen in love with Keats; perhaps we should not be so scornful, because no commentator can write on Keats without becoming deeply involved with his personality. No other figure seems so fey and at the same time so appealing. Coleridge claimed to have felt death in the handclasp of Keats (*TT*, I, p. 325); and the intermingling of that looming death and of the intense ardour of his life makes him an irresistibly sympathetic figure. The sense of enormous human worth along with radical incompleteness teases every commentator's mind and leads to a subliminal urge, all but universal, to become the advocate of this brave and tragic figure. It is not merely fortuitous, it is on the contrary immensely symbolic, that what is perhaps the most important book ever written on Keats – I refer to Walter Jackson Bate's magisterial *John Keats* – is neither to be defined as a biography nor as a work of criticism. Its essential nature is indicated by its inspired title, *John Keats*.[11] Not *John Keats*; *A Biography*; not *John Keats*; *The Achievement of his Poetry*. Not these, nor any modification supplied by a subtitle, simply *John Keats*.

But John Keats did not become John Keats until he assumed his masks. The motto of Descartes was '*larvatus prodeo*' – 'masked, I come forth'; that very motto should certainly be claimed by Keats, for John Keats did not come forth until he was masked. Taken without his masks, Keats was scarcely a figure to be envied. As the present writer observed in a review of Marjorie Levinson's *Keats's Life of Allegory*, which reconfigures the contexts of the poet's activity:

> Levinson's Keats is as an author a poor figure, weak, constrained, and buffeted by inadequacy – 'a man profoundly "entoiled" in social and psychic double-binds'. Keats is here seen as societally determined, his poetry almost written for him by his ill-educated, embarrassed, Cockney situation.[12]

Even his burning letters, which at first glance would seem to be exempt from this proviso with respect to the necessity of masking, witness that truth. For though the letters do not speak from the Yeatsian mask, they speak from the Yeatsian will, and they look toward that will's need to effectuate itself by mask. Indeed, almost nowhere in the annals of poetry do we encounter so revealing and detailed a discrepancy between the state of wanting to be a poet and the actual achieving of great poetry as we do in the short span of Keats's intellectual activity. The will to be a poet before he had acquired the techniques and understandings necessary to that outcome is an irreducible part of the cultural entity John Keats. 'O Poesy!', he exclaims in his early poem *Sleep and Poetry*, 'for thee I hold my pen / That am not yet a glorious denizen / Of thy wide heaven–' (lines 47-9: *PJK*, p. 70).

Almost no other figure provides so revealing a record of embryonic activity as does Keats. As a single example, one may point to *Endymion*. The word 'stretched' in its epigraph, 'The stretched metre of an antique song', takes on ironic function; for Keats seems determined to stretch everything here to its absolute limit, the patience of a reader no less than the seemingly endless wordage of the poem. 'The Authors intention', observed Shelley ruefully of *Endymion*, appeared to be 'that no person possibly get to the end of it'.[13] Roland Barthes' hope of a writerly reader here encounters rough seas; and the more than four thousand lines of the poem dramatically indicate how preoccupied the poet is with smelting out the metal for the Mask of Hellas rather than trimming and fitting it to the actual contours of a face. The verbiage of *Endymion* is a long way from the inspired utterance of 'Ode on a Grecian Urn'. Yet the youthful Keats was well aware of the embryonic nature of his effort; and the explanatory preface to his poem is virtually unique in its candid confession of immature performance: 'the reader', says Keats, 'must soon perceive great inexperience, immaturity, and every error denoting a feverish attempt, rather than a deed accomplished' (*PJK*, p. 102).

The dwelling in a region below that of high art, so unmistakably identified here, is apparent in much of Keats's production. Neither 'I Stood on Tiptoe', the first entry in the 1817 volume, nor *Sleep and Poetry*, the last, is in formal terms much of a poem. Paradoxically, however, one can look back from the great later poetry and discern in these two ventures – neither of which, in Barthian terminology, is much more than a string of lexias – profound shapings for what comes to be great poetry. Both poems bulwark the claim made above about the necessity and authenticity of imperfect effort in the total spectrum of John Keats.

Yet it is not in terms of imperfect effort, but in terms of supreme achievement, that the masks of John Keats engage our lasting interest. Let us for a moment try to keep in mind two configurations, one, the Mask of Camelot, and the other that series of conventional understandings, analogies, dates, psychological guesses, and social agreements that form for us the suppositious figure known as the man John Keats. The man John Keats is for us merely a literary construct, a text. We can assume, with as much right as we accept the rest of the sheaf of assumptions that make up the text called the man John Keats, that he had certain characteristics; specifically, being in his early twenties, he was wracked by sexual passion. The assumption is fortified by other data that we variously tag as Fanny Brawne, love poems, love letters, and the sexuality of consumptives. If we turn to the Mask of Camelot, we see that its central male figure, a young man named Porphyro, is defined in his being and activity wholly by sexual passion.

It is important to understand that the man John Keats and the figure Porphyro share a common phenomenological reality: each is precisely an intentional object of our mentation; neither is anything more. That the figure Porphyro stands in direct relation to the man Keats is evident, and lambent electricity plays back and forth between them. For instance, Cowden Clarke remembered,

> Keats reading to him in 1819 from the *Eve of St. Agnes* and saying, when they came to the passage where Porphyro listens to the midnight music in the castle hall below, that the last line of it 'came into my head when I remembered how I used to listen in bed to your music at school':

> > The boisterous midnight, festive clarion,
> > The kettledrum, and far-heard clarinet,
> > Affray his ears, though but in dying tone:–
> > The hall-door shuts again, and all the noise is gone'.[14]

But the mask, Porphyro, though directly related to the man John Keats, takes shape as the opposite. The man John Keats was racked by loss, apprehensive of early death, harassed by unjust penury, reviled by scornful reviewers, and denied the full bliss of his passion. Though he told Fanny Brawne that 'the very first week I knew you I wrote myself your vassal'[15], and sometime after September 1819 became engaged to her, the outcome of the love was famously disappointing. But as might be expected from so ardent a nature as that of John Keats, disappointment mingled itself with a virtually palpable intensity of passion:

> O, let me have thee whole, – all, – all – be mine!
> That shape, that fairness, that sweet minor zest
> Of love, your kiss, those hands, those eyes divine,
> That warm, white, lucent, million-pleasured breast. –
> Yourself – your soul – in pity give me all,
> Withhold no atom's atom or I die (lines 5-10: *PJK*, p. 492).

This enormous pressure of sexual passion, however, was so demanding in terms of Keats's psychic economy, especially inasmuch as the ratio of continuing bliss to deprivation was so unsatisfactory, that he turned on his own nature and came to regret the fact that he loved:

What can I do to drive away
Remembrance from my eyes? for they have seen,
Aye, an hour ago, my brilliant queen!
Touch has a memory. O say, Love, say,
What can I do to kill it and be free
In my old liberty?

Where shall I learn to get my peace again?

  O, for some sunny spell
To dissipate the shadows of this hell! (lines 1-6, 30, 44-45: *PJK*,
pp. 492-93).

One thing he could do and did to dissipate the shadows of that hell was to transfer his longing for love to the Mask of Camelot. There all the frustration of the man John Keats was negated by the supreme fulfilment of Porphyro. In the poem just quoted, 'What can I do to drive away', Keats had allowed his longing once again humiliatingly to inundate his frustration:

O, let me once more rest
My soul upon that dazzling breast!
Let once again these aching arms be placed,
The tender gaolers of thy waist!

O, the sweetness of the pain!
Give me those lips again!
Enough! Enough! it is enough for me
To dream of thee! (lines 48-51, 56-59: *PJK*, pp. 493-4).

But of course it was not enough. To have consummation reduced to a dream is not enough for anyone with blood in his veins. Fulfilment, however, so absent here, becomes totally present in the masked world of 'The Eve of St. Agnes'. There, the precious life blood of the man John Keats is indeed embalmed and treasured up on purpose to a life beyond life. The gorgeous world of that poem is invoked entirely in the service of an extended trope of passion triumphing over all obstacles and hindrances. The man, John Keats, outside this greatest realization of the Mask of Camelot, is reduced to the sustenance afforded by dream; within the great poem, in polar opposition, dream is transformed into the splendour of eternal reality. As the present writer has elsewhere said, in words that perhaps may stand without change or amendment:

the final stanza of 'The Eve of St. Agnes' is a spectacular triumph and vindication of the Godlike power of the imagination:

> And they are gone: ay, ages long ago
> These lovers fled away into the storm.
> That night the Baron dreamt of many a woe,
> And all his warrior-guests, with shade and form
> Of witch, and demon, and large coffin-worm,
> Were long be-nightmar' d. Angela the old
> Died palsy-twitch'd, with meagre face deform,
> The Beadsman, after thousand aves told,
> For aye unsought for slept among his ashes cold.

The brilliant achievement of the poem as a whole has been the creation of a world, in all its tactile, auditory, and visual splendour. This world deliberately replaces the 'real' world and constitutes its own place and time. Real time ceases and real place is annulled. But now, with the last stanza, another place supervenes and another time begins. The other place, however, is indefinite: they are 'fled away into the storm'. They are gone, gone, however, not into another delimited space but of the poem's delimited space – that is, they are 'gone' from 'here' into the infinite. And the time indication that begins the new series likewise marks the displacement from 'here'; the 'there' it invokes is also indefinite – it is a 'goneness', not an arrival. That is to say, the fact that they are gone, 'ay, ages long ago', stops the lovers' time by the device of starting mundane time within the world of the poem. The lovers, in short, have gone 'ages long ago' not into another chronology but into eternity.[16]

What, one asks, is eternity? It is certainly something outside any specific indication of temporal placement, such as 'St. Agnes Eve, ah bitter chill it was' or 'That night the Baron dreamt'. The 'ages long ago' in which the lovers departed is itself a moment in time, but it exists only *within* the world of the Baron and Angela and the Beadsman. It has no pertinence to the eternity of the lovers:

The infinite and the eternal can be indicated only negatively, and this the poem does by its almost miraculous device of transforming its own original world, which was from the outset as time-free as the Grecian urn, into the mundane and corruptible world of 'reality'. The lovers, eternally the same, are gone 'ages long ago'; but the mundane clock begins to tick in the evacuated and suddenly mortal world they leave behind: 'Angela the old/ Died palsy-twitch'd, with meagre face deform'. Coldness has been the matrix of the poem's excitement and has been the validating contrary to the heat of passion:

Beyond a mortal man impassion'd far
At these voluptuous accents, he arose,
Ethereal, flush'd, and like a throbbing star

But now coldness becomes the absolute of the evacuated world and the symbol of death. The word *cold* that is the poem's last word confirms but also transforms the 'bitter chill' invoked by the poem's very first line: 'The Beadsman, after thousand aves told, / For aye unsought for slept among his ashes cold'. The invocation of false eternity as an endless progression of time – 'For aye unsought for' – is the validating contrary of the true eternity of the lovers' intensity. 'Aeternitas non est successio sine fine sed nunc stans', runs the scholastic definition – 'Eternity is not succession without end, but a standing'.[17]

The way the Keatsian flame of passion burns through a world defined by the co-ordinates of cold is one of the great realizations in all poetry. And there is nothing anywhere like the wondrous description of Porphyro's tumescence, marvellously explicit but without any lubricity at all: 'At these voluptuous accents, he arose, / Ethereal, flushed, and like a throbbing star'. (lines 317-8: *PJK*, p. 315).That is precious life blood in very truth! It is treasured up by means of a mask that provides the most radical opposition for the harried dissatisfaction of the man John Keats, trying to dissipate the shadows of his hell.

So much for that great poem. It is not possible, in a brief essay, to indicate the full panoply of what Keats achieved through the Mask of Camelot, much less to indicate the even larger range of wonders uttered through the Mask of Hellas. Suffice it to say that the supreme mask of 'The Eve of St. Agnes' was summoned by a will exerting itself very early. That will linked sexual need and the vision of the medieval. 'Hadst thou liv'd when chivalry / Lifted up her lance on high', he asks in an early poem, 'Tell me what thou wouldst have been?' (lines 41-3: *PJK*, p. 45). This speculative surveying of the ground of imaginative possibility is replaced, in an almost equally early poem called 'Specimen of an Induction', by a pure expression of will: 'Lo! I must tell a tale of chivalry / For large white plumes are dancing in mine eye' (lines 1-2: *PJK*, p. 47). What impelled his will toward such prospective masking was his dissatisfaction, especially his dissatisfaction with his small stature, which he feared would make him unattractive to women. In an even earlier poem than the ones just cited, he poignantly says, 'Had I a man's fair form, then might my sighs / Be echoed swiftly through that ivory shell / Thine ear, and find thy gentle heart'. But trapped in his minute physical frame, he then says sadly, and for the eventual achievement of 'The Eve of St. Agnes', revealingly: 'But ah! I am no knight whose foeman dies; / No cuirass glistens on my bosom's swell' (lines 1-3, 5-6: *PJK*, p. 44). Through his genius in forging his golden masks, however, Keats eventually did become a being more intense than the embarrassingly small and harried man he saw himself to be; he became the flaming Porphyro, secure forever in the attainment of his love.

Brenda Webster, in her *Yeats; A Psychoanalytic Study*, observes that 'Mask-wearing is expressed by active striving, and through his heroes and beasts Yeats steadily increased his capacity to replay emotional traumas with himself in control, to turn passive suffering into active mastery. Later, in *A Vision*, Yeats schematized his feelings about his evolution from limp and dreamy aesthete to mask-wearing, powerful poet'.[18] Though no one would suggest that the ardent and wonderful man who was Keats is in many ways to be compared to the limp and dreamy aesthete who was the early Yeats, in the largest structure of will and mask they can indeed be compared; for in each case the mask created an augmented personality to replace the earlier personality vitiated and made unsatisfactory by circumstance.

Marcel Mauss, in a probing survey of the way in which the modern idea of the self evolved from the primitive masks of tribal ritual, provides testimony to the deep roots of a virtually universal tendency for masking to be the pathway to higher personality. The great social anthropologist, after discussing tribal manifestations, accepts the Latin word for mask, *persona*, as the linchpin of his discussion. Noting that the Roman emphasis derived from a much stronger preoccupation in Etruscan experience ('The Etruscans had a civilization of masks',[19] he says flatly), Mauss develops the idea of *persona* through Roman law rather than through the more familiar use of *persona* as dramatic mask. Nevertheless, the mask, which originates in tribally organized situations where there is no concept of person, leads eventually to person as our most refined idea of the fullest individual life.

It did so in its own way in the life and work of Keats. Everywhere the mask in Keats transforms the lesser life outside the poem into richer life within it. For a concluding instance, the perfect world of the immortal nightingale, which is a variant of the Mask of Hellas – the bird is nominated at the outset as 'light-winged Dryad of the trees', and Bacchus, Lethe, and the blushful Hippocrene are all on call – that perfect world takes note of the unsatisfactory life outside, where Keats has had to witness his beloved brother Tom's incremental death by consumption: 'Here, where men sit and hear each other groan; / Where palsy shakes a few, sad, last, gray hairs, / Where youth grows pale, and spectre-thin, and dies' (lines 7, 24-6: *PJK*, p. 369-70). Those references invoke the actual world of the man John Keats. The world seen through the mask, on the contrary, lavishes on our senses

'The coming musk-rose, full of dewy wine, / The murmurous haunt of flies on summer eves' (lines 49-50: *PJK*, p. 371). It is such poetry, uttered through the golden mask of Hellas (*persona* comes from *per sonare*, to sound through) that allows Keats, as Arnold said, to be ranked with Shakespeare himself.

Notes

1   John Milton, *Prose Selections*, ed. Merritt Y. Hughes (New York: Odyssey Press, 1947), p. 207.

2   Heinrich Heine, *Historisch-kritische Gesamtausgabe der Werke*, ed. Manfred Windfuhr. Dusseldorfer Ausgabe (Hamburg: Hoffman und Campe, 1973-), VIII, I, p. 126.

3   Thomas McFarland, *William Wordsworth; Intensity and Achievement* (Oxford: Clarendon Press, 1992), p. 93.

4   W. B. Yeats, *A Vision, a reissue with the author's final revisions* (1956: New York: Macmillan, 1969), p. 91.

5   Yeats, *A Vision*, p. 104.

6   Yeats, *A Vision*, p. 86.

7   W. B. Yeats, *Autobiographies* (London: Macmillan, 1955), p. 189.

8   W. B. Yeats, *Collected Poems* (London: Macmillan, 1961), p. 106.

9   Roland Barthes, *S/Z*, trans. Richard Miller, preface by Richard Howard (New York: Hill and Wang, 1974), pp. 211-12.

10   *The Poetical Works of Matthew Arnold*, ed. C. B. Tinker and H. F. Lowry (London, New York, Toronto: Oxford University Press, 1950), p. 2.

11   Presumably emulating Bate's example, Robert Gittings also uses merely the title *John Keats* for his own, later and culminating study of the great poet (London: Heinneman, 1968).

12   *TLS*, 4,478, (Jan 27-Feb 2, 1989), p. 90.

13   *The Letters of Percy Bysshe Shelley*, ed. Frederick L. Jones (Oxford: Clarendon Press, 1964), II, p. 117.

14   Walter Jackson Bate, *John Keats* (Cambridge, Mass.: The Belknap Press of Harvard University Press, 1963), pp. 19-20.

15   Bate, *John Keats*, p. 430.

16   Thomas McFarland, *Originality and Imagination* (Baltimore and London: John Hopkins University Press, 1985) pp. 145-6.

17   McFarland, *Originality and Imagination*, p. 146.

18   Brenda S. Webster, *Yeats; A Psychoanalytic Study* (Stanford: Stanford University Press, 1973), p. 3.

19   Marcel Mauss, *Sociology and Psychology: Essays*, trans. Ben Brewster (London, Boston and Henley: Routledge & Kegan Paul, 1979), p. 79.

13 Locationary Acts: Blake's *Jerusalem* and Hölderlin's *Patmos*

ANGELA ESTERHAMMER

'Rien n'aura eu lieu que le lieu'.
Mallarmé.

The English language offers a beguiling (if etymologically spurious) affinity between *location* and *locution*, place and utterance, that can help engage William Blake's *Jerusalem* and Friedrich Hölderlin's *Patmos*, two poems that unite a focus on place with a distinctive illocutionary or performative dimension of language. The significant interaction between place and utterance in these texts is also encapsulated in the ambiguity of the word *address*, in which the nominal sense of location (one's address) is bound up with a verbal sense of relationship (*how* one is addressed or approached, primarily in writing or dialogue). One could also point to the term *positing*, a putting-in-place that now typically connotes an effect of language, particularly the language of literature. A scientist, using mathematical or natural languages, may posit the existence of black holes, just as a novelist may posit the existence of Northanger Abbey or of Victor Frankenstein's creature. And if to posit is to *give* something a place, our languages also allow us to describe action as a *taking place*, as *avoir lieu* or *stattfinden*. In this discussion, I would like to explore connections among all these concepts – the act of utterance, dialogic interaction or address, and the creation of places – with the goal of identifying some distinctively Romantic ways in which, even across national boundaries, utterance itself takes, and makes, place.

The ultimate paradigm for the creation of place through utterance, which is never quite forgotten nor forgettable in Romantic literature, is God's creation of the world through acts of speech. The scene of creation by the word in the first chapter of Genesis presents the deity as a stable (if inscrutable) consciousness who uses utterance to bring phenomena into existence, then brings them into relationship with himself by naming and blessing them. Significantly, the God of Genesis has no need for an

178

audience nor for accepted verbal formulas to ensure the performative effect of his words, let alone to legitimate or confirm his own identity.[1] His utterances are neither conventional nor dialogic. If anything, they rely on and reveal the nature of speech itself, as an entity that is both spiritual and material. It exists both within the speaking consciousness (as concept or structure) and outside of it (as voice, breath, vibration). Thus we might posit that, when God speaks, the material or sensible aspect of the signifier takes on an ultimate exteriority and becomes objectified as a place uttered or 'outered' from him. Dialogic interaction only becomes possible as a result of God's initial creative utterances, which bring the heaven and the earth, Eden, and humankind into being as places to which God can address himself.

The Book of Revelation, the main precursor text for both Blake's *Jerusalem* and Hölderlin's *Patmos*, responds to Genesis by heralding the creation of a new heaven and earth. Here, too, utterance has a crucial role in creation, although the verbal dimension of Revelation is often eclipsed by the book's spectacular visual effects. Northrop Frye identifies the words of God in Revelation 21:5, 'Behold, I make all things new', as the ultimate antitype of 'Let there be light'[2] – that is, as a new world-creating performative that echoes and revises the original creative word. If the words of God effect the creation of a specific place – the new Jerusalem – and the words of the writer, John of Patmos, repeat that act of creation as an experience shared with a reading audience, these creative utterances are again presented as the words of a stable consciousness whose own place is specifically determined: God speaks from the heavenly throne, and John is granted a vision of heaven from his vantage point on the isle of Patmos. In contrast to Genesis, however, speech acts in Revelation take place in a multivocal and dialogic context. The first verse of the book asserts that vision is passed on in a communicative chain from God, to Jesus, to an angel, to John, and by John to God's servants. Unlike the words of God in Genesis, the speech acts of Revelation are from the beginning directed to and intended for an audience (or rather for several audiences), and they establish reflective and typological relationships between a new and an old earth, and a new and an old Jerusalem.

This interlocutory and relational context foreshadows the role of performative utterance in *Jerusalem* and *Patmos*. In re-creating for themselves the vision presented in Revelation, Blake and Hölderlin again make all things new. Above all, the new and distinctively Romantic quality of their writing lies in the way both create place through language – not, as God or even John does in Revelation, by referring to a place outside of the self, but by locating themselves in relation to other consciousnesses. The address and dialogue already contained in Revelation become constitutive elements of the creation of place in Romantic poetry, since it is only by placing themselves in relation to an addressee (whether God, a human being, or even another text) that Blake and Hölderlin can evoke the places their titles name. Apocalyptic places in Romantic poetry are neither places perceived as external to the subject, nor the places from which objective visions can be perceived. Rather, they coalesce in the spaces that the very concepts of vision and utterance have opened up between subject and object, seer and vision, speaker and addressee. Jerusalem and Patmos come into existence there where networks of dialogic and hermeneutic relationships are established – that is, in/as the texts themselves. The interactive elements in the representational mode of Revelation are here developed into a fully performative phenomenology.

In beginning *Jerusalem* with an address 'To the Public', Blake is in line with the publishing conventions of his time, according to which a prefatory address 'To the Reader' or a concluding advertisement directed 'To the Public' often appeared in books or tracts. But when he goes on to address subsequent chapters of the poem 'To the Jews', 'To the Deists', and 'To the Christians', his prefaces come to resemble Christ's prefatory addresses in the Book of Revelation to 'the seven churches which are in Asia'. Just as Christ addresses praise or admonition to each of the churches, Blake prefaces each of his four chapters with a prose characterization of each audience and its achievements or errors. Christ's representation of the seven churches depends on his identity as a uniquely privileged knower, and readers of Revelation are implicitly asked to accept that his account of the churches is an objective and accurate one. He begins each address with an assertion of his secure, eternal identity (e.g., 'These things saith the Amen, the faithful and true witness, the beginning of the creation of God' [Rev. 3:14]), which is followed in every case by the authoritative formula, 'I know thy works'. Blake's prefaces, however, imply no such objective knowledge on the part of the observing consciousness. Blake addresses groups that are defined by ideology, rather than by history or geography, groups that have been or are being named by him rather than having named themselves. The Deists Blake addresses in Chapter Three of *Jerusalem* would hardly accept his definition of Deism as Natural Religion, from which 'all the Destruction . . . in Christian Europe has arisen' (plate 52; E201)[3] – indeed, this is a reversal of the charge that a Deist like Tom Paine levelled against Christians. Whereas Christ in Revelation identifies each church by its geographical address (Ephesus, Smyrna, Philadelphia, and so on), Blake's addresses create the place where the addressee is located. Thus Blake locates the Deists 'in the State named Rahab' (plate 52; E200), playing on the ambiguity of 'state' as both psychological disposition and physical location. The sense of physical and political place is emphasized by his association of Deism with the 'Laws of . . . Babylon'. Rather than pre-existing the text, let alone being represented objectively within it, the addressees of Blake's prefaces only come into being through the writing of *Jerusalem*, and the act of locating them in relation to the speaker is part of the project of creating a place named Jerusalem as the habitation of Blake's Christians.

The creation of places happens with overwhelming frequency in this poem, and many aspects of place would need to be explored – including the continuous transformation of places, characters, and psychological states into one another, Blake's idiosyncratic use of 'states' to refer at once to geographical, political, ethical, and psychological places, and the process by which *spaces* are opened up and made into *places* by being named, endowed with attributes, and inhabited by characters. Blake's use of places, or at least place-names, is also one of the most alienating aspects of reading *Jerusalem*, since names are often piled up in the kind of impenetrable passage that V. A. De Luca called a 'wall of words', whereby the poet seems to claim an ability to give existence and meaning to places by positing or simply enunciating their names.[4]

> And the Forty Counties of England are thus divided in the Gates
> Of Reuben Norfolk, Suffolk, Essex. Simeon Lincoln, York Lancashire
> Levi. Middlesex Kent Surrey. Judah Somerset Glouster Wiltshire.
> Dan. Cornwal Devon Dorset, Napthali, Warwick Leicester Worcester
> Gad. Oxford Bucks Harford. Asher, Sussex Hampshire Berkshire
> Issachar, Northampton Rutland Nottgham. Zebulun Bedford Huntgn Camb
> Joseph Stafford Shrops Heref. Benjamin, Derby Chesire Monmouth
> And Cumberland Northumberland Westmoreland & Durham are
> Divided in the Gates of Reuben, Judah Dan & Joseph (16.43-51; E160).

It is difficult to know what meaning or illocutionary force to ascribe to a passage like this, unless it is that the very utterance of the names, each after his kind, is to forge relationships among them and bring forth a new spatial structure in the reader's mind.

At several points in the poem, Blake's characters literally create places out of verbal utterances. First, a negative example: toward the end of *Jerusalem*, the Daughters of Albion take a 'Falshood' that their sister Gwendolen has hidden in her left hand behind her back, and make it into the land of Canaan. In uttering her Falshood, Gwendolen counsels her sisters to assert the dominance of the Female Will, to involve all humanity in a religion of chastity and warfare and enclose it within the limits of physical nature. Terrified of being overcome by Los and the Sons of Albion, the Daughters take this Falshood and make it into a space:

> it grew &, grew till it
> Became a Space & an Allegory around the Winding Worm
> They named it Canaan & built for it a tender Moon
> Los smild with joy thinking on Enitharmon & he brought
> Reuben from his twelvefold wandrings & led him into it
> Planting the Seeds of the Twelve Tribes & Moses & David
> And gave a Time & Revolution to the Space Six Thousand Years
> He calld it Divine Analogy[.] (84.32-85.7; E243).

In a demonic parody of the world-creating utterance of God, here it is the false counsel uttered by a female that shapes the biblical Promised Land and the six-thousand-year space of human history, places that all the while retain their identity as forms of language, as 'Allegory' and 'Divine Analogy'.

The positive or, in Blakean parlance, 'apocalyptic' contrary to this creation of place is Los's building of Golgonooza, the City of Art, which is Blake's most specific counterpart to the heavenly Jerusalem described in Revelation. In Chapter One of the poem, Los and his Labourers create Golgonooza out of reified emotions and illocutionary acts:

> The stones are pity, and the bricks, well wrought affections:
> Enameld with love & kindness, & the tiles engraven gold
> Labour of merciful hands: the beams & rafters are forgiveness:
> The mortar & cement of the work, tears of honesty: the nails,
> And the screws & iron braces, are well wrought blandishments,
> And well contrived words, firm fixing, never forgotten,
> Always comforting the remembrance: the floors, humility,
> The cielings, devotion: the hearths, thanksgiving[.] (12.30-7; E155).

These positive and negative examples of creation through utterance are abbreviated and literalized instances of the constructionist project of the entire poem, which ends, famously, with the naming of Jerusalem itself: 'And I heard the Name of their Emanations they are named Jerusalem' (99.5; E259). Like the speech acts with which Los builds Golgonooza (forgiveness, blandishments, thanksgiving), and like Gwendolen's false counsel to her sisters, the poet's naming of Jerusalem is a discursive act.

The name 'Jerusalem' is established through dialogue: because the poet has once heard it, he can repeat it to others. It echoes back from him. But the previous examples of characters who create place through utterance cast a shadow over Blake's last act of naming. Does the creation of Jerusalem partake more of Gwendolen's Falshood, the lie that forms the Promised Land and the history of the world, or of Los's construction of a City of Art? Even on its own, the final line of the poem is strangely unstable. It is hard to determine where the poet is located when he hears and repeats the name of Jerusalem – inside Jerusalem, so as to know it intimately, or outside, so as to view it objectively? He seems to be in two places at once: inside, because at the climax of the poem Jerusalem overspreads all nations and is identified as the Emanation of all human forms; outside, because the poet still appears to be a viewer rather than a participant in the poem's final scene, where, like John of Patmos, he hears Jehovah speak from his holy place and sees before him a pageant of living forms.

Blake's creation and discovery of Jerusalem depends on this claim to an authority that is both subjective and objective. A dramatic illustration of the text's conflicted declarative force is found in the preface to Chapter Two, where Blake appears ready to ground the claim made by his title-page, that Jerusalem is the Emanation of Albion, in independent research findings that reveal Britain to be 'the Primitive Seat of the Patriarchal Religion' (plate 27; E171). Yet his move to make his claim dependent on external evidence ('If it is true: my title-page is also True') is abruptly abandoned in favour of outright declaration ('It is True, and cannot be controverted'). Readers are asked to accept that the guarantor of truth is not evidence but the act of declaration itself. The ambiguity of the preface to Chapter Two is mirrored on a larger scale by the poem as a whole, which begins with a title page that already declares the identity of Jerusalem as 'The Emanation of The Giant Albion', and ends with an identification of Jerusalem that is apparently motivated (if not 'proven') by the series of visions the poet has just related. The final line is 'legitimated', if at all, by the language and action of the poem, which is based on the identification posited by its title, which is legitimated only in the poem's conclusion, and so on and on in a hermeneutic, but perhaps also a vicious, circle.

This tension between referentiality and performativity is the tension that J. Hillis Miller comes back to again and again in his recent book on speech acts and topography, identifying it as the aporia of performative language itself, which claims a cognitive and a rhetorical basis at once. It claims to report or describe, but also to posit or found.[5] A simultaneous reporting ('And I heard the Name of their Emanations') and positing ('they are named Jerusalem') is what takes place in Blake's final line, the two actions separated just enough to cause uneasiness over which has priority or legitimacy. Throughout the poem, this undecidability is heightened by the dialogic context within which the poet locates states and addressees in relation to himself, even while he remains unstably positioned both inside and outside Jerusalem.

The self-positing and self-positioning of the subject is a still more radical activity in Hölderlin's *Patmos*, which resembles *Jerusalem* in adopting the name of a place as its title and in highlighting discursive address, in addition to being approximately contemporary with Blake's poem (the title pages are dated 1803 and 1804, although both poets continued to revise the texts after this date). In centring on place and on dialogic address, *Patmos* is also typical of Hölderlin's oeuvre as a whole. The majority of his mature poems, having titles like 'Heidelberg', 'Stuttgart', 'The Neckar', 'The Rhein', 'The Archipelagus', 'Homeland', and 'Sung under the Alps', evoke either specific places or an intense conception of home. Many of his earlier poems of the 1790s, on the other hand, follow the eighteenth-century practice of using a dedication or address as title (e.g., 'To Neuffer', 'To Diotima', 'To the Aether', 'To Our Great Poets'), so that they open up a dialogic situation from the very beginning. A combination of the two elements obtains in several of Hölderlin's most important poems, so that their title is the name of the place and immediately below the title is a dedication. This is the case with *Patmos*, sub-titled 'To the Landgrave of Homburg'. The address to the Landgrave (who is himself identified not by name, but by the title that connects him with a place), and the poet's positioning of himself in relation to his addressee, informs whatever meaning the title 'Patmos' eventually assumes.

The experience of Hölderlin's poem, in other words, is threefold, consisting in the interrelated acts of locating Patmos, locating an addressee, and locating the self. The first stanza (which acts as a frame or preface for the main action of the poem, the spiritual journey that will bring the poet toward Patmos), situates itself by direct address – not to the Landgrave of Homburg, but to God. It begins by positing the nearness of God and ends with a prayer for whatever is necessary for a safe journey to the far places where friends live. The immediate perlocutionary effect of this prayer is to remove the poet from his home and reposition him in Asia Minor:

> So sprach ich, da entführte
> Mich schneller, denn ich vermuthet
> Und weit, wohin ich nimmer
> Zu kommen gedacht, ein Genius mich
> Vom eigenen Hauß' (II, p.165).[6]

> (So I spoke, when more swiftly
> Than ever I had expected,

And far as I never thought
I should come, a Genius carried me
From my own house) (p. 463).

The poet's ensuing struggle to get his bearings and determine his geographical location parallels a hermeneutic effort to locate himself in relation to other texts and other consciousnesses. What begins as a description of a visionary journey to Patmos quickly becomes a performative project whereby the text itself constructs the relationships that *constitute* Patmos. Even in geographical terms, the journey involves establishing a relative position. Once the poet finds himself in Asia Minor, in the neighbourhood of the mountains Tmolus and Messogis, the river Pactolus, and the Taurus range, he discovers he must retreat westward again from this lavish, dazzling, exotic landscape to a more spiritual island. More important, though, is the fact that he never actually reaches Patmos at all. Rather, his account of the journey gives way to the expression of his *desire* to arrive there:

Und da ich hörte
Der nahegelegenen eine
Sei Patmos,
Verlangte mich sehr,
Dort einzukehren und dort
Der dunkeln Grotte zu nahn (II, p.166).

(And when I *heard*
That of the near islands one
Was Patmos,
I greatly *desired*
There to be lodged, and there
To approach the dark grotto) (p. 465; my italics).

In the Bible Patmos is a place that, when actually visited, gives access to visions, but in Hölderlin's time there is only the desire to visit Patmos and the re-creation of it through interpretation of scriptural texts, including the Gospel of John and Revelation. No longer a fixed location, Hölderlin's Patmos is a *locution* – a place he *hears of*, as Blake hears the name Jerusalem.

Patmos, then, is a place built out of desire and echoing voices – or, alternatively, out of love and hermeneutics. The fifth stanza establishes it as a place of compassion for shipwrecks, exiles, and refugees, a place that gladly hears the approach of strangers, a place whose voices echo back their laments. This attribute, in turn, makes possible an identification between the seer John, who fled to Patmos when his experience as a disciple of Christ was over, and the poet, who flees there in spirit during an age when God/Christ is absent. Once this identification is posited, the poem continues with its story-within-a-story, an embedded narrative of John's experience in the presence of Christ and after Christ's death. The island – or, perhaps better, the *idea* – of Patmos is a connective, a bridge between the present and past of the narrative, a place where the willing listener and the stranger with a story to tell may echo one another's sighs. Similarly, the speaker in Hölderlin's poem is not a unified subject who could travel to Patmos, but rather one who creates himself out of his identification with John and the forlorn disciples, on the one hand, and with fellow interpreters, on the other.

Among his fellow interpreters is the Landgrave of Homburg, Friedrich Ludwig, a pious man who had shown kindness and condescension toward Hölderlin at their recent meeting in Regensburg and had expressed his desire for a poem that would answer the claims of modern biblical interpreters. Hölderlin's initial dedication of the poem to him finally comes to the fore in the penultimate stanza, where he places himself in relation to the Landgrave as one who is also loved by the gods and respects their will:

> Und wenn die Himmlischen jezt
> So, wie ich glaube, mich lieben
> Wie viel mehr Dich,
> Denn Eines weiß ich,
> Daß nemlich der Wille
> Des ewigen Vaters viel
> Dir gilt (II, p. 171).

> (And if the Heavenly now
> Love me as I believe,
> How much more you
> They surely love,
> For one thing I know:
> The eternal Father's will
> Means much to you) (p. 475).

It is apparent from Hölderlin's drafts that this penultimate stanza was actually the first one to be written; indeed, even before Hölderlin's first meeting with the Landgrave, this moment of identification between *I* and *you* had been composed and was waiting to be incorporated into a poem.[7]

Conversely, *Patmos* was first composed as a poem awaiting an addressee: in the first full draft, a space was left beneath the title for a dedication that was not yet there. Hölderlin writes out of a relation between subject and addressee, but it is a relation that exists *in language* before it corresponds to a specific person or an actual experience. In the context of the completed poem, the second-person address comes in only at the end and depends explicitly on the loving relationship between the poet and God that has been negotiated within the text. In other words, Hölderlin's addressee appears as a *product* of the experience of interpretation that *Patmos* enacts – and the poet's own identity is formed in the act of placing himself in relation to this newly-generated addressee. As Johann Christian Friedrich Hölderlin, his very name bears the traces of all those with whom he stands in relation: his two addressees (God and the Landgrave Friedrich) and the object of his interpretation (John/Johannes, the disciple and seer).

This placing-in-relation – which represents at least the prelude to interpretation, if not the experience of interpretation itself – is the essential experience of *Patmos*, to some extent of all of Hölderlin's mature poetry, and perhaps even of a good deal of Romantic poetry. Rather than creating a world through authoritative utterance, the Romantic poet creates a relationship between self and world through discursive utterance. *Patmos* and *Jerusalem* reveal the extent to which utterance not only creates a visionary place, but, for a destabilized (which is to say human) speaker, also creates the place from which vision can be experienced. Even at the end of *Patmos*, what is fixed and existing is the text (*der veste Buchstab*); the poetic self is only positioned in relation to this fixed point, 'following' or orienting itself by it (*Dem folgt deutscher Gesang*).

Both *Patmos* and *Jerusalem*, then, foreground and develop the dialogic structure that is latent in Revelation, and in doing so raise questions that are vital to both Romantic and contemporary thought. If Blake acknowledges (but does not necessarily endorse) the use of effectual language by characters in his poems, and if, in the prefaces to *Jerusalem*, he himself lays claim to the authority of a privileged speaker and knower, his manner of doing so also complicates the issue of authority and language. His work is thus particularly relevant to questions of performativity as they have been formulated by, for instance, J. Hillis Miller or Jean-François Lyotard, who have explored the relative priority of performative language and power.[8] Hölderlin lacks even Blake's problematic declarative voice, and in his work all sources of stability for the speaking subject must be generated by the poetic utterance in its relation to the world. This radical re-establishing of a place from which to speak has made Hölderlin a compelling point of reference for twentieth-century Continental philosophy. It leads Heidegger to ontologize the Hölderlinian notion of place as the clearing opened up by language, while Nancy and Lévinas de-ontologize both Hölderlin and Heidegger and conclude that Being has no place.[9]

While contemporary theory thus takes its cue from the issues raised by Blake and Hölderlin, their rewriting of apocalyptic place is fully representative of Romantic sensibility. This includes, in general, the emphasis on processes and relations that was displacing Enlightenment models of representation and inquiry. The modification of the specular experience of biblical apocalypse into a discursive or dialogic mode of revelation is in sympathy with aspirations (reflected, for instance, in Goethe's *Faust*) to replace the subject-object model of scientific investigation with a more experiential way of knowing. *Patmos*, in particular, resonates with the hermeneutic impulse of Romantic theorists such as Schleiermacher and Coleridge, for whom reading and knowing are essentially relational experiences. P. B. Shelley, among others, speaks for the Romantic re-definition of poetry as relational and self-reflexive when, in *A Defence of Poetry*, he characterizes the historical development of the arts as a gradual convergence of the mode of representation with the thing represented:

> The savage (for the savage is to ages what the child is to years) expresses the emotions produced in him by surrounding objects in a similar manner; and language and gesture, together with plastic or pictorial imitation, become the image of the combined effect of those objects, and of his apprehension of them. Man in society, with all his passions and his pleasures, next becomes the object of the passions and pleasures of man; an additional class of emotions produces an augmented treasure of expressions; and language, gesture, and the imitative arts, become at once the representation and the medium, the pencil and the picture, the chisel and the statue, the chord and the harmony (*SPP*, p. 481).

Jerusalem and *Patmos* go even further in manifesting the self-reflexive self-consciousness of Romanticism. They exemplify an awareness of utterance itself as an event that effects changes in the circumstances in which it takes place, that alters both speaker and addressee, resulting in the paradoxical state whereby the utterance both depends on *and creates* the conditions of its effectiveness. This performative consciousness can be traced through a wide range of Romantic-period texts, from political writing to philosophical arguments about the way language shapes a speaker's thought and world. In practical terms, for instance Tom Paine's awareness of the power of language to alter perception, and thus shift the balance of power, affects both the style and content of his writing; on a theoretical level, performative consciousness is a key feature of the linguistic philosophy of Herder and Wilhelm von Humboldt.

The effect of exploring the phenomenological and performative dimensions of *Jerusalem* and *Patmos* is that the title of each must finally be read as a reference to the speech act that is the poem, but simultaneously re-literalized as the name of a place. The 'wall of words' that is *Jerusalem* is, after all, Jerusalem's wall, or rather the poem's four chapters are four walls in which, as in the heavenly city, Blake would claim, every stone finds its fit place. *Patmos*, on the other hand, is (as in the Bible) the place from which revelation begins, in the sense that the poem's final line brings Hölderlin into the fellowship of interpreters whose utterances constitute 'German song' (which is to say, for Hölderlin, modern Western poetry). This also means that in the Romantic texts the doubleness of the title of the Book of Revelation is fully realized at last, since they demonstrate that a *revelation* is not only that which is seen but the process or event of seeing, and that the vision and the process, the place and the experience, are one.

Notes

1   See Angela Esterhammer, *Creating States: Studies in the Performative Language of John Milton and William Blake* (Toronto: University of Toronto Press, 1994), pp. 42-64; Sandy Petrey, 'Speech Acts in Society: Fish, Felman, Austin and God', *Texte*, 3 (1984), pp. 43-61; J. Hillis Miller, *Topographies* (Stanford: Stanford University Press, 1995), pp. 156-8). All these critics have emphasized the fundamental differences between the speech acts of Genesis 1 and J. L. Austin's definition of the performative as a contextualized, rule-governed utterance.

2   Northrop Frye. *The Great Code: The Bible and Literature* (Toronto: Academic Press, 1982).

3   All quotations from *Jerusalem* are from *The Complete Poetry and Prose of William Blake*, ed. David V. Erdman (Berkeley: University of California Press, rev edn, 1982) and are identified by plate and (where applicable) line numbers.

4   V. A. De Luca. 'A Wall of Words: The Sublime as Text', in *Unnam'd Forms: Blake and Textuality*, ed. Nelson Hilton and Thomas A. Vogler (Berkeley: University of California Press, 1986), pp. 445-77.

5   Miller characterizes his book as exemplifying 'this strange feature of speech acts, that they may create that in the name of which they speak': 'Each chapter, then, contributes a new view of a terrain that always seems to have been there already when we move into it, though the text and its reading, it may be, are performative speech acts bringing the terrain into existence. It is impossible to make a decision about that, since the only way to approach the terrain is through the readings' (p. 5). Miller later makes a similar point about landscapes in the novel: 'Novels themselves aid in making the landscape that they apparently presuppose as already made and finished' (p. 16). He uses this 'strange feature of speech acts' as the basis for a critique of Heidegger (pp. 216-54).

6   German language quotations from *Patmos* are from Friedrich Hölderlin, *Sämtliche Werke*, ed. Friedrich Beissner. 8 vols. (Stuttgart: Kohlhammer, 1946-85) and are identified by volume and page numbers in the text. English translations are from Friedrich Hölderlin, *Poems and Fragments*, trans. Michael Hamburger (Cambridge: Cambridge University Press) and are identified by page numbers in the text.

7   Werner Kirchner, 'Hölderlins Patmos-Hymne: Dem Landgrafen von Homburg überreichte Handschrift', in *Hölderlin: Aufsätze zu seiner Homburger Zeit*, ed. Alfred Kelletat (Göttingen: Vandenhoeck and Ruprecht, 1967), pp. 57-68.

8   See for, instance, Lyotard's analysis of how the linking of phrases 'presents' a universe, or creates the power structures that constitute 'reality'. He suggests that successful performativity, not social context, creates power: 'the phrase *The meeting is called to order* is not performative because its addressor is the chairperson of the meeting. The addressor is the chairperson of the meeting to the extent that the phrase in question is performative', *The Differend: Phrases in Dispute*, trans. Georges Van Den Abbeele (Minneapolis: University of Minnesota Press, 1988).

9   These philosophical positions are summarised and critiqued by Hent de Vries in 'Theotopographies: Nancy, Hölderlin, Heidegger', *Modern Language Notes*, 109 (1994), pp. 445-77. According to the reading proposed in my essay, the place that Romantic poetry reveals has existence, but as an act; it *is* not, but it *happens*.

14 The Romantics: Cosmopolitan or Nationalist?

MARY ANNE PERKINS

Late twentieth-century critical theory has increasingly 'placed' the philosophies of Romanticism as idealist, élitist, inconsistent, and escapist. While some have challenged this representation,[1] many specialists in this field have accepted the characterization of the Romantics as pursuing an impossible principle of unity and devoted to the distortions of a dominant, all-devouring Subject. One of the aspects of Romantic preoccupation which is most likely to provoke the suspicions of twentieth-century hindsight is the promotion of nationalistic ideals. The adoption of Romantic themes, language and ideology by twentieth-century fascist leaders has strengthened this suspicion. A powerful and dark side to Romanticism has been seen to lend itself too easily to evil purposes. Although writers such as Hans Kohn and Carlton Hayes have shown that not all expressions of national identity combine with racism, xenophobia and chauvinism, the suspicion remains and evidence is not lacking to confirm it. A liberal nationalism is now, it seems, a contradiction in terms.

The link between Romanticism and nationalism has been attributed primarily to German thinkers who were the first to associate national cultural ideals and a sense of a unique and glorious history with a national language which both reflected and shaped a superior moral character. An important factor here was the Lutheran renaissance of this period through which an emphasis on the divine Word became associated with the purity of the German language, the *Ursprache*. Fichte, Schelling, Arndt and Jahn all point to Luther as a heroic German archetype who not only opposed Rome, like the Hermann figure of German myth, but extolled the intellectual and moral beauty of the German language and its fitness for the communication of God's Word. In England, S. T. Coleridge declares that 'In Luther's own German writing, and eminently in his translation of the bible, the *German* language commenced. I mean the language as it is at present *written;* that which is called the HIGH GERMAN' (*BL* I, p. 210). Luther had linked nationhood to language and truth in a way which became irresistible to the Protestant nationalisms of the Romantic period. He had shown that worldly mediators between God and the individual conscience are unnecessary; the Word itself was the sole mediator and authority over conscience. This idea, now deeply rooted in European Protestant thought, strengthened the new philosophical emphases of the late eighteenth century on language and its relationship to thought and identity. In this way the origin and evolution of the language of a people, a *volk*, was embued with a spiritual character; it became the medium and the manifestation – the incarnation – of national spirit. Language was explored as a living power which reconciled the polarity of infinite and finite consciousness and carried the divine revelation of a unique mission. Luther's stand against Rome was seen as analogous to German resistance to the imperialism of French culture; here again, it was the authority of the Word, in this case of the German language, which would prevail.

Luther's influence was not the only source of this emphasis on language and literature as the focus of national identity. Germany had to find a basis for unity which could neither be provided by the historical continuity of a Constitution, as in England, nor by the political and social revolution of a free people, as in France. German writers had to look elsewhere for inspiration; J. G. Herder, himself reflecting the Protestant ideals of individual freedom of inquiry, and the sacredness of language, provided the paradigm. The unique spirit of each particular nation, he claimed, is expressed and represented in its history, its culture and, perhaps most of all, in its language.

An inspirational source for Herder, as for his mentor, Hamann, and other Protestant precursors of Romanticism, was the mysticism of Jakob Böhme. This emphasised the divine source of the original gift of human language, given to Adam in Eden. As James McKusick has shown, Böhme's 'explication of the German language presupposes that its words contain traces, or "signatures", of the spiritual essences they represent . . . The German language, and not some dead language of antiquity, represents . . . the paradigm case of a natural language, . . . it is a transparent medium of spiritual truth'.[2] It is a short step from this to the idea that the German people received a unique divine calling, reflected in its own particular language which then mirrored the creative and redemptive activity of the divine Word.

The links between Protestantism, nationalism and language did not remain confined to the propagation of a German language and literature. They became a wider basis of philosophical and political theory. The principle of the divine Word, the *Logos,* at the heart of S. T. Coleridge's search for a unified system is not merely epistemological, moral, and ontological, nor is its significance confined to aesthetics or poetics in relation to national character. The *Logos,* as the incarnation of Will in the form of Reason, becomes the very symbol of nationhood itself through which Coleridge attempts to reconcile a metaphysic of language, a philosophical and political theory of nationhood, with the idea of the nation. The divine Word, for him, is the living Idea of nationhood; that is, the *Logos*, as *Deus alter et idem* [God who is Other and the Same], is both the principle of mediation and reconciliation to unity, on the one hand, and. on the other, that of distinction.[3]

Of course, the term 'Romantic' is not entirely appropriate if applied to this aspect of Coleridge's work which draws on ancient classical and theological sources. Nor can it properly be applied to German Idealist philosophy as a whole. Nevertheless, the extent of cross-fertilization between the great Idealist systems and the ideologies of Romanticism should not be ignored; an obvious example is the parallel (though this should not be overdrawn) between Coleridge's view and Hegel's presentation of the *Logos* as the ideal of the rational will incarnated within the state.

Peter Alter uses the term 'awakeners' for those who believed that 'the existence of a nation was a function of a shared language, and that linguistic uniformity was the precondition of a nation-state'. For these, language provided 'a criterion of differentiation' and became 'a kind of status symbol, the object of a whole variety of scientific and literary enterprises'.[4] Certainly, the Romantics' nationalism is closely linked with their philosophies and histories of language, their etymological searches, their theories of symbolism and poetry. The associations which these 'awakeners' made between the origin, development and relative purity of language and national moral development could all too easily be expanded to support the idea of divine favour for a 'Chosen People'. A. W. Schlegel, for example, claims in his *Lectures on Literature and Art*, 1803-4 that the purity and primitive roots of the German language, even when its debts to Greek and Latin are allowed, are in strong contrast to the composite neo-Latin and English tongues. Languages which are derived in a kind of slavery from the domination of a foreign root, are, he claims, markedly inferior, limited and inadequate. Schlegel develops the idea of language as the key to national character. J. G. Fichte draws on Schlegel's work in his idealization of the early Germans and his claims for the superiority of the German language in comparison with the neo-latin languages .[5]

Fichte, though he cannot rightly be placed in the Romantic camp, substantially contributed to the development of a linguistic chauvinism in his *Speeches to the German Nation*. What distinguishes the Germans from other European peoples of Teutonic descent (such as the Scandinavians) is, he insists, precisely that their language is an original one – which 'broke forth among the same people, has developed continuously out of the actual common life of this people, and into which no element has ever entered that did not express an observation actually experienced by this people'.[6] This, he argues, makes the German people especially fitted to bring philosophy to its highest point,[7] and it is on these grounds that the importation of foreign words is damaging to the 'supersensuous' part of the language.[8]

The difference between Germans and other European branches of the Teutonic root is, he explains, that 'the former retained and developed the original language of the ancestral stock, whereas the latter adopted a foreign language and gradually reshaped it in a way of their own'.[9] The historical continuity which is required for true nationhood, is provided by the continuity of language:

> If we give the name of People to men whose organs of speech are influenced by the same external conditions, who live together, and who develop their language in continuous communication with each other, then we must say: The language of this people is necessarily just what it is, and in reality this people does not express its knowledge, but its knowledge expresses itself out of the mouth of the people.[10]

E.M. Arndt was another who sought to make language the basis for national unity, calling for all who spoke the German tongue in Lorraine, Alsace, Luxembourg, Flanders, to be reunited with the German empire.[11] Friedrich Schiller went so far as to claim that 'Our language will rule the world. Language is the mirror of a nation; when we look in this mirror we are faced with a great and noble reflection of ourselves'. He extolled 'the delicious treasures of the German language, which expresses everything, both the deepest and the most superficial, the spirit, the soul, and which is suffused with meaning'.[12]

The attempt to link theories of linguistic origin and development to national moral character was not confined to German thought. S. T. Coleridge, for example, often compares the merits and demerits of languages as vehicles of poetic or philosophic genius. The French, he asserts, have abandoned the concreteness of poetry for abstractions which distort philosophy.[13] His belief in the association of language with morality is clearly expressed in a note of 1809 in which he plans to write 'Of the apparent defects of a language which arise from the moral defects & false taste of a Nation' (*CN*, III, 3557).

At this point it may appear that the grounds on which Romanticism is placed as a source of the ideology of nationalism have been strengthened rather than challenged; for, until now, I have followed the common practice of ignoring those aspects which can stand as counterweights to the thesis. A different picture emerges from a closer scrutiny of the relationship between the centrality of linguistic studies and theories in this period, and the nationalism, if such it may be called, with which they have been associated.

A new and interesting perspective is gained on this question through the familiar Romantic and Idealist theme of distinction-in-unity. In relation to language, this model contributed to, for example, the consubstantiality of the symbol and its constitutive power. Both 'word' and 'nation' may be understood as symbols embodying the truth of Ideas. The reconciliation of particular with universal, of the many with the One, is the catalyst of their connection. In this case, the motif of the divine Word is used not so much to suggest a unique revelation and calling to a particular people but rather as a paradigm of reconciliation. The unique power of 'living words', particularly of symbols, is their embodiment in particular, finite and concrete form and thought of a universal which cannot be otherwise communicated. If 'an IDEA in the *highest* sense of that word cannot be expressed but by a *symbol* and 'all symbols of necessity involve an apparent contradiction' (*BL*, I, pp. 156-7) then the Idea of nationhood, expressed in a particular nation, must involve the apparent contradictions of the universal (represented by the cosmopolitan ideal), and the particular (represented by the ideal of patriotism).

The principle of individuation which Coleridge finds in the evolution of life, and the 'desynonymization' which, for him, marks the subtle distinctions of a morally and philosophically mature people, both connect with this idea of the necessary uniqueness of national identity. 'As society introduces new relations', he argues, 'it introduces new distinctions, and either new words are introduced or different pronunciations'.[14] Both Herder and Humboldt acknowledged this process. The latter writes, 'the number of synonyms always decreases with the degree of linguistic development';[15] conversely, this linguistic development becomes the paradigm of distinct national identity which is necessary for human social and political progress.

It is here that the nexus of 'word' and 'nation', becomes most interesting, for, with this model in mind, the insistence of the Romantics on the particularity and uniqueness of nationhood can no longer automatically be associated with exclusivity and chauvinism. It must rather be seen as *one* aspect of a struggle to realize both nationhood and a cosmopolitan, humanitarian ideal. The unique history, character and mission of *each* people, particularly as expressed in its evolved language, is seen by, for example, Herder, as the indispensable route to the progress of humanity as a whole. For him, 'a philosophical comparison of language would constitute the best essay on the history and diversified character of the human heart and understanding, for every language bears the stamp of the mind and character of a people'.[16] The study of particular nations is, he argues, the way to an understanding of our common humanity and to the ideals of universal progress and mutual understanding.

Wilhelm von Humboldt is another who links national character and national language, who finds French a language devoid of philosophical concepts and for whom German is closer to the Greek because it reflects what is natural, substantive and rich in contrast to both English and French.[17] Despite his general cosmopolitanism, Humboldt writes of the artifice of French (and, in some respects, English) culture, language, and philosophy which is, he suggests, 'often empty [of substance] and unnatural'.[18]

However, in Humboldt too the link between Word and nation is, on the whole, benign. Again, the principle of *relationship* through distinction-in-unity is at the core. 'Language' he argues, 'cannot be brought into reality by a single individual, but only socially, by the joining of one daring experiment to another . . . language must gain extension in a listener and a responder'. This characteristic of language is expressed by the pronoun, in its differentiation of the second person from the third and the relation of each to the first. For Humboldt, this is an example of how language itself both reflects and *effects* relational activity as an essential quality of humanity:

> Only through the joining, effected in language, of an 'other' to an 'I' do there arise all the profounder and nobler feelings which motivate the whole man, which in friendship and in love and in every communion of mind make the connection between two beings the loftiest and the most intimate of all connections.[19]

For Humboldt, words are 'the intelligible signs by which we determine the differing spheres of particular objects and by which we bring certain portions of our thought to unity, which need to bring themselves together'.[20] Language, he claims, is the medium through which man shapes the world and himself; it is the means by which he becomes aware that he is able to separate himself, as individual, from the external world.[21] Again, Luther's influence is clear: for example, when Humboldt describes language as 'not a work (*ergon*) but an activity (*energeia*)'.[22] Humbolt, like Herder, believes that the study of a nation's language is the key to its history, character, and stage of development.

Friedrich Meinecke has argued, however, that, for Humboldt, 'the national character most worthy of investigation was the one that best reflected the essential nature of humanity'.[23] Clearly, for Humboldt too, the tension between the cosmopolitan ideal and devotion to the fatherland is significant: 'Whoever occupies himself with philosophy and art belongs to his fatherland more intimately than others . . . Philosophy and art are more in need of one's own language, which emotion and reflection have formed and which forms them again in turn'.[24] Yet for Fichte, for Novalis and for himself, Humboldt, the very foundation of Germany's greatness is that it is most representative of, not particular, but universal humanity. Novalis writes, 'German nature is representative of genuine humanity and is therefore an ideal'. 'No nation', he insisted, 'can compete with us in vigorous universalism' – and again – 'German nature is cosmopolitanism mixed with the strongest individuality'.[25] Humboldt claims in his essay on the eighteenth century that the Germans are often criticized because they imitate other nations but that this is in fact an admirable quality which is flawed only by being carried to the extreme.[26]

Friedrich Schleiermacher is another who engages in the struggle to reconcile particular nationhood with a universal cosmopolitan ideal. The strength of his belief in the unique value of the individual is mirrored in his political and social criticism: 'Where', he asks, 'is foresight keeping close watch lest the country be seduced and its spirit corrupted? Where [can be found] . . . the individual character each state should have, and the acts that reveal it?'.[27] For him, the nation question is clearly related to wider philosophical, linguistic and hermeneutical issues. The emphasis which he places on the relational acts of communication and understanding between individuals is extended to the idea of national identity. Again, the model of distinction-in-unity is central. He writes, for example, of the dawning in his mind of his 'highest intuition': 'I saw clearly that each man is meant to represent humanity in his own way, combining its elements uniquely, so that it may reveal itself in every mode, and all that can issue from its womb be made actual in the fullness of unending space and time'.[28] This model is extended to a paradigm of distinct, unique nations uniting in a universal human community; it also parallels his hermeneutical theory. In the process of investigating the nature of understanding, Schleiermacher identifies two factors which, though normally unheeded, operate at the level of ordinary conversation. In addition to the personal message to be communicated (the 'particular element'), there is also a shared language between speaker and hearer, a 'universal element'. These two elements intersect and are interdependent in actual dialogue.[29]

For Schleiermacher, the incarnation of the divine Word provides the paradigm for this relation of the unity of the universal with the distinct and particular finite form. This is the key to understanding his claim that 'Christianity was, and remains, a language-producing power'.[30] Equally, his emphasis on the preservation of the uniqueness of nationalities must be understood in the light of a concept of relationships in which the ideal unity of the whole, whether of life, of love or of language, is dependent for its realization upon the hermeneutical acts of unique individuals. 'Whenever I notice an aptitude for individuality', he writes,

> inasmuch as love and sensitiveness, its highest guarantees, are present, there I also find an object for my love. I would have my love embrace every unique self, from the unsophisticated youth in whom freedom is but beginning to germinate, to the ripest and most finished type of man . . . His unique being and its relation to humanity is the object of my quest. I love him in the measure that I find and understand this individuality, but I can give him proof thereof only in proportion to his understanding of my own true self.[31]

It is neither the part nor the whole which should be the focus but the power, the energy of the relation itself. We would not, writes Schleiermacher, 'charge the failings of lovers to the weakness of love itself'; in the same way, it is not patriotism which makes for 'narrow partisanship', prejudice and contempt for other nations, but the failings of individuals. He insists that 'he who is not imbued with the worth of his own people and does not cling to it with love, will not value these things in another . . . And he who is not enlightened with the calling of his own people, knows not the mission characteristic of other peoples'.[32]

The influence of Fichte is evident: patriotism and cosmopolitanism are only realizable in conjunction, and no knowledge can be separated from this wider context of nationhood; for Schleiermacher even science has its national traits, for 'science depends essentially on language and therefore if it is not in the political sense patriotic, it is at least *volkstumlich*'.[33]

For Germans thinkers of this period, language is, paradoxically, not only the pure vehicle of the spirit of the German people, but also the image of the divine Word for humanity in general. It is characterized by freedom, together with that characteristic which. according to Herder, defines the human – reflective reason. Therefore language must be contemplated philosophically, critically, and must be recognized as always maintaining the character of polarity, of opposition and otherness. When A. W. Schlegel, Fichte and Humboldt link the Germans to the Greeks, the implicit claim to the superiority of the national language is striking. But this link also represents their emphasis on the ideals of philosophy, freedom and the ideal of the city state. The point is that the Greeks were archetypes of *humanity,* and it is this which is set up as the German mission. There are, of course, immense dangers here if the mission for universal humanity is seen as belonging exclusively to a chosen people, and if this mission is nothing less than the salvation of humanity as a whole.

The *displacing* of Romanticism through criticism which recognizes the cosmopolitan and humanitarian ideals of many of the nationalist writers is at one and the same time liberating and anxiety-provoking. The writers during this period of the emergence of European nationalisms cannot, we have seen, simply be dismissed as bigots only interested in the dominance of their own nation as the Chosen People. At the same time, their claims both to cultural, moral and intellectual superiority, often based on the concept of an *Ursprache,* and on the national tongue as the incarnation of a divinely inspired national spirit, clearly are not merely what would now be termed politically incorrect; they have a much more dangerous potential. How is it possible to accept this uncomfortable dichotomy? And how does it bear on wider questions of national character? The questions are important, for if the Romantics' pursuit of national identity is simply dismissed as the cradle of totalitarian, fascist and nationalist extremes, we risk failing to identify the real causes of bigotry and xenophobia by this mis-placement. Their solutions may be flawed, but these thinkers recognized the importance of the apparent dichotomy of nationhood and human community and the importance of the attempt to find a basis of reconciliation.

A passage in Eva Hoffman's *Lost in Translation* presents the question clearly. She writes of the country of her childhood, Poland, that it 'lives within me with a primacy that is a form of love', and then wonders whether the absolute nature of the 'first loves' of the particular 'colors and furrows of reality' is a form of blindness and self-deception. We grow out of our first childish loves, after all; we learn to be 'less indiscriminate and foolish in our enthusiasms'. But she suggests that there is a worse state into which we then risk falling: 'that other absurd, in which we come unpeeled from all the objects of the world, and they all seem equally two-dimensional and stale'. To avoid this, somehow we must 'retain the capacity for attachment, the energy of desire that draws us toward the world and makes us want to live within it'.[34] This, I suggest, is one aspect of what the Romantics perceived; their sense of national identity reflects this vital 'capacity for attachment'.

The suggestions of Ernest Gellner and Eric Hobsbawm that nationalisms will eventually decline or even disappear when the results of industrialization become increasingly global and international, seem suddenly unlikely in the light of recent developments.[35] If nations are here to stay, it will be necessary to increase our understanding of the roots, the development and the manifestations of nationalism. If the twentieth century has focused, above all, on language in the search for new philosophical, literary critical and theological insights, it may be time to re-assess the role of language in both shaping and reflecting the self-conscious identity of modern nation states. It may be possible, without demonizing Romantic nationalisms still further, to explore whether the stimulus of the distinction-in-unity model can help us to get beyond the extremes of, on the one hand, xenophobic and chauvinistic forms of nationalism, and, on the other, a vague cosmopolitanism – even a 'new world order' – which avoids the duties, responsibilities of commitment to the particular and the concrete.

The totalitarian idealism of Marxism with its commitment to a unity of theory which will inevitably be fulfilled in practice appears to have failed to vanquish nationalisms. On the other hand, the endlessly fragmenting and eventually indefinable localities of the postmodern world look just as unlikely to succeed. Perhaps, even if flawed, the Romantic postulate of an analogy between nation and word on the basis of distinction-in-unity may now be worth reassessing. Also, it may be no coincidence – as Schleiermacher's example suggests – that the development of hermeneutics as a discipline, and the emergence of the self-consciousness of national identity occurred at around the same time. The problem of 'otherness' recognized in the hermeneutical task is close to that which Eva Hoffman so vividly conveys in personal terms concerning language and nation. Displaced as a twelve-year-old girl, from post-war Poland to Canada, her ensuing crises of identity are closely bound up both with the 'loss' of language and with a sense of the loss of self. Finally, she adapts, and then finds herself able to observe, as it were from the outside, the process of her partial assimilation. She writes of the obsession with words which accompanied her sense of displacement: 'I gather them, put them away like a squirrel saving nuts for winter, swallow them and hunger for more. If I take in enough, then maybe I can incorporate the language, make it part of my psyche and my body. I will not leave an image unworded, will not let anything cross my mind till I find the right phrase to pin the shadow down . . . The thought that there are parts of the language I'm missing can induce a small panic in me, as if such gaps were missing parts of the world or my mind – as if the totality of the world and mind were coeval with the totality of language'.[36] Separated from her national identity and from her first language, she experienced a driving need to place herself in relation to another. There is a world of difference between these personal confessions and the high, philosophical language of the German Romantics; yet there is a common thread of insight into the closely interdependent reality of language, identity, selfhood and nationhood. As mere conceptual recognition this is neither positive nor negative but neutral. As *idea* (in the dynamic, ontological sense in which Schelling, Hegel or Coleridge distinguish idea from concept) 'nation' can be *either* positive or negative. This will partly depend on the contingencies of human and national identity and relations, but partly too, I suggest, on the extent to which individuals are willing and able to explore self-critically the history of the idea of nationhood in so far as it has shaped their own consciousness and experience. Although theirs is the period in which the modern nation-state emerged, the Romantics powerfully demonstrate that 'nation' is not merely identifiable with 'state' as a political entity, and that the cultural and historical aspects of nationhood are inextricably interwoven with the self-consciousness which develops contemporaneously with language. It may be important to recognize the likelihood, if this is the case, that attempts to combat the extremes of nationalism require a much broader base than political means alone.

Notes

1   Kathleen Wheeler has drawn attention to the anticipation of 'deconstructive gestures' in Romantic irony ('Coleridge and Modern Critical Theory', in *Coleridge's Theory of Imagination Today*, ed. Christine Gallant (New York: AMS Press, 1989), p. 100; and A. J. Harding has pointed out the neo-Romantic elements of New Criticism in 'Imagination, In and Out of Context', also in Gallant, p. 129.

2   James C. McKusick, *Coleridge's Philosophy of Language* (New Haven and London: Yale University Press, 1986), pp. 9-10.

3   'The only possible Unity of a Nation', Coleridge asserts, 'is Will = Reason'. This unity was to be found in Christ, the divine Word, divine Reason, for 'Christ, as the filial Godhead . . . is essentially & from everlasting was Will = Reason'. 'The Son is, relatively to the Father, the Distinctity in the One: relatively to the Sabaoth the Unity in the Distinctities' (*CN*, IV, 5078).

4   P. Alter, *Nationalism* (London: Edward Arnold, 1985), p. 60.

5   A. W. Schlegel, *Vorlesungen über schöne Litteratur und Kunst* (1803-4) is the source for most of these ideas. His *Geschichte der romantischen Literatur* contains others. For detailed references see, Xavier Leon, *Fichte et son temps* (Paris: Colin, 1922-27), II, pp. 422-433; III, pp. 67-68.

6   J. G. Fichte, *Addresses to the German Nation,* ed. G. A. Kelly, trans. R. F. Jones and G. H. Turnbull (New York: Harper and Row, 1968) p. 53.

7   'So we may say that genius in foreign lands will strew with flowers the well-trodden military roads of antiquity, and weave a becoming robe for that wisdom of life which it will easily take for philosophy. The German spirit, on the other hand, will open up new shafts and bring the light of day into their abysses, and hurl up rocky masses of thoughts, out of which ages to come will build their dwelling . . . the German spirit is an eagle, whose mighty body thrusts itself on high and soars on strong and well-practiced wings into the empyrean, that it may rise nearer to the sun whereon it delights to gaze'. Fichte, *Addresses,* pp. 73-74.

8   Fichte, *Addresses*, p. 53-54.

9   Fichte, *Addresses*, p. 47.

10   Fichte, *Addresses*, p. 49.

11   E. M. Arndt, *Geist der Zeit* (2nd edn), III, p. 313.

12   *Schillers Nachlass* in *Schiller. Schriften*, ed. K. Goedeke, Historisch-Kritische Ausgabe, vol. 11, (Stuttgart, 1871) p. 41.

13   See e.g., *TT*, I, p. 75, where Coleridge suggests that the French have replaced poetic concreteness with abstractions; and *TT*, I. p. 234n: 'I hate the flimsiness of the French language: – my very organs of speech are so anti-Gallican that they refuse to pronounce intelligibly their insipid tongue' (from *A Memoir of Charles Mayne Young* [1871], p. 115). While the German language is superb with regard to grammar and philosophy, it is unfitted for poetry (*CN*, II, 2431). Furthermore, 'German is inferior to English in modifications of expression of the affections"; although he acknowledged that German was superior 'in modifications of expression of all objects of the senses' (*TT*, I, p. 383). 'It may be doubted' he wrote, 'whether a composite language like the English is not a happier instrument of expression than a homogeneous one like the German. We possess a wonderful richness and variety of modified meanings in our Saxon and Latin quasi-synonyms, which the Germans have not' (*TT*, I, p. 320).

14   *The Philosophical Lectures of Samuel Taylor Coleridge*, ed. K. Coburn (London: Pilot Press, 1949) p. 369.

15   Wilhelm von Humboldt, 'Des achzehnte Jahrhundert', *Gesammelte Schriften* (1903), II, p. 74.

16   *Herder's Sämmtliche Werke*, ed. B. Suphan, 33 vols. (Berlin, 1877-1913), XIII, p. 363. Quoted in translation by Carlton J. H. Hayes, 'Contributions of Herder to the doctrine of nationalism', *The American Historical Review*, 32 (1927), p. 726.

17   *Der Briefwechsel zwischen Friedrich Schiller und Wilhelm von Humboldt* (Berlin: Aufbau-Verlag, 1962), II, p. 56. The correspondence with Schiller took place between 1794-1797.

18   *Der Briefwechsel*, II, p. 56.

19   'On Duality' (1827), in *Gesammelte Schriften*, VI, pp. 26-6: *Humanist without Portfolio*, pp. 336-7.

20   *Der Briefwechsel*, II, pp. 206-7.

21   *Der Briefwechsel*, II, p. 207.

22   W. Humboldt, *Linguistic Variability and Intellectual Development*, trans. Georg C. Buck and Frithjof A. Raven (Coral Gables, Florida: University of Miami Press, 1971), p. 27. In *Luthers deutsches Sprachschaffen* (Berlin: Akademie-Verlag, 1962) E. Arndt has pointed out in this connection (see e.g. p. 19), showing that already, in his commentaries on the Psalms of 1513-14, Luther establishes a substantial identity of speech and action. See also P. Meinhold *Lutherssprachphilosophie* (Berlin, 1958), pp. 9 & 12 for more on this subject of spoken communication as energy, power, and act.

23   Friedrich Meinecke, *Cosmopolitanism and the National State*, trans. R. B. Kimber (Princeton: Princeton University Press, 1970), pp. 42-43.

24   Letter to Goethe written from Paris on 18 March 1799, quoted in Meinecke, *Cosmopolitanism*, p. 42.

25   *Novalis Schriften*, ed. E. Heiborn (Berlin, 1901), II, pp. 16 & 70; also *Friedrich von Hardenberg (Novalis): Eine Nachlese aus den Quellen des Familienarchivs etc* (Gotha, 1873), p. 69, quoted in Meinecke, *Cosmopolitanism*, p. 55.

26   According to Herder, 'this imitation appears primarily to be a high-minded striving for idealistic diversity, since it does not arise from a lack of strength but only from the lack of circumscribed nature, and it is the absence of such limitation that frees the

understanding in the formation of judgements and the will in the development of strength' (quoted in Meinecke, *Cosmopolitanism*, p. 45).

27   *Schleiermacher's Soliloquies,* trans. H. L. Friess (Chicago: Open Court, 1926), pp. 58-9.

28   *Schleiermacher's Soliloquies*, p. 31.

29   See e.g., F. D. E. Schleiermacher, *Hermeneutics: The Handwritten Manuscripts* ed. Heinz Kimmerle, trans. James Duke and Jack Forstman (Missoula, Montana: Scholars Press, 1977).

30   Schleiermacher, *Hermeneutics*, MS 1 p. 50.

31   *Schleiermacher's Soliloquies*, p. 46.

32   *Predigten,* in *Schleiermacher. Sämmtliche Werke.* (Berlin, 1834), II, i, p. 233; quoted in K. Pinson, *Pietism as a Factor in the Rise of German Nationalism* (New York: Columbia University Press), p. 101.

33   Pinson, *Pietism*, p. 179, quoting from F. D. E. Schleiermacher, *Sämmtliche Werke,* 33 vols. (Berlin, 1835-64), III, xxvi, p. 58.

34   Eva Hoffman, *Lost in Translation. A Life in a New Language* (London: Minerva, 1991), p. 75.

35   It is interesting to note that J. G. Herder was equally convinced that nationalism would be replaced by European federalism.

36   Hoffman, *Lost in Translation*, pp. 216-217.

15 Romantic Displacements: Representing Cannibalism

PETER J.KITSON

I

Recently a number of critics of Romanticism have explored the thought and literature of the period in the context of Britain's imperial history, bringing to bear, with differing degrees of theoretical sophistication, some of the insights of contemporary post-colonial thought.[1] The period roughly coincided with the sustained historical process that was to culminate in Britain's domination of roughly one quarter of the surface of the globe by the later nineteenth century. The acceleration in this material process that had begun in the sixteenth century brought with it a sustained awareness of human variety and difference, both cultural and physical as well as a growing anxiety about the status of European civilization. Increasingly, subjects of the metropolitan centre sought to define themselves against a non-white and non-Christian 'other'. This construction of an imperial subjectivity coincided with the growth of the sciences of human taxonomy, which we recognize today as the beginnings of the 'race idea'. Frantz Fanon, some time ago, demonstrated how colonial subjects are produced by colonial ideology and discourses.[2] Other post colonial theorists have argued that this subject was characterized as 'other' through discourses such as primitivism and cannibalism, establishing the binary separation of colonizer and colonized and, at the same moment, confirming the naturalness of the colonizing culture and its ideology. Cannibalism, one might say, is the most notorious process of colonial 'othering', both as an alleged practice and as a critical construct. It is clear that cannibalism was used as process by which imperial Europe distinguished itself from the subjects of it colonial expansion while concomitantly demonstrating a moral justification for that expansion. This essay discusses the use of the cannibal trope in a number of Romantic period works in an attempt to investigate how this process of 'othering' or displacing functions in both colonial and domestic writing. The process is not confined to the colonial encounter itself, but is apparent in a number of separate but overlapping discourses. Rather than simply functioning as a psychic adjunct to the

204

material process of nineteenth-century colonial expansion, I argue that the cannibal trope is used to shore up a white Christian subjectivity against the anxieties that haunted the Romantic self, during a period when extreme hunger and starvation made the prospect of 'white cannibalism' a very real possibility, or, at least, a very palpable fear. This anxiety is particularly pronounced in the practice of survival cannibalism at sea. When using the word 'cannibal' anthropologists usually denote the social practice of the eating of human flesh in the form of a ritual.[3] The eating of human flesh is then a socially significant act, which is a part of a larger system of signs. Cannibalism in Levi-Strauss's terminology is thus confined to the sacred. This is the subject of most anthropological work on the topic. By and large anthropologists do not find the subject of the other main type of cannibalism, survival cannibalism, to be a fruitful area of debate, despite the fact that survival cannibalism is well-documented and clearly occurs, whereas there is scepticism about the extent and significance of ritual or social cannibalism. My concern in this essay is with these two forms of cannibalism, ritual and survival and their representation in Romantic period texts.

There have been at least four influential explanations for ritual cannibalism which derive from Enlightenment discussions of the subject.[4] The first stresses the importance of the word or symbol over the deed. This argues that ritual cannibalism was occasioned by a desire for social vengeance. Montaigne claimed, in his essay 'Des cannibales' (first published in 1580), that the Tupinamba Indians were cannibals for reasons of revenge and they were thus easily assimilated into an aristocratic code of honour.[5] They could thus serve as a foil to point out the deficiencies of European civilisation. Similarly, Daniel Defoe's 'Man Friday' is a cannibal for reasons of vengeance. His people 'no eat mans but when make the war fight'. Neither the Tupinamba of Brazil nor the Amerindian Friday enjoyed the eating of human flesh *per se* and thus they were capable of nobility and redemption, capable of being assimilated within a European code of honour. This view of cannibalism survives in the work of contemporary anthropologists such as Marshall Sahlins and Peggy Reeves Sunday who argue that the practice is a part of the broader cultural logic of life, death and reproduction.[6] This was also the thrust of Tzvetan Todorov's *The Conquest of America* (1984) which argued that Hernán Cortéz was able to defeat the Aztecs because he mastered their sign system of ritual sacrifice. The Aztecs, hampered by a religious literalism, were not able to improvise, mistaking the thing for the thing signified, whereas their Spanish invaders were ironic and adaptable.[7]

The second major explanation for social cannibalism became current during the Enlightenment. This argued that the practice resulted from food shortage, especially protein deficiency, and was most obvious on island economies and in South America, where livestock was limited. Both Voltaire and Diderot put forward this view. In his *Essay on the Principle of Population* (second edition, 1803), the Reverend Thomas Malthus identified cannibalism as one of the necessary checks on population expansion, similar in function to war and dearth. Malthus believed that cannibalism 'undoubtedly prevailed in many parts of the new world' and that it had its origin in 'extreme want, though the custom might afterward be continued from other motives'. It is possible that revenge and rancour might also provide explanations for the phenomenon but 'the goad of necessity' is paramount.[8] This view has been revived in contemporary anthropological thought. Marvin Harris, for instance, explains Aztec cannibalism as a utilitarian resort to protein deficiency.[9] This idea tended to detract from the heroic nature of Montaigne's cannibal but it also removed the moral stigma, as all civilisations were potentially cannibalistic.

The third cannibal hypothesis argued that the practice resulted from a form of racial degeneration. This view was assimilated in the nascent Enlightenment sciences of ethnology and anthropology. The eighteenth-century natural historian, Buffon, accounted for human variety in terms of a process which he called degeneration and which he described as occurring through the influence of climate and environment. Humanity was originally white with European features but it degenerated into various other races. The most influential theorist of race in the period, J. F. Blumenbach, following Buffon, argued that human variety this process of 'degeneration' evidenced not just by skin colour but also by the totality of human anatomy, especially the shape of the skull. Blumenbach argued, in 1775, that the originary race of human beings were white and beautiful and that all present varieties descended from this people with the European or Caucasian as the least degenerate and the Ethiopian and Mongolian (or Calmuck) as the most degenerate.[10] Thus the figure of the 'cannibal' in the Romantic period and beyond becomes an instance of racial and moral degeneration.[11] From being an arbitrary mark of difference indicating savagery, cannibalism came to represent a natural sign of racial or class depravity. This hypothesis was available in Kant's writings on race and is typified by Hegel's comment in *The Philosophy of History* that 'the eating of human flesh is quite compatible with the African principle; to the sensuous Negro, human flesh is purely an object of the senses, like all other flesh'.[12] Although not specifically mentioning cannibalism, Coleridge, in later years, speculated about how the African's physical characteristics were symbolic of a moral degeneration.[13] This view the young Darwin applied to the alleged cannibalism of the natives of Tierra del Fuego in his *Journal of Researches into the Geology and Natural History of the Various Countries* (1846)[14] and which chimes in with his developed notions of race in *The Descent of Man* (1860).[15] Cannibalism like blackness and the shape of the skull came to be regarded as a signifier inscribed on the body itself of a degenerate race. Cannibalism thus acquires the status of an inherent racial characteristic, a specifically racial lust, rather than simply being a savage or barbaric practice, and one that is associated not just with Africans but also with the Irish and the lower classes. This is certainly the case in later nineteenth-century fictions, such as H. Rider Haggard's *King Solomon's Mines* (1885) and *She* (1887), and H. G. Wells's *The Time Machine* (1895) and *The Island of Dr Moreau* (1898), and, more ambiguously, Joseph Conrad's *Heart of Darkness* (1902).

The final hypothesis to explain the phenomenon, and the most controversial, is one of straightforward denial. As Geoffrey Sanborn has recently shown accounts sceptical of the existence of cannibalism were available from the early eighteenth century.[16] Allegations of cannibalism among the Africans had been made in William Snelgrave's pro-slavery *A New Account of some Parts of Guinea, and the Slave-Trade* in 1734. Snelgrave's claims were challenged in John Atkins's *A Voyage to Guinea, Brasil, and the West-Indies* (London, 1735). Atkins doubted that, outside of the exigencies of famine, 'whether there be any such men on the face of the Earth'.[17] Atkins's scepticism was echoed later in the century by Enlightenment men such as Joseph Banks and Captain Cook (until they were convinced by his own observation of evidence of Maori cannibalism), and most notably, in the early nineteenth century, by Sir John Barrow, the second secretary to the Admiralty, in a series of ironic reviews of travellers tales and voyages for the *Quarterly Review*.[18] This sceptical explanation suffered from the apparently substantial flow of empirical data throughout the nineteenth century that supposedly established the existence of the phenomenon within the bounds of certainty. It was, however, unexpectedly revived in recent years by William Arens's anthropologically iconoclastic *The Man-Eating Myth: Anthropology and Anthropophagy* (1979). Arens surveyed the famous case studies of cannibalism from classical times to the present with a coruscating irony, in particular discussing the alleged cannibalism of the Aztecs, which is often taken for granted. Arens famously concluded his work by stating that he 'was dubious about the actual existence of this act as an accepted practice for any time or place'.[19] Arens argued that he could find no reliable eye-witness account of the practice existing at any time. Standard accounts mostly had a clear motive for stigmatising certain societies as cannibal, and the texts in question were usually heavily revised and mediated for a particular audience, often being full of the kinds of inconsistency that made them seem unreliable. Frequently these texts were redacted or second-hand texts. For Arens the imputation of cannibalism was simply a way of denigrating a society's cultural achievements. This was certainly true for the Spanish who destroyed a sophisticated and highly civilised Aztec culture. It functioned as a way of creating a boundary between the civilized and the savage and that boundary was always fluid. This stigmatization had occurred from early times when the Greeks first designated those who lived beyond the Black Sea as 'Anthropophagi' (literally eaters of human beings): as much a term of moral as political geography. The early Christians of the second century BC were also said to be, in Andrew MacGowan's phrase 'the ancient cannibals *par excellence*'.[20] This may also have been due to a misunderstanding of the nature of the Eucharist. Arguably the first literary allusion to the Eucharist is a cannibal scene, the eating of Eumolpus in Petronious's *Satyricon*. This use of 'cannibal' to demonize is common. *The Guardian* in 1982 reported the fears of Argentine soldiers that they would be eaten if captured by the British. As Jan Nederveen Pieterse concludes, 'Cannibalism is an allegory which establishes a centre and a periphery within a moral geography'.[21]

Arens's work has led to a lively debate within anthropological and literary studies. Marshall Sahlins, among others, has instanced eye-witness accounts of cannibalism in Fiji and New Zealand, witnessed by no less an authority than James Cook (who, it is often alleged, was himself a victim of Polynesian cannibalism).[22] It is thus very likely that cannibalism has been practised as a socially symbolic act in some cultures but that the imputations of cannibalism to a society crucially includes much more than a simple descriptive statement. The very term 'cannibal', as Peter Hulme subtley demonstrates, relates to the linguistic morphology of the word 'Carib'. The word was used to describe the people of the Antilles, which passed into Spanish as 'Cannibal' and thence into other European languages. Gradually 'cannnibal' (eater of human flesh) became distinct from 'Carib' (native of the Antilles). This process was completed in English in 1796 (the first *OED* entry for the word). Columbus who was himself responsible for the confusion remained sceptical as to whether the Caribs were, in fact, cannibals. Hulme's own position is rather complex. Although he does not validate or deny the imputations of cannibalism to West Indian societies he accepts the existence of cannibalism as a discursive practice: '*Cannibalism* does exist. It exists as a term within colonial discourse to describe the ferocious devouring of human flesh practised by some savages'.[23]

Unlike the ritual variety, survival or famine cannibalism, sometimes referred to as 'white cannibalism', appears to need no explanation other than of necessity. It is universally admitted to occur and is well documented. We have reports of its occurrence in periods of famine from ancient times onwards. Celebrated instances include the *Medusa* shipwreck (versified by Byron in *Don Juan* Canto II); the ill-fated Donner Party of 1846 (stranded on its migration westward on the Rocky Mountains); the final expedition of Sir John Franklin in 1845 to discover the North-West Passage, the siege of Leningrad, the case of the last voyage of the Yacht the *Mignonette* in 1884 (where two seamen were sentenced to death for killing and eating their young ship mate Richard Parker) which lead to the celebrated case of *Regina v Dudley* tried by Lord Coleridge; and the Andes Plane Crash of 1972.[24] By and large post-colonial critics of cannibalism have been overly concerned with the site of the colonial encounter between two cultures and have not yet given a similar sustained critical analysis of the use of the cannibal trope in domestic discourses.[25] When we look at the use of the figure in certain Romantic period discourses we can see how it similarly haunted by anxieties of empire.

II

Cannibalism as a fact and a figure is chiefly prominent in five overlapping discourses of the writing of the Romantic period: political writing, pro-and anti-slavery literature, colonial fictions, shipwreck narratives, and Gothic fiction. In this essay I will briefly discuss the first four of these forms of writing, indicating how they exploit the cannibal trope in ways that reveal the tensions that underlay it use.[26] I am also concerned to see how such representations fit into the post-Enlightenment anthropological discourses of cannibalism that I have just outlined. Allegations of cannibalism, real or metaphorical, were not simply ethnic slurs, they also operated in a wide field of signification. For Edmund Burke, for instance, the practice of cannibalism appeared to have no racial signification, although it did relate to conceptions of nationality. Cannibalism was a sign of the savage and unnatural. This seems to be the case in his descriptions of the North American Indians employed by the British to scalp the colonists in the American War of Independence.[27] Burke also famously attacked the revolutionaries in France as adhering to a cannibal philosophy'. They are unnatural monsters who 'make no scruple to rake with their bloody hands in the bowels of those who came from their own'. In his *First Letter on a Regicide Peace* of 1796 he defined the French mob as cannibal: 'By cannibalism, I mean their devouring, as a nutriment of their ferocity, some part of the bodies of those they have murdered; their drinking the blood of their victims, and forcing the victims themselves to drink the blood of their kindred slaughtered before their faces'. The French government was thus represented as a 'cannibal republic'.[28] Burke's rhetoric here eerily pre-empts Freud's collective myth of the origins of civilization in *Totem and Taboo*, where the band of brothers kill and eat the father to assimilate his strength and wisdom, and to share out his women, thereafter proscribing the act as taboo.[29] Equally familiar, perhaps, is James Gillray's caricature of September 1792, '*Un Petit Souper a la Parisienne – or – A Family of sans-Culotts refreshing after the fatigues of the day*'. The cartoon is a response to the news of the September Massacres and presents the Parisian family engaged in an unnatural cannibal feast. The image is dependent on the conflation of two discourses: that of survival cannibalism and the Burkeian political discourse that locates the centre of political and moral deformity within the family. This image also has strong generic links with the Gothic and the unnatural family in such novels as Lewis's *The Monk* (1797) and the story of the Scottish cannibal family of Sawney Beane.[30]

Of course the same rhetoric was open to radical and well as conservatives. Thomas Paine in *The Rights of Man* could describe primogeniture as a system of cannibalism by constraint: 'Aristocracy has never more than *one* child. The rest are begotten to be devoured. They are thrown to the cannibal for prey, and the natural parent prepares the unnatural repast'.[31] Like Burke's cannibals, those of Paine prey on the family and the body politic. Paine here locating, as Burke, the origins of political deformity in the family. Coleridge, looking back on his period of radical dissent in 1803, also recalled his alleged use of the cannibal trope as an index of political and moral savagery. In a letter to Sir George and Lady Beaumont, he adverted, perhaps imaginatively, to a political address:

> Speaking in public at Bristol I adverted to a public Supper which had been given by Lord – I forget his name, in honour of a victory gained by the Austrians, & after a turbid Stream of wild Eloquence I said – "This is a true Lord's Supper in the communion of Darkness! This is a Eucharist of Hell! A sacrament of Misery! – over each morsel & each Drop of which the Spirit of some murdered Innocent cries aloud to God, This is *my* Body! & this is *my* Blood! (*CL*, II, p. 1001).

In this satanic, inverted Last Supper, Coleridge envisages the victims of the counter-revolution devoured by the European coalition against the

Republic. Here the Eucharist is treated not as symbolic, but as literal, whereby the counter-revolution devours the victims of its atrocities, rather than symbolically celebrating, affirming and incorporating Christ's message as the Protestant understanding of the Eucharist would have it. In 1795 Coleridge's radical tract the *Conciones ad Populum* had attacked the tactics of Major John Butler (the subject of Burke's censures) who, in 1788, led an expedition of 400 Loyalists and 500 Indians in a massacre of the settlers of Wyoming Valley. Coleridge tells how '*English* Generals invited the Indians "to banquet on blood": the savage Indians headed by an Englishman attacked' the 'American paradise'. Again the point is that of Montaigne, that the 'savage' Indians are less truly 'savage' than the barbaric English: the 'banquet of blood' perhaps recalling the Eucharist. In Shelley's *Laon and Cythna* (1817), it is a similar triumph of the counter-revolution itself that leads to a literal and symbolic cannibalism:

> There was no corn – in the wide market place
> All loathliest things, even human flesh, was sold;
> They weighed it in small scales – and many a face
> Was fixed in eager horror then.[32]

Shelley's horror at this market in human flesh is complicated by his vegetarianism, which has a close relationship with his political opinions.[33] In all such examples it is usually the figurative aspect of cannibalism that is to the fore. But as always a troubling sense of literalness haunts the representation. We know that in times of siege and famine humans were driven to literal cannibalism. There were times of famine (though seldom actual strarvation) in France during the Revolution. A few years before Shelley wrote *Laon and Cythna*, Napoleon's *Grand Armée* had resorted to cannibalism in the disastrous retreat from Moscow. None of the examples from political discourse are, as yet, racialized, nor do they appear to be indicate a resort to necessity, due to scarce resources. Rather the 'white cannibals' of Burke, Paine, Coleridge and Shelley suggest that their unnatural feeding is as much an expression of their depraved lust as a resort to need, and therefore morally inexcusable. Here cannibalism is a barbaric practice, resulting from a moral but not yet, perhaps, a physical or somatic degeneration, despite the implied degeneracy of the lower classes as indicated in Burke and Gillray's caricatures of the cannibal *sans culottes*.

III

It is the area of colonialism and the debate over the slave trade where the cannibal trope is most visibly employed. I have already mentioned William Snelgrave's allegations of cannibalism against the Africans and John Atkins's sceptical rebuttal of 1735. The vehemently racist Edward Long, in his *History of Jamaica* (1774), repeated the allegation. He describes Angolan 'custom' of 'butchering a vast number of human victims . . . feasting on human flesh, and preferring it to any other'.[34] Long's fellow West-Indian, the more moderate Bryan Edwards, in his *The History, Civil and Commercial, of the British Colonies in the West Indies* (1793) also believed cannibalism was widespread in the West Indies and he detailed the drinking of the planters' blood during the slave revolts.[35] Of course the imputation of cannibalism to the African was a handy justification for slavery. Long's *History* argued that the African was a separate species from the rest of humanity and therefore the African's cannibalism was just another sign of their bestiality. Various travel accounts such as that of Robert Norris described the horrors of the Kingdom of Dahomey in the period. Dahomey was notorious for its excessive practice of human sacrifice. Norris reported, in his *Memoirs of the Reign of Bossa Ahádee* (1788), how the victims of the sacrifice 'is almost wholly devoured, as all the mob below will have a taste of it'.[36] Norris was notorious as a participant in the slave trade who aided first the opponents of abolition before being bribed by the merchants of Liverpool to act in defence of the trade.

This kind of rhetoric was also available to the opponents of the trade who frequently employed the metaphor of cannibalism and the topos of 'blood as sugar' in their writing. William Fox argued that in every pound of West Indian sugar we 'may be considered as consuming two ounces of human flesh'.[37] Robert Southey's sonnets on the slave trade make the same point to the consumer: 'O ye who at your ease / Sip the blood-sweeten'd beverage'.[38] One of the most interesting uses of this kind of rhetoric is in Coleridge's 'Lecture on the Slave Trade' given at Bristol in 1795. Coleridge is here keen to deconstruct the binary opposition of savagery and civilization which fuels the economy of the cannibal trope: 'the Savage eagerly seizes every opportunity of intoxication – and hence the polished Citizen lies framing unreal Wants and diverts the pains of Vacancy by the pestilent inventions of Luxury' (*LPR*, p. 236). Here, in the time-honoured tradition from Montaigne's 'Des cannibales' onwards, civilised (or 'polished') life is shown to be in no way superior, and in many ways inferior, to so-called savage life. Coleridge's 'Lecture' constitutes an indictment of contemporary manners, leading to his powerful attack on fashionable sensibility. What Coleridge does is to reverse the qualities the civilized European ascribes to the savage African, in this case the common identification of the African with the cannibal:

> Gracious Heaven! at your meals you rise up and pressing your hands to your bosom ye lift up your eyes to God and say O Lord bless the Food which thou hast given us! A part of that Food among most of you is sweetened with the Blood of the Murdered. Bless the Food which thou hast given us! O Blasphemy! Did God give Food mingled with Brothers blood! Will the Father of all men bless the Food of Cannibals – he food which is polluted with the blood of his own innocent Children? Surely if the inspired Philanthropist of Galilee were to revisit earth and be among the feasters as at Cana he would not change Water into Wine but haply convert the produce into the things producing, the occasioned into the things occasioning!
>
> (*LPR*, p. 248).

He accuses the European of cannibalism which travel accounts from Columbus onwards had attributed to the savage races. In Bhabha's essay 'Signs Taken for Wonders' we are given, as an example of the 'hybridisation' of colonial writing, the instance of the Missionary who reports the case of the Indian who accepts the Hindu translations of the gospels but refuses to take the Sacrament of the Lord's Supper because the Europeans eat dead cow's flesh: '*How can the word of God come from the flesh-eating mouths of the English?*'. Thus, argues Bhabha, 'the trace of what is disavowed is not repressed but repeated as something *different* – a mutation, a hybrid'.[39] Hayden White, in an argument based on Freud's treatment of cannibalism and incest in *Totem and Taboo*, demonstrates how European taboos of cannibalism, nakedness, community of property, lawlessness and sexual promiscuity are common in European reports of the savage. He argues that, 'this may be, in the European commentators, a projection of repressed desires onto the lives of the natives . . . but if it is such it is desire tainted by horror and viewed with disgust'.[40] Coleridge's question relating to the grace, 'Will the father of all men bless the Food of Cannibals', in implicating the European in act of cannibalism, pre-empts White's theory of taboo and repression; arguably, it functions in the same way as Bhabha's notion of hybridity, it turns 'the gaze of the discriminated back upon the eye of power'.[41] The ex-slave Olaudah Equiano does something similar, in his *Interesting Narrative* (1789), when he remembers, upon embarking on the slave ship, how he asked his fellow slaves 'if we were not to be eaten by those white men with horrible looks, red faces, and long hair'.[42] In an analogous incident, the explorer Mungo Park records in his *Travels in the Interior of Africa* (1799) how when he attempted to save the life of a young African boy (who had been shot through the leg) by suggesting amputation everyone started with horror supposing him 'a sort of a cannibal for proposing so cruel and unheard of an operation'.[43]

For an outsider, and for many an insider, the sacrament of the Eucharist condoned cannibalism, the very atrocity that the West has displaced onto the other. As Peter Hulme brilliantly speculates on the fourth Lateran Council's literalist interpretation of the Eucharist in 1215, 'boundaries of community are often created by accusing those outside the boundary of the very practice on which the integrity of that community is founded'.[44] At a self-conscious level the cannibalistic trope functions to deconstruct Coleridge's audience's ideas of civilization and savagery. For the Unitarian Coleridge a true, contemporary miracle that the 'inspired Philanthropist of Galilee' might perform would be to make the eighteenth-century consumer aware of the production processes of sugar, 'he would not turn Water into Wine but haply convert the produce into the things producing, the occasioned into the things occasioning' giving us 'instead of sweetmeats Tears and Blood, and Anguish–and instead of Music groaning and the loud Peals of the Lash' (*LPR*, p. 248). In fact Jesus would do no more today than that which 'truth-painting Imagination' achieves. In Timothy Morton's words, 'the blood sugar topos reverses consumption into production'.[45] Certainly Coleridge's 'Lecture' is as much concerned with defining his own Unitarian version of dissent in attacking the sacraments and outlining the modern day miracles of a messiah who is nor more than an 'inspired philanthropist'. Nevertheless its author does try to make his audience aware of both the horrors of the slave trade and of the processes of representation itself. Ultimately in this lecture, Coleridge is trying to refute that the two radical indicators of savagery, absence of language and cannibalism, apply to the African.

IV

Robert Southey believed in the existence of cannibalism, especially in the South American context. His *History of Brazil* (1810-19) carefully collected the accounts of cannibalism in that area. The *History* includes the standard instances of Brazilian cannibalism, in particular, those by Hans Stadten and Jean de Lery, important founding descriptions of the practice and key sources for Montaigne's famous essay. Southey's earlier epic poem, *Madoc* (1805), used the colonial encounter between twelfth-century Welshmen and the New World Aztec civilization as a means of exploring, or affirming, early nineteenth-century imperialist attitudes. The Aztecs, in his account, were ritual cannibals. Southey's poem describes how Madoc, the youngest son of Owen Gwyneth, leaves his native land after the throne was usurped by David. David is a strong but Machiavellian ruler whose alliance with the Saxons is regarded by Madoc as a threat to the racial and religious purity of the Welsh. Madoc and his band thus emigrates to Florida where they found a settlement. This brings the Welsh into conflict with the indigenous Indians, the Aztecs. Unlike the Spanish, Madoc's motives are pure 'not of conquest greedy, nor of gold'.[46] The Aztecs are twice defeated in battle by the superior weaponry of the Welshmen, before migrating to found their Mexican Empire. The poem closes with Southey's anticipation of their conquest by 'the heroic Spaniard's unrelenting sword' (II.xxv.395) apparently without any irony. In the nineteenth-century context Madoc's group represents Protestant English colonialism, the kind of ethos Southey celebrated in his *Life of Nelson* (1817): like Madoc a 'Lord of the Ocean'. Both the Saxons and the Aztecs, with their superstitions and priestcraft, in this scheme of things, can be seen as different representations of European Catholicism. Following the accounts of the Spanish historians of the Conquest, such as Bernal Diaz del Castille's *The Conquest and Discovery of New Spain*, Southey depicts the Aztec as cannibals for reasons of superstition, a comparatively unusual explanation for the practice in the Romantic period.[47] They enslave the native tribe of Indians, the Hoamen, and use them as sacrifices. In what may be another parodic reference to the Eucharist the Aztec priest claims the children of the Hoamen. They are said to 'lay them on the altar of his God/ Pluck out their little hearts in sacrifice, / And with his brotherhood in impious rites, / Feast on their flesh!' (I.vi. 51-3). The Gods in the Aztec pantheon are devourers of human flesh and blood. Part 2 Canto 10 of the poem describes the festival when the Aztec God Tezcalipoca appears in human form:

> Lo! as Tezozomoc was passing by
> The eternal fire, the eternal fire shot up
> A long blue flame. He started; he exclaim'd,
> The God! the God! Tezcalipoca's Priest
> Echoed the welcome cry, The God! the God!
> For lo! his footsteps mark the maize-strewn floor.
> A mighty shout from all the multitudes
> Of Atzlan rose; they cast into the fire
> The victims, whose last shrieks of agony
> Mingled unheeded with the cries of joy (II. x. 206-16).

It is clear that in the form of their religion, with its blood sacrifice, idolatry and superstition, the Aztecs are meant to recall the practices of Catholic Church, which Southey, as a Protestant Englishman, finds superstitious and repulsive. The reader is meant to draw a comparison between this Aztec worship and the form of Christianity that Madoc fled his home to escape. The usurper David is criticized for making an alliance with the Saxons. Part 1, Canto 15 of the poem describes an excommunication, whereby the great Saxon Prelate, 'the mitred Baldwin', attempts to excommunicate the dead and buried Cyveilioc the Prince of Powys for his refusal to take part in the Crusades.

> Let him feel the curse
> At every waking moment, and in every act,
> By night and day, in waking and in sleep!
> We cut him off from Christian fellowship;
> Christian sacraments we deprive his soul;
> Of Christian burial we deprive his corpse;
> And when that carrion to the Fiends is left
> In unprotected earth, thus let his soul
> Be quench'd in hell (I.xv.47-55).

Madoc responds that although Gwynedd may bow its neck to 'the yoke of Rome', Baldwin can tell his Pope he shall not strike a topsail 'for the breath of all his maledictions' (I.xv.111, 115). The reader is surely meant here to draw an analogy between David's Catholic-oppressed Gwynedd and the Aztec Empire. Similarly we are encouraged to see the Aztec's imperial ambitions as reflected in the Crusades of Catholic Europe against the allegedly barbarous nations. So too when King David's bride-to-be is described 'as a sacrifice to/To that cold king-craft' (I.ix.55-6), we are made to draw a comparison between her plight and those of the Aztec sacrificial victims. Again the implication is that Catholic Europe is worse than the barbarous Aztec because it has perverted the truth, while the Aztecs have been *directly* corrupted by the Devil himself, in the form of one of his demons, the Snake God which Madoc will slay. However when attempting to represent Madoc's benevolent imperialism Southey is no more convincing. The Welshmen, although they claim not to be motivated by gain, do colonize the lands of others. In this case the peaceful Hoamen, the third term of the colonial encounter, welcome them. Ultimately Madoc wins every encounter through force of arms. The Hoamen are easily converted to Madoc's anticipated Protestant Christianity. His religion is primarily Christological in the Protestant tradition:

But who can gaze
Upon that other form, which on the rood
In agony is stretch'd? ... his hands transfix'd,
And lacerate with the body's pendent weight;
The black and deadly paleness of his face,
Streak'd with the blood which from that crown of scorn
Hath ceased to flow; the side wound streaming still;
And open still those eyes, from which the look
Not yet hath pass'd away, that went to Heaven,
When, in that hour the Son of Man exclaim'd,
Forgive them, for they know not what they do! (II.vii.30-40).

Southey would no doubt intend his readership to see in this sacrificial account a positive counterpoint to the ritual human sacrifices of the Aztec. However, both Madoc's God and the Aztec's Tezcalipoca require bloody sacrifices. Theologically both are sacrifices to appease an angry deity. Both are figuratively cannibal Gods. The only thing that gives Madoc's Christian account any validity is his military success, his 'conquering arm'. In response to Madoc's prayer, Queen Erillyab of the Hoamen answers:

My people, said the Queen, their God is best
And mightiest. Him to whom we offered up
Blood of our blood and of our flesh the flesh,
Vainly we deem'd divine; no spirit he
Of good or evil, by the conquering arm
Of Madoc mortal proved (II.viii.103-8).

Southey's attempts to disentangle Anglican Protestantism from Catholic and Aztec superstition here collapses into representational confusion. His desire to draw the boundary between civilized and degenerate by, in Hulme's formulation, 'accusing those outside the boundary of the very practice on which the integrity of that community is founded'[48] simply becomes a statement that Western Protestant might is right and Aztec ritual weak and wrong.

V

Finally I would like to briefly comment on the issue of survival cannibalism, or 'white cannibalism'. As A. W. Brian Simpson and others have pointed out, this was not an exotic or furtively-discussed subject but, indeed, a 'socially accepted practice' among sailors for which there was a wide variety of sources and narratives.[49] Such cannibalism was presented as not cannibalism at all, but a response to extreme circumstances, it was not an instance of lust, revenge, or superstition and was not ceremonial or ritualistic. This facing of the cannibal, however, does not derive from the colonial encounter *per se*, that Hulme and others have focused upon, but from narratives and discourses that are more domestic in orientation. What should be appreciated is that eighteenth-century European societies, especially in times of warfare, were subject to period of famine and the concomitant resort to survival cannibalism. The superstitions and taboos that surrounded the eating of human flesh were all the more potent and powerful because of the very real possibility that one might, in certain circumstances face extreme hunger and starvation. Rather than focusing on the element of aggression (as Hulme and other post-colonial critics) this kind of writing relates more to anxieties that, at base, Europeans will resort to the same base primitive urges that characterise the savage.[50]

The most notable example of this situation in the literature of the Romantic period is surely to be found in Canto Two of Byron's *Don Juan* (1819). As well as the accounts of the Medusa wreck of 1819 and the controversy surrounding them, Byron also drew on Sir J. G. Dalyell's *Shipwrecks and Disasters at Sea* (1812) which contains several accounts of sailors resorting to cannibalism, depicted as a last resort. The vessel in which Juan is travelling is shipwrecked, the crew and passengers take to a long boat and, after much suffering, resort to cannibalism; first Juan's spaniel and then his tutor, Pedrillo are eaten by the crew. Byron's treatment owes much to the scandal of the wreck of the French frigate *La Méduse* in 1816 which ran aground of the West African coast due to the criminal incompetence of its Royalist Captain. The survivors took to a raft and later resorted to cannibalism. An event portrayed by Géricault's famous painting *The Raft of the Medusa*. Géricault refrained from depicting cannibalism itself (though this was featured in some of the preliminary sketches for the work), yet he hinted at it in his depiction of the father who holds the body of his dead son, which alludes to Reynolds's and Fuseli's versions of Dante's representation of Ugolino, condemned to cannibalism in Hell.[51] For Géricault the survivors were heroes rather than degenerates. Byron's treatment of the incident, however, is grimly ironic, pointing out the discrepancy between the primary animal needs of humanity and its rationalizations of such desire, 'But man is a carnivorous production'. On the seventh day afloat, 'the longings of the cannibal arise / (Although they spoke not) in their wolfish eye' (lines 575-6; *BCPW*, V, p. 111). The survivors decide in time-honoured fashion to draw lots for 'flesh and blood / and who should die to be, his fellow's food'. The sailors use Julia's love letter to Juan for this purpose.

The lots were made, and mark'd, and mix'd and handed,
   In silent horror, and their distribution
Lull'd even the savage hunger which demanded,
   Like the Promethean vulture, this pollution;
None in particular had sought or plann'd it,
   'Twas nature gnaw'd them to this resolution,
By which none were permitted to be neuter–
And the lot fell on Juan's luckless tutor.

He requested to be bled to death:
   The surgeon had his instruments, and bled
Pedrillo, and so gently ebb'd his breath,
   You hardly could perceive when he was dead.
He died as born, a Catholic in faith,
   Like most in the belief in which they're bred,
And first a little crucifix he kiss'd,
And then held out his jugular and wrist.

The surgeon, as there was no other fee,
   Had his first choice of morsels for his pains;
But being thirstiest at the moment, he
   Preferr'd a draft from the fast-flowing veins:
Part was divided, part thrown in to the sea,
   And such things as the entrails and the brains
Regaled two sharks, who follow'd o'er the billow–
The sailors ate the rest of poor Pedrillo
                 (lines 593-616; *BCPW*, V, pp. 112-3).

In representing the incident with a mixture of grim irony and extreme pathos, Byron uses the motif of sacrifice. Pedrillo is sacrificed, but this time the victim consents through the use of that symbol of chance, the lottery. Like Southey's Aztec rituals, Pedrillo's sacrifice is related to Christ's, although in a more sympathetic and poignant manner. In this case the sacrifice is individual, the result of necessity and not the result of a social system: 'None in particular had sought or plann' d it'. The scene is still horrific and those who partake of the feast go 'raging mad'. Juan, of course, does not feast. Having refused earlier to eat his spaniel for sentimental reasons he feels unable to 'dine with them on his pastor and his master' (line 624; *BCPW*, V, p. 113).

Commenting on this scene, Philip Martin questions why Byron apparently sanctions the superstition, derived from Dalyell but not from the *Medusa* narratives, that those who eat human flesh become degenerate and mad, a practice which 'sorts so badly with the post-Enlightenment scepticism exhibited' in his work as a whole.[52] As Sanborn points out this superstition indicates that 'white people who ate human flesh would either go mad and die or develop a lifelong addiction to the substance'.[53] For Martin, Byron's shipwreck is not descriptive but an example of Byron's political discourse. Thus although Byron's account of cannibalism is ostensibly an Enlightenment version, we can see how the distinction between ritual and survival cannibalism breaks down.[54]

However the presentation of survival cannibalism is, indeed, usually ritualistic. In an important discussion of the representations of the death of James Cook, Gananath Obeyesekere argued that Cannibalism, although it existed in the South Seas, was in fact a British fantasy exported onto the Polynesians, a projection of European aggression.[55] Obeyesekere, exploiting the Freudian notion that cannibalism is a form of oral aggression deriving from the primal scene, argues that Europeans displaced their own cannibal obsessions onto non-white societies.[56] In the culture of seafarers, like Cook, shipwreck, starvation and survival cannibalism were regular phenomena, represented in countless ballads of the sea.[57] In this seafaring culture cannibalism became a reality, so much that sailors began to accept the literal idea of consuming the body and blood of a victim chosen by lots. Thus the Europeans shifted their cannibalism onto that of a society characterized by pronounced anthropophagy. Obeyesekere argues that the British had a developed discourse and practice of cannibalism, which involved ritual sacrifice (the business of the drawing of lots and the selection of a victim) followed by the convention of the feasters going mad from their repast. This discourse was probably far removed from the reality. In Conrad's strange Nietzschean tale 'Falk: A Reminiscence' (1903), the narrator is very disappointed when the survival cannibal Falk tells him that that these conventions are not true: the sailors did not draw lots for their victims but preyed off each other as individuals with the strongest surviving in the end.

What we therefore have in these writings is a series of overlapping discourses relating to politics, race, theology (chiefly regarding the Eucharist), colonialism, popular fictions and folklore. As H.L. Malchow comments in his discussion of popular cannibalism, 'the nineteenth-century image of the racial cannibal was built upon, interwoven with, and sustained by domestic discourse'.[58] It may be that the rigid distinction between survival cannibalism and ritual cannibalism is not justified anyway and that the attempt to maintain it is a form of ethnocentrism which exports all the worst aspects of the European's psyche on to the colonial other. Cannibalism, as both taboo, fact and metaphor is so common in Western literature and culture that it encourages us to think in terms of reversal. Our myths of sacrifice are validated by our culture, their myths are primitive and degenerate. Although a signifier of barbarity for other cultures in the Romantic period, for many years the cannibal feast was the central symbol at the heart of Western Christian thought and practice. The recognition that Europeans in the period were figurative cannibals (Christologically) and often literal cannibals (in times of famine and disaster) had to be abjected onto that which became other to quell the anxiety that the self was prey to savage desires. This resort to cannibalism, however understandable in the circumstances, must nevertheless be inflected with implications of primitive lusts and presentments of punishment. Eating people was therefore right, or at least allowable, but only if the consumption conforms to certain discursive practices.

Notes

1   Edward Said, *Orientalism* (London: Routledge and Kegan Paul, 1978); *Culture and Imperialism* (London: Chatto and Windus, 1993); Nigel Leask, *British Romantic Writers and the East: Anxieties of Empire* (Cambridge: Cambridge University Press, 1992); Alan Richardson and Sonia Hofkosh, ed. *Romanticism, Race and Culture, 1780-1834* (Bloomington and Indianapolis: Indiana University Press, 1996); Tim Fulford and Peter J. Kitson, *Romanticism and Colonialism: Writing and Empire, 1780-1830* (Cambridge: Cambridge University Press, 1998); Alan Bewell, *Romanticism and Colonial Disease* (Baltimore and London: John Hopkins University Press, 1999).

2   Frantz Fanon, *Black Skins: White Masks*. Translated by Charles Lam Markmann (1952: London: Pluto Press, 1968).

3   Peter Hulme, 'The Introduction: The cannibal scene', in *Cannibalism and the Colonial World*, ed. Francis Barker, Peter Hulme and Margaret Iversen (Cambridge: Cambridge University Press, 1998), pp. 1-38. Peter Hulme, *Colonial Encounters: Europe and the Native Caribbean 1492-1797* (London, and New York: Routledge, 1986); Bill Ashcroft, Gareth Griffiths and Helen Tiffin, *Key Concepts in Post-Colonial Studies* (London and New York: Routledge, 1998), pp. 29-30.

4   See Geoffrey Sanborn, *The Sign of the Cannibal: Melville and the Making of a Postcolonial Reader* (Durham and London: Duke University Press, 1998), pp. 20-73.

5   See Frank Lestringnant, *Cannibals: The Discovery and Representation of the Cannibal from Columbus to Jules Verne*. Trans. Rosemary Morris (London: Polity Press, 1997), pp. 53-67.

6   Peggy Reeves Sunday, *Divine Hunger: Cannibalism as a Cultural System* (Cambridge: Cambridge University Press, 1986); Marshall Sahlins, *Islands of History* (Chicago: University of Chicago Press, 1985); *How Natives Think: About Captain Cook, For Example* (Chicago: University of Chicago Press, 1995).

7   Tzvetan Todorov, *The Conquest of America*. Trans. Richard Howard (Ithaca: Cornell University Press, 1984).

8   T. R. Malthus, *An Essay on the Principle of Population* 2 vols (2nd edn, London: J. Johnson, 1803: London: Everyman, 1927), I, pp. 34, 38, 44. See, Frank Lestringnant,

Cannibals (London: Polity Press, 1997), pp. 144-52; Sanborn, *The Sign of the Cannibal*, pp. 38-46.

9   Marvin Harris. *Cannibals and Kings: The Origins of Culture* (New York: Random House, 1977).

10   Johann Friedrich Blumenbach, *De Generis Humani Varietate Nativa* (3rd edn Göttingen: Apud Vandenhoek et Ruprecht, 1795), in *The Anthropological Treatises of John Friedrich Blumenbach*, trans and ed. Thomas Bendyshe (London: The Anthropological Society, 1865), p. 269. See Peter J. Kitson, ed. *Theories of Race,* Vol 8, *Slavery, Abolition and Emancipation: Writings in the British Romantic Period,* ed. Peter J. Kitson and Debbie Lee (London: Pickering and Chatto, 1999), pp. vii-xxvi. Hannah Augstein, ed, *Race: The Origins of an Idea, 1760-1850* (London: Thoemmes Press, 1996).

11   As H. L. Malchow argues, in the nineteenth century 'growing colonial discourse . . . objectified the idea of cannibalism as an inherent racial characteristic rather than merely a barbaric practice'. *Gothic Images of Race in Nineteenth-Century Britain* (Stanford: Stanford University Press, 1996). p.48.

12   Emmanuel Chukwudi Eze. ed. *Race and the Enlightenment: A Reader* (Oxford: Blackwell. 1997). pp. 38-64. 134. David Lloyd, 'Race Under Representation', *Oxford Literary Review*, 13 (1991), pp. 62-94; Nicholas Hudson, 'From "Nation" to "Race": The origins of Racial Classification in Eighteenth-Century Thought', *Eighteenth-Century Studies*, 29 (1996), pp. 247-64.

13   See J. Haeger, 'Coleridge's Speculations on Race', *Studies in Romanticism*, 13 (1974), pp. 333-57; Patrick J. Keane, *Coleridge's Submerged Politics: The Ancient Mariner and the French Revolution* (Columbia and London: University of Missouri Press, 1994).

14   See Sanborn, *Sign of the Cannibal*. pp. 38-9.

15   For Darwin, see Adam Lively, *Masks, Blackness, Race and the Imagination* (London: Chatto and Windus, 1998), pp. 99-124.

16   Sanborn. *Sign of the Cannibal*. pp. 30-38.

17   John Atkins. *A Voyage to Guinea, Brasil and the West Indies* (London: C. Ward and R. Chandler, 1735), p. 123.

18   Sanborn, *Sign of the Cannibal*, pp. 33-38.

19   William Arens. *The Man-Eating Myth: Anthropology & Anthropophagy* (Oxford and New York: Oxford University Press, 1979). p. 8. Although a number of specialised studies of early societies would now seem to have placed the matter of the existence of cannibalism among human societies beyond reasonable doubt, the debate continues. The publication of Christy Turner and Jacqueline Turner's *Man Corn: Cannibalism and Violence in the Prehistoric American South-West* (Salt Lake City: University of Utah Press, 1999) caused a controversy by presenting evidence of cannibalism among the tenth-century Anasazi people of today's New Mexico. See Paul Henley's review 'A Generous Quantity of Fat', *London Review of Books* (September, 1999), pp. 24-6. For an informed, recent review of the debates in contemporary anthropological and cultural works see C. Richard King, 'The (Mis) Uses of Cannibalism in Contemporary Cultural Critique', *Diacritics*. 30.i (2000), pp. 106-23.

20   Andrew McGowan, 'Eating People: Accusations of Cannibalism Against Christians in the Second Century', *Journal of Early Christian Studies*, 2 (1994), pp. 413-42 (p. 438). See also, Heidi Zogbaum, 'Cannibalism in the New World: A Case Study in Stigmatization', *Meanjin*, 53 (1994), pp. 734-42.

21   Jan Nederveen Pieterse, *White on Black: Images of Africa and Blacks in Western Popular Culture* (New Haven and London: Yale University Press, 1992), pp. 113-23 (p. 116). In Claude Rawson's more sophisticated formulation, 'Cannibalism, it seems, is what others do, except metaphorically', Claude Rawson, '"Indians" and Irish: Montaigne, Swift, and the Cannibal Question', *Modern Language Quarterly*, 53 (1992), pp. 299-363 (p. 358). See also, Preserved Smith, *A Short History of Christian Theophagy* (London and Chicago: Open Court Publishing Co., 1922).

22   Marshall Sahlins, 'Cannibalism: An Exchange', *New York Review of Books*, 26. iv (22 March, 1979), pp. 46-7. For Arens's recent unrepentant reassessment, see his 'Rethinking anthropophagy', in Barker, Hulme, and Iversen, *Cannibalism and the Colonial World*, pp. 39-64; Noel Elizabeth Currie, 'Cook and the Cannibals: Nootka Sound, 1778', in Donald W. Nichol and Margarete Smith, ed. *Lumen*, XIII (Academic Edmonton, 1994), pp. 71-78.

23   Hulme, *Colonial Encounters*, p. 85. For the debate about Hulme's sceptical reading of New World depictions of cannibalism, see Myra Jehlen, 'History Before the Fact; or, Captain John Smith's Unfinished Symphony', *Critical Inquiry*, 19 (1993), pp. 677-92; Peter Hulme, 'Making No Bones: A Response to Myra Jehlen' *Critical Inquiry*, 20 (1994), pp. 179-86; Myra Jehlen, 'Response to Peter Hulme', *Critical Inquiry*, 20 (1993), pp. 179-86, 187-91.

24   Sanborn, *Sign of the Cannibal*, pp. 38-46; A. W. Brian Simpson, *Cannibalism and the Common Law: The Story of the Tragic Last Voyage of 'Mignonette' and the Strange Legal Proceedings to Which It Gave Rise* (Chicago: University of Chicago Press, 1984); Hans Askenasy, *Cannibalism from Sacrifice to Survival* (Amherst: Prometheus Books, 1994); Reay Tannahill, *Flesh and Blood: A History of the Cannibal Complex* (London: Hamilton, 1975); Scott Cookman, *Ice Blink: The Tragic Fate of Sir John Franklin's Lost Polar Expedition* (London, 2000).

25   Recent exceptions to this are H. L. Malchow's study of the Gothic novel, *Gothic Images of Race*, and Geoffrey Sanborn's discussion of Melville's treatment of cannibalism in *The Sign of the Cannibal*.

26   For the use of the subject in Gothic writing, see Malchow, *Gothic Images of Race*, pp. 41-123.

27   Burke made attempts in Parliaments to censure the military commanders that gave the orders to the North American Indians perpetrating atrocities against the colonists. See *Annual Register* (1778), 'History of Europe', p. 111; *Annual Register* (1778), 'History of Europe', p. 113; Robert Macfarlane, *The History of the Second Ten Years of the Reign of George the Third* (London, 1782), p. 379.

28   Edmund Burke, *Three Letters . . . on the Proposals for Peace with the Regicide Directory of France* (1796), in *The Works of the Right Honorable Edmund* Burke. 9 vols (London, 1884), V, pp. 140, 211-2, 273, 287, 309.

29   For a Freudian analysis of the rhetoric of the Revolution, see Lynn Hunt, *The Family Romance of the French Revolution* (London and New York: Routledge, 1992): 'Only by killing him [Louis XVI] could they overcome their own weaknesses; only by eliminating a great criminal could they purify the community; only by eating the king could the people become sovereign themselves', pp. 53-88 (p. 59).

30   For a recent discussion of such imagery in the context of colonial dietary discourses, see Bewell, *Romanticism and Colonial Disease*, pp. 131-60.

31   Thomas Paine, *The Rights of Man* (1791-92: Harmondsworth; Penguin, 1969), p. 104.

32   *The Complete Works of Percy Bysshe Shelley*, ed. Nevill Rogers. 4 vols (Oxford; Oxford University Press, 1975), II, p. 236.

33   See Timothy Morton, *Shelley and the Revolution in Taste* (Cambridge: Cambridge University Press, 1994).

34   Edward Long, *History of Jamaica* (London: T. Lowndes, 1774), II, p. 373.

35   Bryan Edwards, *The History, Civil and Commercial, of the British Colonies in the West Indies.* 3 vols (London: B. Crosby, 1788). See Malchow, *Gothic Images of Race*, pp. 16-31.

36   Robert Norris, *Memoirs of the reign of Bossa Ahádee, King of Dahomy* (London: W. Lowndes, 1789), p. 126.

37   William Fox, *An Address to the People of Great Britain, on the Propriety of Abstaining from West India Sugar and Rum* (London: M. Gurney, 1791), p. 2.

38   Robert Southey, *Poems by Robert Southey* (Bristol: J. Cottle, 1797; Oxford: Woodstock, 1989), p. 35.

39   Homi K. Bhabha, *The Location of Culture* (London and New York: Routledge, 1994), pp. 116. 110.

40   Hayden White, *Tropics of Discourse: Essays in Cultural Criticism* (Baltimore and London: John Hopkins University Press, 1978), p. 187.

41   Bhabha, *Location of Culture*, p. 112.

42   Olaudah Equiano, *The Interesting Narrative and Other Writings*, ed. Vincent Carretta (London and New York: Penguin, 1995), p. 55.

43   Mungo Park, *Travels into the Interior of Africa* (1799: London: Eland, 1983), p. 77. Park was sceptical about allegations of cannibalism, believing that 'the accounts which the Negroes give of their enemies ought to be received with great caution', however, he did accept that the inhabitants on Maniana, 'indulge themselves with unnatural and disgusting banquets of human flesh'. *Travels*, p. 166.

44   Hulme, *Colonial Encounters*, p. 85. 187-91.

45   Timothy Morton, 'Blood Sugar', in Kitson and Fulford, *Romanticism and Colonialism*, pp. 87-106 (p. 92).

46   Robert Southey, *Madoc*, II.i.5. *Poems of Robert Southey*, ed. Maurice H. Fitzgerald (Oxford: Henry Frowde, 1909), p. 521. Further references to the poem will be cited in the text by Part, Canto and line number.

47   See Sanborn, *Sign of the Cannibal*, pp. 53-61.

48   Hulme, *Colonial Encounters*, pp. 85. 187-91.

49   Simpson, *Cannibalism and the Common Law*, p. 145; Keith Huntress, *A Checklist of Narratives of Shipwrecks and Disasters at Sea to 1860* (Ames: Iowa State University Press, 1979). For the best recent discussion of this, see Sanborn, *Sign of the Cannibal*, pp. 38-46.

50   As Malchow argues, '[C]annibalism an important – perhaps the most important element of nineteenth-century racial discourse, . . . nevertheless drew deeply on popular domestic European culture – that is, from the 'white cannibalism' of the madman, the criminal, the mob, the sailor, and the harpylike female', *Gothic Images of Race*, p. 6. This is also the general thesis of Frank Lestrignant's *Cannibals*.

51   See Dante, *Inferno*, XXXIII, lines 76-8. Lorenz Eitner, *Géricault's Raft of the Medusa* (London: Phaidon Press, 1972), pp. 45-6.

52   Philip Martin, *Byron: a Poet Before his Public* (Cambridge: Cambridge University Press, 1982), pp. 208-13 (p. 208).

53   Sanborn, *Sign of the Cannibal*, p. 45. Dalyell describes how in the shipwreck of the slave-ship *Thomas* in 1797, 'Those who indulged their cannibal appetite to excess, speedily perished in raging madness'. *Shipwrecks and Disasters at Sea.* 3 vols (Edinburgh, 1812), III, p. 357. This notion of the white cannibal's addiction to

human flesh is interestingly played upon in Antonia Bird's grimly-ironic film
Ravenous (1999).

54 For a discussion of Byron's depiction of cannibalism at sea in relation to his source,
see, Sanborn, *Sign of the Cannibal*, pp. 40-6.

55 Gananath Obeysekere, '"British Cannibals": Contemplation of an Event in the Death
and Resurrection of James Cook, Explorer', *Critical Inquiry*, 18 (1992), pp. 630-54.
See also *The Apotheosis of Captain Cook: European Mythmaking in the Pacific*
(Oxford and Princeton; Princeton University Press, 1992). For a recent restatement
of Obeysekere's ideas, see 'Cannibal feasts in nineteenth-century Fiji; seamen's
yarns and the ethnographic imagination', in *Cannibalism and the Colonial World*,
ed. Barker, Hulme and Iversen, pp. 63-86. See also Jack Forbes, *Columbus and
Other Cannibals: The Wétiko Disease of Exploration, Imperialism and Terrorism*
(New York: Autonomedia, 1992) which argues that Western civilization creates the
discourse of cannibalism as result of a psychosocial condition resulting from its own
exploitations and consumption.

56 The most notable discussion of cannibalism as a sublimation of this impulse occurs
in Eli Sagan's *Cannibalism: Human Aggression and Cultural Form* (New York,
Harper Torchbooks, 1974).

57 See, Simpson, *Cannibalism and the Common Law*; Sanborn, *Sign of the Cannibal*,
pp. 38-46.

58 Malchow, *Gothic Images of Race*, p. 42. For a discussion of the relationship between
contemporary consumerism and cannibalism, see Dean MacCannell, 'Cannibalism
Today', in *Empty Meeting Grounds: The Tourist Papers* (London and New York;
Routledge, 1992), pp. 17-73. See also, Deborah Root, *Cannibal Culture: Art,
Appropriation, and the Commodification of Culture* (Boulder: Westview, 1996), and
King's incisive review of MacCannell and Root in 'The Mis(Uses) of Cannibalism'.

Index